THE OXFORD HISTORY OF MUSIC

INTRODUCTORY VOLUME

THE OXFORD
HISTORY OF MUSIC

INTRODUCTORY VOLUME

EDITED BY
PERCY C. BUCK

M.A., Mus. Doc. Oxon.
Hon. M.A., Trinity College, Dublin
King Edward Professor of Music in the
University of London

GENERAL EDITOR
Sir W. H. HADOW

NEW YORK
COOPER SQUARE PUBLISHERS, INC.
1973

Originally Published 1929 by Oxford University Press
Reprinted by Permission of Oxford University Press
Published 1973 by Cooper Square Publishers, Inc.
59 Fourth Avenue, New York, New York 10003
International Standard Book Number 0-8154-0482-4
Library of Congress Catalog Card Number 73-82351

Printed in the United States of America

EDITOR'S PREFACE

THE Oxford History of Music originally appeared in the years 1901–5, and its publication was greeted on all sides as an event of importance in English musical life. But it must be difficult, if not impossible, for the present generation of students to realize what the volumes meant to those whose student days fell before that date.

It is nowadays a commonplace of all education that the true understanding of any subject can only be derived from the study of how it came to be what it is. And even in those days this truth received a certain lip-service. The word 'genetic' had not, possibly, acquired a very firm foothold in the jargon of pedagogy, but musical students were expected to know, and were frequently examined in, the outlines of the history of their art. And there were even, here and there, voices of wise men crying in the wilderness—notably that of Sir Hubert Parry—that true genetic knowledge did not consist in dates, anecdotes, and facts, but in a first-hand familiarity with the actual compositions of the past. But to the ordinary student a knowledge of the past was only to be reached through the then available histories of music, and the writers of these, by their ingenuous custom of purloining and re-writing the material of their predecessors, had thoroughly justified the Napoleonic epigram that history is 'fable agreed upon'. Almost any middle-aged musician will now admit that, as a student, he looked on the history of music as an unpleasant necessity of the Examination School, and that his knowledge of the subject was, like that of most of his examiners, derived solely from text-books, éked out by articles from Grove's *Dictionary*, and possibly supplemented by a superficial acquaintance with some of the less trustworthy examples to be found in that monument of inaccuracy known as Boyce's *Cathedral Music*.

There were, however, excuses to be offered on all sides. In the first place, the music of bygone ages was not procurable in print, or was only procurable at a cost which to the student— who then, as always, 'hadde but litel gold in cofre'—was prohibitive. Nor was it possible, save on the rarest occasions, to hear performances of such music. Furthermore, such specimens of old music as could be bought were, in the main, edited and brought up to date by 'scholars' who thought them crude and quite frankly said so; and the performance of them, when they did get a hearing, was in the hands of singers and conductors who were merely experimenting in the dark. Nowadays, for a few pence, any student can, thanks to Dr. Fellowes, buy any madrigal as the composer wrote it, and also, thanks to the English Singers, can hear it performed as the composer intended; after which he will know, from the inside, more about the work of Weelkes and Wilbye than was known by the greatest expert of fifty years ago.

Lastly, there is the excuse that the actual teaching as to the nature of music of the past was founded on misconception of it. The teaching was definite, but it was definitely wrong. The one definition, for example, of the counterpoint of the period, which was paraded *ad nauseam*, was that it was a combination of melodies. Every student can now discover, with his own eyes and ears, that the essence of the matter was the combination of rhythms, and that the melodies were left, as a rule, to look after themselves. 'Modes', again, were looked on as, and were actually said by the most learned teachers to be, synonymous with 'keys', notwithstanding all the varied harmonic imputations which the word 'key' carries to a modern mind. Every student can now understand, if he will take the minimum of trouble, that a mode is a melodic limitation, and that the history of composition, from the days of pure plainsong to the birth of the *Forty-eight*, is a history of the cession of modal characteristics under the pressure of the evolution of a harmonic system in which they were unworkable.

It is in no way derogatory to the value of the other volumes of the *Oxford History* to say that, to the students of a generation ago, the first two volumes of the series came as a revelation and a gift beyond price. Here for the first time the whole apparatus of Tudor music, the origin and growth of its laws, the scope and usage of its conventions, were traced and laid bare, with copious illustrations, by a brilliant scholar whose mind was steeped in it. The processes of early musical development which had hitherto presented themselves to students as crude and inexplicable conundrums were seen to have been intelligent, and often bold, attempts at the solution of problems which would have confronted ourselves, had we been living at that period. Professor Wooldridge earned, and was accorded, the gratitude of a generation.

It has, however, come to be felt at the present day—and the mere existence of such a feeling is in itself a witness to the enlightenment the original work created—that the method of treatment adopted by Professor Wooldridge was, to a large extent, too one-sided. The student of his volumes is liable to gather the impression that throughout the Middle Ages music was in a state of chaos, and that the great men were those who nursed the art through its growing pains and infantile complaints, steered it through shoals and quicksands, and slowly and painfully forged a medium in which we can now express musical ideas which are moving and profound. But are we justified in assuming that for centuries musicians felt themselves to be struggling in the dark after something dimly conceived to be possible, never imagining that they had attained to a means of expressing the human feelings of joy and beauty in a form felt, at the time, to be entirely adequate ? It is an axiom of the modern historian that, however backward the development of any branch of human life may seem when scrutinized by a later generation, to its own contemporaries it is always ' modern '. A thousand years hence the Professor Wooldridge of the period will doubtless write a volume in which he will try to persuade his own sceptical generation that *L'Après-midi d'un Faune* and *Pétrouchka* were actually thought to be, by music-lovers of the present day, adequate and moving embodiments of living beauty. Those who knew Professor Wooldridge know that, so far from controverting this axiom, he would have claimed it as the fundamental belief of his historical creed ; and they know that his volumes were purposely written to lay bare the anatomy of his subject, and not to inquire into the functions of its heart. Consequently they believe that there is room, in the interests of students, for an attempt to show that at all times there has existed an art of music which, however uncouth it may appear to listeners in a later stage of musical development, the music-lovers of its own period found adequate for the expression of their aspiration and the solace of their sorrow.

The present volume, therefore, is intended to be an introduction to the study of the history of music. The six volumes of the *Oxford History of Music* provide the student with ample material for the study of the evolution of what we, at this moment, call modern music. This introductory volume is meant to remind him that music always has, at the moment, been modern. It is an attempt to supply, so far as the best available knowledge can supply, an answer to the questions which will always be asked by those who believe that music could never have persisted and survived unless its contemporary appeal had been to the human heart. To the mere examination-student Greek music may well seem to be a bewildering accretion of incomprehensible terms, and it can only be saved from becoming a dead branch of archaeology by the remembrance that, to the living Greek, it served to express the whole gamut of his emotions. Jewish music, again, may appear to the present-day student a formal and artificial thing, created by convention and sustained by tradition ; but even the most casual reader of the Old Testament must realize that, in its day, it could stir and quicken the pulse of man.

It will be ample justification for the present volume if the minds of its more serious readers are stimulated to the further elucidation of the problems with which it deals. The charge has already been made that the histories of a generation ago did not solve, or even attempt to solve, the various problems on which the grasp of history depends. The function of an historian was to give an *ex cathedra* verdict on such issues as arose, and piety demanded that he should complacently hand on the verdicts of his predecessors. But the fact that our own generation, in its wiser scepticism, has shaken off the methods of the parrot does not imply that it has succeeded in solving all the problems by any surer means. A generation of students has yet to arise that will, by the patient study of historical records, gradually fill in the missing pieces in the mosaic of musical history.

To the student who combines historical aptitude with a love of music there is an almost illimitable field of research. What was the exact conspectus of music in the *Quadrivium*? What sort of music would you have heard from the minstrels' gallery of Lancaster Castle if you had dined with John of Gaunt? How did a composer get his works circulated and performed? What kind of a tune was that of the Clerk of Oxenford, when he said

> I wol with lusty herte fresshe and grene
> Seyn you a song to glade you, I ween.

The truth is, we have all of us succumbed to the view of history as a mass of facts, and not of human impulses. We know that while our cathedrals were echoing to the austerities of Taverner and Tallis the peasantry were dancing outside to the gay rhythms of the wandering minstrel; and we have, thanks to recent research, some glimmering of the parallel development of learned and unlearned music. But it is little more than a glimmering. The march from Paris to Versailles, with the 'Marseillaise' to exhilarate and sustain the spirit, is to this day an almost photographic reality to us, because the

'Marseillaise' still has the power to tingle our blood. But which of the most learned of musical historians can, in imagination, join in the surging crowds who, in the Peasants' Rising of 1381, marched to London singing the rebel songs founded on *Piers Plowman*? And which of us, from our knowledge of the music of Adam de la Hale, can guess wherein lay the seductiveness of Troubadour music—a seductiveness so great and so politically significant that it led to the horrors of the Albigensian crusades?

It would be easy to fill many pages with questions of absorbing interest, on the human side, to any serious student of musical history. And such questions are not necessarily unanswerable. It may fairly be claimed that in this book some of the problems have been brought a little nearer their solution, but its main plea of justification lies in the fact that it is a reminder, as necessary now as ever, that at every moment of history music always has been, is now, and in the future can only survive by being, the expression of the deepest feelings of the human race.

P. C. B.

HARROW, *August* 1928.

CONTENTS

CHAPTER VII

CHAPTER VIII

CHAPTER IX

LIST OF ILLUSTRATIONS

GREEK MUSIC

By Cecil Torr

Amongst the ancient Greeks the word Music meant a great deal more than it means now. When they called a man 'unmusical' they meant he was a 'philistine', not merely callous to music, but callous to the allied and associated arts. According to Plato, Music and Gymnastics made a liberal education; these two arts gave men faultless minds in faultless bodies, and fitted them for life in peace or war. Gymnastics included wrestling, running, leaping, &c., and music included the rhythmic movement of the body in response to melody. Plato treats this rhythmic movement as one of the three main things in music, and playing and singing as the other two; but Aristotle thought that playing was unworthy of free men and should be left to hirelings.[1]

Though in those times Music meant much more, it also meant much less. The ancient Greeks knew nothing of counterpoint or orchestration and were content with melody alone. Melody is really the essential thing—the others are mere adjuncts—and by fixing their whole minds on that one thing they gave it a perfection that modern Europeans cannot understand. The modern diatonic scale had only major tones and minor tones and diatonic semitones, and the tempered scale has nothing but mean tones and mean semitones; but the ancient scales had quarter-tones and a dozen other intervals that were less than semitones; and with such intervals a melody could have much greater subtlety. Small intervals are not unknown

---

[1] Plato, *Republic*, ii. 376 E; *Alcibiades*, i. 108 C, D; *Crito*, 50 D; *Laws*, ii. 673 A, B; Aristotle, *Politics*, viii. 6. 5, 7. 1.

in Oriental music even now, but the modern Oriental has not
the genius of the ancient Greek for taking full advantage of
them, nor has the modern European any such capacity.   Hearing nothing now but semitones and multiples of semitones, the
ear has grown less sensitive and lost its power of distinguishing
small intervals and taking pleasure in them.

This is really the main difference between our modern music
and the music of the ancient Greeks.   We divide the octave
into twelve equal intervals and use many notes at once according
to fixed rules, whereas they divided it into many unequal intervals and rarely used more than one note at a time.   And this
may be the reason why modern music has less effect on the
emotions.   With ancient music the effect was marvellous, if we
can credit what the ancient writers say.   Dorian music made
men brave and steadfast, Phrygian made them headstrong,
Lydian made them slack and sentimental, &c. ; and philosophers
thought that Dorian should alone be used.[1]

The ancient Greeks classified their music as Lydian, Phrygian,
Dorian, Aeolian, and Iastian, which last term is equivalent to
Ionian.   These were the names of two foreign nations and three
tribes of the Greeks themselves.   Herodotus (i. 142–51) speaks
of thirty Greek cities on the western coast of Asia Minor and
the adjacent islands, and he says that these cities were grouped
in three confederacies, six Dorian cities in the south, twelve
Ionian cities in the north, and twelve Aeolian cities between.
The territories of the Lydians and the Phrygians were only
a little way inland, and perhaps extended to the sea before the
Greeks intruded.   The five names seem to show that all Greek
music had its origin in the western parts of Asia Minor : at any
rate they show that it was classified in this way by a person
well acquainted with those parts.

This person would probably be Pythagoras.   He lived at
Samos, one of the twelve Ionian cities, until about 530 B.C. when

---

[1] Plato, *Republic*, iii. 398 E--399 C ; Aristotle, *Politics*, viii. 5. 8, 7. 8-10;
Athenaeus, xiv. 19, 20, 624 C-625 E.

he and his followers migrated into southern Italy and spread his theories there. Some of the ancient writers say that his theory of music was borrowed from the Egyptians; and he could easily have gone to Egypt, as it was only four or five days' run from Samos in the sailing vessels of those times. Other ancient writers say that he invented his theory himself. However that may be, it is certain that he knew the fundamental fact : namely, that with strings of equal thickness and of equal tension the pitch of the notes was governed by the length of the strings. Thus if the lengths were in the ratio of 1 to 2 they made an octave; if the ratio was 2 to 3 they made a perfect fifth; if it was 3 to 4 they made a perfect fourth; if it was 8 to 9 they made the tone that is the difference between the perfect fourth and perfect fifth; and if it was 243 to 256 they made the semi-tone that is the difference between two of these tones and a perfect fourth. The intervals can easily be calculated from the ratios by means of logarithms. If an octave is divided into 1,200 equal parts a mean semitone will have 100 of them, a mean tone will have 200, and so on; and the number in any other intervals is approximately given by the formula 4,000 $(\log x - \log y)$, where x and y are the lengths of the strings. If the lengths are 2 and 3 the interval is 702, not 700; if they are 3 and 4 it is 498, not 500; if they are 8 and 9 it is 204, not 200; and if they are 243 and 256 it is 90, not 100.

The ratios were studied systematically. A ratio of 1 to 2 is the same thing as a ratio of 2 to 4, and this gives ratios of 2 to 3 and 3 to 4. Then 2 to 3 (or 4 to 6) gives 4 to 5 and 5 to 6, and 3 to 4 (or 6 to 8) gives 6 to 7 and 7 to 8. Then 4 to 5 (or 8 to 10) gives 8 to 9 and 9 to 10, while 5 to 6 (or 10 to 12) gives 10 to 11 and 11 to 12. Then 8 to 9 (or 16 to 18) gives 16 to 17 and 17 to 18, and so on with the rest. Six-and-twenty of these ratios are used by Ptolemy (*Harmonica*, ii. 14) in setting out his own scales and the scales that he ascribes to Archytas and Eratosthenes and Didymus; and thirteen of the twenty-six are less than semitones. Reckoning a mean semitone as 100, the ratio 18 to 19 makes 94; 19 to 20 makes 88; 20 to 21 makes 85; 21 to 22 makes 80; 23 to 24 makes 74; 24 to 25 makes 71; 27 to 28 makes 63; 30 to 31 makes 57; 31 to 32 makes 55; 35 to 36 makes 49; 38 to 39 makes 45; 39 to 40 makes 44; and 45 to 46 makes 38. This last ratio is in one of Ptolemy's own scales, and may not be of great antiquity—he was writing in A.D. 140 or thereabouts— but he gives the ratio of 39 to 40 in a scale of Eratosthenes and the ratio of 27 to 28 in a scale of Archytas; and Eratosthenes was in his prime a little before 200 B.C. and Archytas a little after 400 B.C.

At first sight all these ratios seem to be a matter of mathematics rather than of music; but music and mathematics really are the same thing here. The ratios are in accordance with the structure of the human ear—as Helmholtz demonstrated in his *Tonempfindungen*—and the same results can be obtained by hearing as by calculation, provided that the hearing is acute enough.

Instead of reckoning intervals by ratios, Aristoxenus and his followers reckoned them by fractions. Dividing a fourth into sixty equal parts, he reckoned intervals as six, eight, nine, twelve, &c., of these sixtieth parts.[1] A sixtieth part of a fourth is 8·3 if a mean semitone is taken as 100, and six sixtieths are 49·8, eight are 66·4, nine are 74·7, twelve are 99·6, and so on. The ratio 35 to 36 gives 48·9, the ratio 77 to 80 gives 66·4, the ratio 23 to 24 gives 73·9, the ratio 17 to 18 gives 99·3, and so on. And thus the fractions give approximately what the ratios give exactly, and give it in a more convenient form. But twelve sixtieths (99·6) are so nearly a mean semitone, and twenty-four (199·2) are so nearly a mean tone, that many people think that Aristoxenus must have known the tempered scale. The ancients

---

[1] Aristeides, *De Musica*, i, pp. 20, 21 ; Ptolemy, *Harmonica*, ii. 14. In his extant work, *Harmonica Stoecheia*, i, p. 25, Aristoxenus speaks of twelfth parts of tones, that is, thirtieth parts of fourths.

did not think so. Euclid proved that six tones are greater than an octave; and when the Aristoxenians talked of six tones to the octave, Ptolemy's comment was that they should either have accepted what was proved, or invented something else to take its place; and he would hardly have said that, if they had invented something else in the shape of a tempered scale.[1] The fact is that the Aristoxenians were walking in the footsteps of Pythagoras just as much as the Pythagoreans themselves: the only difference was that they were walking slipshod.

Aristoxenus was one of Aristotle's own disciples, and therefore was no fool; and if he had discovered the tempered scale, he would have gone on logically to its consequences, unlike the modern musicians who still parade the ancient terminology though they have nothing to which it corresponds. The piano and all keyed instruments are made with equal temperament, and it surely is ridiculous to keep to five black keys and seven white now that we have dropped the system on which the seven and five were based. They ought to have black keys and white alternately all through so that music could be written in a simpler form.

The old Greek notation was arranged for one-and-twenty notes within the octave, each of the seven original notes being followed by two supplementary notes. And as the compass was three octaves and a third, there were seventy notes in all.

Two letters were assigned to every note, one set of letters being prescribed for instruments and another set for voices. Apparently the two sets were not used concurrently, as in singing with an accompaniment all through. In songs the melody ran on, but the words did not necessarily begin at the first note or finish at the last, and there might be breaks between; and the lettering for instruments was used in these places and the lettering for voices in the rest.[2]

[1] Euclid, *Sectio Canonis*, prop. 9; Ptolemy, *Harmonica*, i. 9.
[2] Aristeides, *De Musica*, i, p. 26, says that the lettering for instruments

This is the lettering for voices, taking the notes in order of ascent :

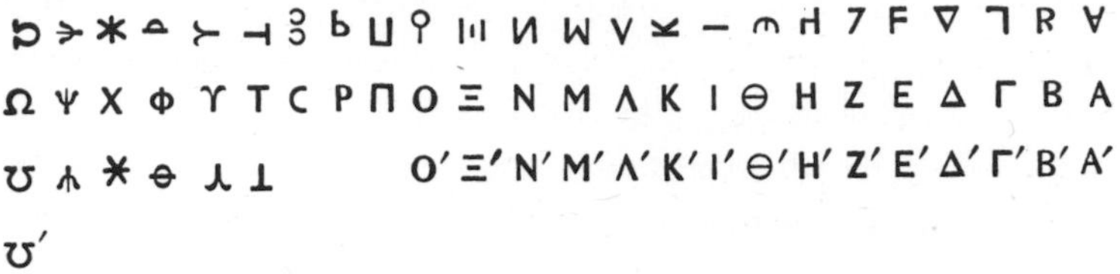

And this is the lettering for instruments :

Thus in the lettering for voices the common letters of the alphabet are taken in their natural order from Α to Ω. Next beyond the common Ω comes ∀, a modified Α, beginning the alphabet again with every letter modified. And next before the common Α comes Ʊ, a modified Ω, finishing the alphabet with another set of modifications. In the lettering for instruments the modifications are introduced in groups of three, the object being to associate each pair of supplementary notes with the original note to which they properly belonged. The lettering for voices omits the letters σ, ρ, π and passes on from ⊥ to Ο′, Ξ′, Ν′ &c., for the sixteen highest notes ; and in both letterings these sixteen highest notes are distinguished only by an accent from the notes an octave lower down. It looks as if these sixteen notes were added at a later time.

Alypius describes the letters carefully in setting out the scales. In his *Eisagogê Musicê* he sets out five-and-forty scales of eighteen notes apiece, not merely writing down the letters,

was used for τὰ ἐν ταῖς ᾠδαῖς μεσαυλικά, or interludes, and ψιλὰ κρούματα, or 'bare twangs', i. e. instrumental notes unaccompanied by voices. For an example see p. 24, lines 19 to 21.

but describing every letter every time that it occurs. Thus A
and V are Alpha and Alpha upside down, and Ⱶ and ⅄ and ⅄
and ⅂ are the left and right halves of Alpha looking up and
looking down. But he must have been mistaken in deriving ⊌
and ⊓ from ⊓ instead of H, and also in deriving ⅂ from ⊓, as
this would naturally be ⅁, a modification of Δ that matches
the adjacent ◁ and ⋀, and clearly / and \ are modifications of
N and И, not accents as he says. In the lettering for instruments two of the half Alphas are attached to Z and the other
two to ⅃, although the letters elsewhere come in groups of three.
And there is an anomaly in the lowest notes as well: they end
with T ⅄ ⴲ ✕ ◁ ⅁ just as the lettering for voices ends with
⊣⅄ ⸽ ✕ ⋗ ꝺ. This looks as if the lettering for instruments was
invented at a time when the scale did not extend beyond two
octaves, Ɛ to Z.

This notation can be simplified by transcribing the ancient
letters into modern letters in the following way:

voice

e	e^1	e^2	f	f^1	f^2	g	g^1	g^2	a	a^1	a^2	b	b^1	b^2	c	c^1	c^2	d	d^1	d^2	e	e^1	e^2

Instr

Ω Ψ X Φ Υ T C P ⊓ O Ξ N M ⋀ K I Θ H Z E Δ Γ B A

| f | f^1 | f^2 | g | g^1 | g^2 | a | a^1 | a^2 | b | b^1 | b^2 | c | c^1 | c^2 | d | d^1 | d^2 | e | e^1 | e^2 | f | f^1 | f^2 |

O′ Ξ′ N′ M′ ⋀′ K′ I′ Θ′ H′ Z′ E′ Δ′ Γ′ B′ A′

| g | g^1 | g^2 | a | a^1 | a^2 | | b | b^1 | b^2 | c | c^1 | c^2 | d | d^1 | d^2 | e | e^1 | e^2 | f | f^1 | f^2 |

K′ ′⅄′ И′ ⊓′◁′⋀′< ′V′ >′⊏′⊔′⊐′N′ /′\′

υ′

g

Z′

In a degenerate form of ancient music there were notes of equal pitch, like our A sharp and B flat. In setting out a scale of semitones, Gaudentius puts ⌐, ⊢, ⵠ, b, ⵕ, ιιι in the scale with ⊣, Ⴑ, N as ὁμότονα, while Aristeides puts ⌐, ⊣, ⵠ, Ⴑ, ⵕ, И in the scale with ⊢, b, ιιι as συμφωνίαι. But the origin of these *symphones* or *homotones* is plain enough. The old notation provided for a pair of supplementary notes after each of the original notes, putting ⊢ (υ) and ⊣ (τ) between ⌐ (φ) and ⵠ (σ), b (ρ) and Ⴑ (π) between ⵠ (σ) and ⵕ (ο), &c. But when the scale was limited to semitones, there was only one supplementary note between φ and σ, only one between σ and ο, &c. ; and as these supplementary notes were placed about half-way between, it did not really matter whether they were known as υ or τ, as ρ or π, &c. Gaudentius, however, has selected the letters that come first, υ after φ, ρ after σ, ξ after ο, &c., while Aristeides has selected the letters that come second, τ, π, ν, &c.[1]

With that degenerate scale it was impossible to play such music as the hymns discovered at Delphi. These have passages where *e* is followed by e^1 and e^1 by e^2, and others where c^2 is followed by c^1 and c^1 by *c*. If e^1 and e^2 were notes of equal pitch, and so also c^2 and c^1, there would merely be a repetition of one note, not two notes in succession with the second a little higher or lower than the first. It also was impossible to play the scales that had a^1 and a^2, b^1 and b^2, &c., in succession.

According to Alypius the scales were formed of eighteen notes apiece; and there were forty-five scales in all, or fifteen scales of three types each—diatonic, chromatic, and enharmonic. In the chromatic and enharmonic types the letters were just the same ; and in the diatonic type they also were the same, with the exceptions of notes 4, 7, 10, 14, and 17. Putting the diatonic notes for these in brackets, the entire system is reducible to this :

---

[1] Gaudentius, *Eisagogé*, 22 ; Aristeides, *De Musica*, i, p. 27.

	1	2	3	4	(4)	5	6	7	(7)	8	9	10	(10)	11	12	13	14	(14)	15	16	17	(17)	18
HYPO-DORIAN	f	g	g¹	g²	(a²)	c	c¹	c²	(d²)	f	f¹	f²	(g²)	a²	g	g¹	g²	(a²)	c	c¹	c²	(d²)	f
HYPO-IASTIAN	f²	g²	a	a²	(b)	c²	d	d²	(e)	f²	g	g²	(a)	b	g²	a	a²	(b)	c²	d	d²	(e)	f²
HYPO-PHRYGIAN	g	a	a¹	a²	(c)	d	d¹	d²	(f)	g	g¹	g²	(a²)	c	a	a¹	a²	(c)	d	d¹	d²	(f)	g
HYPO-AEOLIAN	g²	a²	b	b²	(c²)	d²	e	e²	(f²)	g²	a	a²	(b)	c²	a²	b	b²	(c²)	d²	e	e²	(f²)	g²
HYPO-LYDIAN	a	b	b¹	b²	(d)	e	e¹	e²	(g)	a	a¹	a²	(c)	d	b	b¹	b²	(d)	e	e¹	e²	(g)	a
DORIAN	a²	c	c¹	c²	(d²)	f	f¹	f²	(g²)	a²	b¹	b²	(c²)	d²	c	c¹	c²	(d²)	f	f¹	f²	(g²)	a²
IASTIAN	b	c²	d	d²	(e)	f²	g	g²	(a)	b	c	c²	(d)	e	c²	d	d²	(e)	f²	g	g²	(a)	b
PHRYGIAN	c	d	d¹	d²	(f)	g	g¹	g²	(a²)	c	c¹	c²	(d²)	f	d	d¹	d²	(f)	g	g¹	g²	(a²)	c
AEOLIAN	c²	d²	e	e²	(f²)	g²	a	a²	(b)	c²	d	d²	(e)	f²	d²	e	e²	(f²)	g²	a	a²	(b)	c²
LYDIAN	d	e	e¹	e²	(g)	a	a¹	a²	(c)	d	d¹	d²	(f)	g	e	e¹	e²	(g)	a	a¹	a²	(c)	d
HYPER-DORIAN	d²	f	f¹	f²	(g²)	a²	b¹	b²	(c²)	d²	e¹	e²	(f²)	g²	f	f¹	f²	(g²)	a²	b¹	b²	(c²)	d²
HYPER-IASTIAN	e	f²	g	g²	(a)	b	c	c²	(d)	e	f	f²	(g)	a	f²	g	g²	(a)	b	c	c²	(d)	e
HYPER-PHRYGIAN	f	g	g¹	g²	(a²)	c	c¹	c²	(d²)	f	f¹	f²	(g²)	a²	g	g¹	g²	(a²)	c	c¹	c²	(d²)	f
HYPER-AEOLIAN	f²	g²	a	a²	(b)	c²	d	d²	(e)	f²	g	g²	(a)	b	g²	a	a²	(b)	c²	d	d²	(e)	f²
HYPER-LYDIAN	g	a	a¹	a²	(c)	d	d¹	d²	(f)	g	g¹	g²	(a²)	c	a	a¹	a²	(c)	d	d¹	d²	(f)	g
	1	2	3	4	(4)	5	6	7	(7)	8	9	10	(10)	11	12	13	14	(14)	15	16	17	(17)	18

Each of these scales is constructed of an octave, notes 1 to 8, containing a tone, notes 1 and 2, and two fourths, notes 2 to 5 and 5 to 8. After the second fourth there is a third fourth, notes 8 to 11, and also a second octave repeating the first octave higher up, this octave likewise containing a tone, notes 8 and 12, and two fourths, notes 12 to 15 and 15 to 18. This tone and the fourth fourth, notes 8 and 12 to 15, overlapped with the third fourth, notes 8 to 11, note (14) being the same as note 11.

The first fourth (notes 2 to 5) was called the highest (*tetrachordon hypatón*), as the Greeks said 'high' where we say 'low', the second (notes 5 to 8) was called the midmost (*tetrachordon mesón*), the third (notes 8 to 11) was called the joined (*tetrachordon synémmenón*) as it joined on to the second, the fourth (notes 12 to 15) was called the disjoined (*tetrachordon diezeugmenón*) as there was a tone between it and the second, and the fifth (notes 15 to 18) was called the extreme (*tetrachordon hyperbolaeón*). The names of the notes were : 1. *proslambanomenos*, 2. *hypaté hypatón*, 3. *parhypaté hypatón*, 4. *lichanos hypatón*, (4) *diatonos hypatón*, 5. *hypaté mesón*, 6. *parhypaté mesón*, 7. *lichanos mesón*, (7) *diatanos mesón*, 8. *mesé*, 9. *trité synémmenón*, 10. *paranété synémmenón*, (10) *diatonos synémmenón*, 11 *nété synémmenón*, 12. *paramesé*, 13. *trité diezeugmenón*, 14. *paranété diezeugmenón*, (14) *diatonos diezeugmenón*, 15. *nété diezeugmenón*, 16. *trité hyperbolaeón*, 17. *paranété hyperbolaeón*, (17) *diatonos hyperbolaeón*, 18. *nété hyperbolaeón*.

In the Lydian scale notes 1 to 8 are the same as notes (4) to 11 in the Hypo-Lydian, and (4) to 11 in the Lydian are the same as 1 to 8 in the Hyper-Lydian. These three scales therefore seem to come from one with five successive fourths, *b–e*, *e–a*, *a–d*, *d–g*, *g–c*; and the other scales, Aeolian, Phrygian, &c., have the same connexion with those that are distinguished from them by the prefixes Hypo and Hyper. Moreover, notes 8 to 11 in any scale are the same as notes 12 to 15 in the scale that comes next but one before it in the list; and thus it was an easy matter to pass from one scale to another.

According to Aristeides, much smaller scales were used in very early times : three of an octave each, one with a tone more, one with a tone less, and one with two tones less. His statement is that the Dorian scale then was g, a, a^1, a^2, d, e, e^1, e^2, a ; the Phrygian was the same, but with g in place of a, the Lydian was e^1, e^2, a, b, b^1, b^2, e, e^1, the Mixo-Lydian was e, e^1, e^2, g, a, a^1, a^2, e, the Syntono-Lydian was e, e^1, e^2, a, c, and the Iastian was e, e^1, e^2, a, c, d. (All the notes in these six scales are in the ordinary Hypo-Lydian scale, notes 5 to 18.) He quotes Plato for the six names, Mixo-Lydian, Syntono-Lydian, &c. ; and Plato certainly speaks of the six as if they were the only scales in use in his time. Heracleides, however, uses the five ordinary names ; and he lived at the same time as Plato. There was much squabbling over names. Heracleides said that Dorian, Iastian, and Aeolian were the original Greek scales, and Lydian and Phrygian came in afterwards, whereas Aristoxenus said that Iastian and Hypo-Iastian were derived from Phrygian, Aeolian and Hypo-Aeolian were derived from Lydian, and Hyper-Dorian, Hyper-Iastian and Hyper-Phrygian were all derived from Mixo-Lydian. Heracleides probably was right in saying that national names did not necessarily imply a national type of music.[1]

The essential difference between the scales did not arise from pitch, but from the great variety of intervals they would admit. For example, eleven of the fifteen scales do not contain the notes b^1 or e^1. Iastian has b, b^1, b^2, and Lydian has e, e^1, e^2, while Hyper-Iastian and Hypo-Lydian both have b, b^1, b^2, and e, e^1, e^2. Consequently these were the only scales in which composers could employ the smallest intervals of all, b–b^1, b^1–b^2,

[1] Aristeides gives these six scales, De Musica, i, pp. 21, 22, and quotes Aristoxenus on p. 23 as to the ordinary scales ; but his quotation goes beyond the statement in the extant work of Aristoxenus, Harmonica Stoecheia, ii, p. 37. Heracleides (of Pontus) is quoted by Athenaeus, xiv. 19-21, 624 C–626 A. As to Plato see Republic, iii. 398 E–399 A.

e–e^1, e^1–e^2 : which intervals were only about an eighth part of a tone. Again, Dorian has b^2 and Aeolian has e^2, while Hyper-Dorian and Hypo-Aeolian both have b^2 and e^2. Consequently these four scales, and the four already mentioned, are the only scales admitting the next smallest intervals, b–b^2, b^2–c, e–e^2, e^2–f. These are somewhat less than quarter-tones, being fractions of b–c and e–f, whereas c–c^1, c^1–c^2, d–d^1, &c. are rather more than quarter-tones, being fractions of c–d, d–e, &c. (Reckoning a mean semitone as 100, b–c and e–f are 90 each, whereas c–d, d–e, &c. are each 204.) Phrygian does not admit these lesser quarter-tones, but only the larger quarter-tones, c–c^1, c^1–c^2, d–d^1, &c ; nor can the lesser quarter-tones be found in Hypo-Phrygian or Hyper-Phrygian, Hypo-Dorian or Hyper-Lydian; and Hypo-Iastian and Hyper-Aeolian have no quarter-tones at all, but only semitones.

Composers would get quite another type of music from these scales with semitones than from the Phrygian with its quarter-tones or from the Iastian or the Lydian with their eighth parts of tones. And the difference would not depend entirely on the size of the intervals, but partly on their frequency. For instance, the proportion of eighth parts of tones to quarter-tones or semitones is one to four in the Iastian scale, two to three in the Lydian, three to two in the Hyper-Iastian and four to one in the Hypo-Lydian; and as these other intervals were quarter-tones in the Lydian and Hypo-Lydian, and semitones in the Iastian and Hyper-Iastian, the nature of the music must have depended very largely on the choice of scale. And this is probably the reason why such different emotions were aroused by music in one scale and by music in another.[1]

Euclid gives the method of setting out the ordinary diatonic scale. In his *Sectio Canonis*, proposition 19, he says, "Take

---

[1] In his *Modes of Ancient Greek Music* the late Mr. D. B. Monro identified the modes (ἁρμονίαι) with the keys, but did not perceive that different keys had different scales with very different intervals.

a string, length a to x, and divide it into four equal parts at d and a and a: then a–d will be a fourth, ratio 4 to 3, and a–a and a–a will be octaves, ratio 2 to 1. Halve d–x at d: then d–d will be an octave, ratio 2 to 1. Reduce a–x by one third of its length, making e: then a–e will be a fifth, ratio 3 to 2. Double e–x at e: then e–e will be an octave, ratio 2 to 1. Reduce e–x by one third of its length, making b: then e–b will be a fifth, ratio 3 to 2. Double b–x at b: then b–b will be an octave, ratio 2 to 1." Thus, if the length of the string is 144, a comes at 144, b at 128, d at 108, e at 96, a at 72, b at 64, d at 54, e at 48, and a at 36. Each octave therefore has two tones, a–b and d–e, with one fourth, e–a, and one third, b–d. He speaks of these nine notes as 'fixed' and the other nine as 'movable'; and in proposition 20 he says, " Increase a–x by one eighth of its length, making g, and increase g–x by one eighth of its length, making f: then a–g and g–f will be tones, ratio 9 to 8. Increase f–x by a third of its length, making c: then f–c will be a fourth, ratio 4 to 3. Increase c–x by half its length to f: then c–f will be a fifth, ratio 3 to 2. Double c–f at c: then c–c will be an octave, ratio 2 to 1. Reduce d–x by a quarter of its length, making g: then d–g will be a fourth, ratio 4 to 3." Thus c will come at $121\frac{1}{2}$, f at $91\frac{1}{8}$, g at 81, c at $60\frac{3}{4}$, f at $45\frac{9}{16}$, and g at $40\frac{1}{2}$. The net result is that the intervals a–b, c–d, d–e, f–g, g–a, &c., will all be tones, ratio 9 to 8, and b–c, e–f, &c., will be leimmas,[1] ratio 256 to 243.

Euclid speaks of the notes by their names, *proslambanomenos*, *hypatê hypatôn*, &c., and in saying that c, f, g, c, f, g are movable notes he is referring to the second note in each of the fourths b–e and b–e and the second and third notes in each of the fourths e–a and e–a. The movement could have been effected by bringing in the supplementary notes, a^1, a^2, b^1, b^2, &c. Suppose that a–a^1, c–c^1, d–d^1, f–f^1, g–g^1 had the ratio

---

[1] The earliest Pythagoreans called a *leimma* a *diesis*, and in saying that a *diaschisma* was half a *diesis* they probably meant it was a quarter-tone, but the name *diesis* was usually applied to quarter-tones and other very small intervals. A *leimma* and an *apotomê* together made a tone.

36 to 35 and $b-b^1$, $e-e^1$ had the ratio 64 to 63 (see below) and take 128, 121½, 108, 96 as the length of strings for b, c, d, e, the lengths for b^1, c^1, d^1, e^1 will then be 126, 118⅓, 105, 94½. Thus, while the fourth, b, c, d, e, has the ratios 256 to 243, 9 to 8, and 9 to 8, that is, a leimma of 90 followed by two major tones of 204 apiece, the fourth, b^1, c^1, d^1, e^1, has the ratios 16 to 15, 9 to 8, and 10 to 9, that is, a diatonic semitone of 112 followed by a major tone of 204 and a minor tone of 182, and the fourth, b^1, c, c^1, e^1, has the ratios 28 to 27, 36 to 35, and 5 to 4, that is, two intervals of 63 and 49 followed by a major third of 386, and this is the fourth that Ptolemy describes as the enharmonic tetrachord of Archytas.

Tones could be divided by reckoning their ratios as 18 to 16 in place of 9 to 8, and thereby bringing in the ratios 18 to 17 and 17 to 16. As there were five tones in an octave, these ratios would bring in five supplementary notes, and as the tones were $a-b$, $c-d$, $d-e$, $f-g$, $g-a$, these supplementary notes would belong to a, c, d, f, g. Now, the scales show that a^2, c^2, d^2, f^2, g^2 were the only supplementary notes that had to stand a fourth or a fifth away from one or other of the original notes: so these must represent the supplementary notes that were inserted in the middle of each tone. Two more such notes could then have been inserted in each tone by doubling the ratios 18 to 17 and 17 to 16, and thereby bringing in the ratios 36 to 35, 35 to 34, 34 to 33, and 33 to 32. But the notation shows that only one more supplementary note was inserted in each tone; and as a^1 came between a and a^2, c^1 between c and c^2, and so on, the ratios 36 to 35 and 35 to 34 were those that fixed the five notes a^1, c^1, d^1, f^1, g^1. If the intervals $b-c$ and $e-f$ are treated in the same way, one supplementary note will be obtained by doubling the ratio 256 to 243 and bringing in the ratios 512 to 499 and 499 to 486, and then another by doubling the ratio 512 to 499 and bringing in the ratios 1024 to 1011 and 1011 to 998; and the first of these two notes will be b^2 or e^2 and the second will be b^1 or e^1. The net result is that an octave will have strings of these lengths, the figures being multiplied in order to get rid of fractions :

e, 3072	f, 2916	g, 2592	a, 2304
e^1, 3033	f^1, 2835	g^1, 2520	a^1, 2240
e^2, 2994	f^2, 2754	g^2, 2448	a^2, 2176
b, 2048	c, 1944	d, 1728	e, 1536
b^1, 2022	c^1, 1890	d^1, 1680	
b^2, 1996	c^2, 1836	d^2, 1632	

Having some doubts about the working of a scale constructed in this way, the present writer fixed the pitch of e at 324 double vibrations per second, and thus obtained the following pitch for the ensuing notes, the rate of vibration varying inversely as the length of the strings :

b, 243	c, 256	d, 288	e, 324
b^1, 246·12	c^1, 263·31	d^1, 296·23	
b^2, 249·33	c^2, 271·06	d^2, 304·94	

Having done this, he ordered a set of tuning-forks giving these vibrations. The forks were made for him by Messrs. Valantine & Carr at Sheffield and tested by them on their tonometer and were tested afterwards by the late Mr. Hipkins on the Ellis tonometer. (This was in 1896.) Excepting b, b^1, b^2, the notes all come out clearly at intervals that can easily be recognized ; and the sequence is exceedingly melodious. But when b or b^1 or b^2 is sounded by itself, there is some difficulty in saying which of them it is, although the difference is obvious enough when they are sounded in succession.

In the above reckoning the ratio 256 to 243 in b–c and e–f has been treated in exactly the same way as the ratio 9 to 8 in c–d, d–e, &c. ; but this may not be quite correct, as 2016 and 3024 (not 2022 and 3033) appear to be the proper lengths of string for b^1 and e^1. With 2016 for b^1 there will be the ratio 4 to 5 in g^1–b^1, the ratio 5 to 6 in b^1–d^1, the ratio 6 to 7 in b^1–d, the ratio 7 to 8 in d–e^1, the ratio 9 to 10 in d^1–e^1, the ratio 15 to 16 in e^1-f^1, the ratio 27 to 28 in e^1-f. As all these ratios were in use, there must have been some notes in the positions that would produce them. And it may be noted that, with b^1 at 2016, there is the same difference between b-b^1 (ratio 63 to 64) and a-a^1 (ratio 35 to 36) as between a minor and a major tone.

As already stated, the usual method of dividing intervals was to take a length of string midway between the lengths that formed the interval—for instance, 17 between 18 and 16—but there must have been some small adjustments to make a scale yield all the intervals that were required. Seven well-known intervals result from moving b^1 and e^1 from 2022 and 3033 to 2016 and 3024, and presumably a like result would follow from moving b^2 and e^2 from 1996 and 2994 into some neighbouring place; but the present writer has failed to find that neighbouring place.

Few pieces of the old Greek music are in existence now. There are three inscribed on stone, some fragments written on papyrus and three complete pieces in ordinary manuscript. Two others have been printed; but these may not be genuine.

The excavations at Delphi disclosed a number of inscriptions on the walls of the Treasury of the Athenians; and two of these inscriptions are hymns to Apollo with music. The notes are in the spaces between the lines of words, each note above the syllable to which it belongs; and when the syllable has two notes it is spelt accordingly, βωμοιοῖσι for βωμοῖσι, ταούρων for ταύρων, and so on. The first hymn has the lettering for voices, and the notes are Ⅎ or d^1, Φ or g, Y or g^1, O or b, M or c, Λ or c^1, K or c^2, I or d, ⊖ or d^1, Γ or f, B or f^1, ʊ or g, ⅄ or g^1, ✷ or g^2. Excepting b and f^1, all these notes come in the Phrygian scale: see p. 9. The second hymn has the lettering for instruments, and the notes are Γ or e, L or e^1, Ⅎ or g, C or a, ᴗ or a^1, Ɔ or a^2, K or b, ⋎ or b^1, < or d, V or d^1, Ɛ or e, ⊔ or e^1, Z or g, ʃ or g^1, ⅃ or a. Excepting b and b^1

and g^1, these notes are in the Lydian scale. Some of the notes come in much oftener than others, especially in the second hymn. In that hymn 40 per cent. of the notes are either e or e^1, 22 per cent. are d or d^1, 18 per cent. are a or a^1, and the remaining 20 per cent. takes in the other nine notes. In the first hymn 30 per cent. of the notes are c or c^1 or c^2, 25 per cent. are g or g^1, 18 per cent. are d or d^1, 12 per cent. are f^1, and the remaining 15 per cent. takes in the other six notes.

Both hymns have suffered from the collapse of the wall on which they were inscribed. The first hymn has broken into two large bits and a few little bits, and the second is almost all in little bits. The following lines are from one of the big bits of the first : [1]

```
   Γ      ℧ ⅄ ℧
ΚΑΥΤΑΜΕΓΑΛΟΠΟΛΙΣΑΘΘΙΣΕΥΧΑΙΕ

  Κ  Λ  Μ   Ο    Κ  Λ  Κ  Γ   ℧ ⅄ ℧
ΙΦΕΡΟΠΛΟΙΟΝΑιΟΥΣΑΤΡΙΤΩΩΝΙΔΟΣΔΑ

 Θ  Γ    Μ     Γ Β  Γ  Λ Κ   Γ Ο Μ Γ
ΟΝΑΘΡΑΥΣΤΟΝΑΓΙΟΙΣΔΕΒΩΜΟΙΟΙΣΙΝΑ

 Κ  Μ  Λ Κ Λ   Μ       Λ Μ  Ο    Κ
ΑΙΣΤΟΣΑΙΕΙΘΕΝΕΩΝΜΗΡΑΤΑΟΥΡΩΝΟΜΟΥ

 Λ   Γ Μ ℧ Θ  Ι   Θ  Γ   Θ    Υ Ο  Μ Λ Μ
ΟΥΔΕΝΙΝΑΡΑΨΑΤΜΟΣΕΣΥΛΟΜΠΟΝΑΝΑΚΙΔΝ

 Ο Υ Ο     Μ   Λ Μ   Λ Κ  Λ Μ
ΤΑΙΛΙΓΥΔΕΛΩΤΟΟΣΒΡΕΜΩΝΑΕΙΟΛΟΙΟΙΣ

  Μ  Υ Ο  Μ   Λ  Μ  Γ  Λ Κ Γ   Μ
ΛΕΣΙΝΩΙΔΑΑΝΚΡΕΚΕΙΧΡΥΣΕΑΔΑΔΥΘΡΟΥ

  Κ Λ Μ   Ο Υ Ο Μ Λ  Μ    Ο Φ ℧
ΘΑΡΙΣΥΜΝΟΙΣΙΝΑΝΑΜΕΛΠΕΤΑΙΟΔΕΤ

  ⅄ Γ   ℧  Θ   Γ         ⅄       ℧
ΩΩΝΠΡΟΠΑΣΕΣΜΟΣΑΘΘΙΔΑΛΑΧΩΝ
```

This may be transcribed as follows:

$$f \qquad g\ g^1\ g$$

ἴθι,) κλυτὰ μεγαλόπολις ᾿Αθθίς, εὐχαιε-

$$c^2 \quad c^1\ c\ b \qquad c^2\ c^1\ c^2 \quad f \quad g\ g^1\ g$$

ἰσ)ι φερόπλοιο ναίουσα Τριτωωνίδος δά(πε

$$d^1\ f\ c \qquad f\ f^1\ f \quad c^1\ c^2\ f\ b\ c \quad f$$

δ)ον ἄθραυστον· ἁγίοις δὲ βωμοιοῖσιν ῾Α-

$$c^2\ c \qquad c^1\ c^2\ c^1 \qquad c \qquad c^1\ c\ b \qquad c^2$$

φ)αιστος αἰείθε(ι) νέων μῆρα ταούρων· ὁμου-

$$c^1\ f\ c\ g\ d^1 \quad d\ d^1\ f \qquad d^1\ g^1\ b\ c\ c^1\ c$$

οὗ δέ νιν ῎Αραψ ἀτμὸς ἐς ῎Υλομπον ἀνακίδν(α-

$$b \quad g^1\ b \qquad c \quad c^1\ c \quad c^1\ c^2\ c^1\ c$$

ται· λιγὺ δὲ λωτοὸς βρέμων ἀειόλοιοις (μέ-

$$c \quad g^1 \quad b\ c \quad c^1\ c \quad f\ c^1 \qquad c^2\ f\ c$$

λεσιν ὠιδαὰν κρέκει, χρυσέα δ᾽ ἀδύθρου(ς κί-

$$c^2\ c^1 \quad c\ b\ g^1 \quad b\ c\ c^1\ c\ b \quad g\ g$$

θαρις ὕμνοισιν ἀναμέλπεται. ὁ δὲ τ-

$$g^1\ f \quad g\ d^1\ f \qquad g^1\ g$$

εχνιτ)ωῶν πρόπας ἐσμὸς ᾿Αθθίδα λαχών

In the hymns that are in manuscript (see p. 20), a note is written over every syllable, and sometimes the same note is written several times successively; but in these hymns on marble there is no such repetition of the written notes, and many of the syllables have no notes above them. Presumably these syllables were sung to the same notes as the syllable next before them. Thus in the fourth line of the above extract c would be repeated twice and c^1 and b once each, making the line run, c^2, c, c^1, c^2, c^1, c^1, c, c, c, c^1, c, b, b, c^2. These lines are not complete; but, roughly speaking, they have ninety of these written notes and thirty blanks. Thirty-seven of the written notes are only a quarter of a tone away from the next

note before them. There are two groups of seven notes each,
$c, c^1, c^2, c^1, c, c^1, c$, and $c, c^1, c, c^1, c^2, c^1, c$, and there are ten
groups of three notes each, c, c^1, c ; c^2, c^1, c^2 ; d^1, d, d^1 ; f^1, f,
f^1 ; g, g^1, g ; c^2, c^1, c ; and in all these groups except the last
the final note is the same as the first. Besides the thirty-seven
quarter-tones there are twelve semitones, two of which are $c-c^2$
and ten are $b-c$. Some of the other intervals seem dispropor-
tionately large; one is an octave, $g-g$, two are fifths, g^1-d^1 and
$c-g$, two are nearly three tones each, $b-f$ and c^2-g, six are
fourths, $c-f$, and so on. And these large intervals are inter-
spersed amongst the smallest. For example, the third of those
lines has two fourths, $f-c$, $c-f$, followed by two quarter-tones,
$f-f^1$, f^1-f, then two tones and a quarter, $f-c^1$, a quarter-tone,
c^1-c^2, two tones, c^2-f, and three tones $f-b$. In round numbers,
40 per cent. of the intervals are quarter-tones, 15 per cent. are
semitones, 40 per cent. range from a tone to a fourth, and
5 per cent. are about three tones or more.

The following lines are from the second of these hymns : [1]

⊏ ⋎ <   ⊏ ⋃ ⊏   Γ   <
ΤΟΤΕΛΙΠΩΓΚΥΥΝΘΙΑΝΝΑΑΣΟΝΕ.......ΣΠΡ
K ⋎ <   ⊏   ˥⊏⋃ ⊏   < ⊏
ΚΑΡΠΟΓΚΛΥΤΑΝΑΤΘΙΔΕΠΙΓΑΑΛ.........ΤΡΙΤΩΩΝΙ

And they may be transcribed as follows :

$e\ b^1\ \ d$ $e\ \ e^1\ e$ e d
τότε λιπὼγ Κυνθίαν ναᾶσον ἐ(πέβα θεὸ)ς πρ(ωτό-

$b\ b^1\ d$ e a $e\ e^1$ e $d\ e$
καρπογ κλυτὰν 'Ατθίδ' ἐπὶ γααλ(όφωι πρῶνι) Τριτωωνί(δος.

There is the same intermixture here of large and little
intervals, and some of the little intervals are smaller still,
being only eighths of tones, not quarters. Thus the first of
these lines has a tone, $d-e$, followed by two eighth parts

---

[1] *Bulletin, &c.*, vol. 18, plate 12 *bis*, and vol. 17, page 606, fragment 9.

κατολοφύρομαι, κατολοφύρομαι,
ματέρος αἶμα σᾶς, ὅ σ’ ἀναβακχεύει ;
ὁ μέγας ὄλβος οὐ μόνιμος ἐν βροτοῖς·
ἀνὰ δὲ λαῖφος ὥς
τις ἀκάτου θοᾶς τινάξας δαίμων
κατέκλυσεν δεινῶν πόνων ὡς πόντου κ.τ.λ.

And the papyrus has :

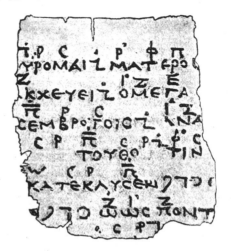

The notes are Φ or *g*, C or *a*, P or *a*[1], Π or *a*[2], I or *d*, Z or *e*,
E or *e*[1], which are notes (4), 5̇, 6, 7, 8̇, 12, 13̇, in the Lydian
scale. There is a mark like a Z dividing the verses, and there is
always a dot above this Z and a dot behind the note that
follows. Thus there is a Ż to divide κατολοφύρομαι from
ματέρος, and a P· to give the note for μα : so also a Ż to divide
ἀναβακχεύει from ὁ μέγας, and an I· to give the note for ὁ ;
and again a Ż to divide βροτοῖς from ἀνά, and an I· to give the
note for ά. But evidently the scribe was puzzled by the half
verse ἀνὰ δὲ λαῖφος ὥς and completed it with τις ἀκάτου θοᾶς,
putting a Ż above the line to divide θοᾶς from τινάξας, and a
Φ· to give the note for τι, as though this were the beginning of
another verse. And having thus lost the guidance of the metre,
he makes a long scrawl after κατέκλυσεν, and tries to start

another verse at ὡς πόντου by adding Ż and I· above the line. Apparently there was a dot and dash ∸ to mark the first note of the fourth foot in every verse. This is distinctly visible above the note for ἐμ in ἐμ βροτοῖς at the end of the third verse, above the note for τοῦ in ἀκάτου θοᾶς, which is treated here as the end of the fourth verse, and above the note for σεν in κατέκλυσεν, as though the scribe were trying to make the fifth verse end with κατέκλυσεν πόνων in order to begin the sixth with ὡς πόντου. There is also a trace of it above the note for φυρ in κατολοφύρομαι at the end of the first verse, but not above the note for βακ in ἀναβακχεύει at the end of the second.

The following piece is part of the inscription on a small stone column found at Tralles in Asia Minor.[1] The column appears to be the pedestal of a statue of a man named Seikelos, and the inscription says that he put it up as a memorial of himself. The song may be transcribed as follows :

$$
\begin{array}{cccccccccc}
\overline{} & \overset{\cdot/}{} & \overset{\div/}{} & & \overline{} & \cdot\cdot & & \overline{} & \overset{\cdot/}{} & \\
a & e & e & c^2de\ \overset{\cdot}{d} & c^2\ d & e\,dc^2 & b & a & bg & a
\end{array}
$$

ὅσον ζῆς, φαίνου· μηδὲν ὅλως σὺ λυποῦ· πρὸς

$$
\begin{array}{ccccccccc}
\cdot\ \cdot\ \cdot & \overline{}\ \overline{} & \overset{\cdot/}{} & \cdot & \cdot\ \cdot & & \overline{} & \overset{\div/}{} \\
c^2e\,d & c^2dc^2\ \overline{a} & bg & a & c^2b & d & e & c^2 & a\,a\,af^2e
\end{array}
$$

ὀλίγον ἐστὶ τὸ ζῆν· τὸ τέλος ὁ χρόνος ἀπαιτεῖ.

The notes are nos. (4), 5, 6, (7), 8, (10), 11, 12, in the Iastian scale. The sign ∸/ is used here, like the sign Z in the papyrus, for marking off the verses; and there is a dash — above the last note of the third foot, just as the papyrus has a dot and dash above the first note of the fourth foot. Thus the words ὅσον ζῆς must form a verse apart, as they answer to the endings of the verses σὺ λυποῦ, τι τὸ ζῆν, ἀπαιτεῖ, and the word φαίνου will likewise form a verse apart. Also, there are dots above the three notes of the second foot, whereas the papyrus has a dot behind the first note of each verse.

---

[1] Bull. de Corres. Hellénique, vol. 7, p. 277 ; vol. 18, plate 13 ; vol. 48, p. 507.

As the position of the dots and dashes is regulated by the metre, they really are superfluous things ; and this is probably the reason why they do not appear in other bits of ancient music. Of course, they may have been omitted in the copying of the pieces that are in manuscript, but they can never have existed in the Delphic hymns, these being originals on marble slabs. Accents also are absent from the words. They were not invented until 200 B.C. or thereabouts, and really were superfluous, as they only marked the intonation that was already in use. As a rule, the accented syllable has the highest note in the word ; and this shows how much the melody was based upon the ordinary intonation.

There are some fragments of Greek music on the back of a bit of papyrus which has a Latin document of A.D. 156 on the front.[1] It gives the beginning of twenty-three lines of music, but no complete lines ; and 1–12, 16–19, 23, have words with the lettering for voices, while 13–15, 20–22, have the lettering for instruments and no words. Lines 1 to 12 contain the notes Φ or g, C or a, O or b, Ξ or b^1, I or d, Z or e, A or f^2, Ʊ or g, ꙋ or a, which are notes 3, (4), 5, 6, (7), 8, 12, 13, (14), in the Hyper-Iastian scale, and lines 13 to 15 contain the notes Γ or e, ꓱ or f^2, F or g, C or a, ꓽ or b^1, < or d, ⊏ or e, \ or f^2, ꓶ or a, which are notes 1, 2, 3, (4), 6, (7), 8, 11, 12, of that same scale but in the other lettering. But they each have another note ∩ which is not mentioned in Alypius or elsewhere. Possibly, however, it may not be a note, but only a symbol, like the Z in the Euripides papyrus. Some of the notes have a dot · or a dash — above them, or a dot and dash combined ∸, and sometimes two or three adjoining notes are connected by a curve below them, as at the end of the song of Seikelos.

Another fragment of papyrus has some remnants of a Christian hymn written on the back of it, probably before A.D. 300. (The front has farm-accounts.) The end of the hymn [2] may be transcribed :

---

[1] *Sitzungsberichte der k. d. Akad. der Wiss.* 1918, pp. 763 ff.
[2] *Oxyrhynchus Papyri*, part 15, no. 1786.

$$b^1 \, \overline{d:e \, \overline{e}^1} \quad :d \, e : \overline{b^1 b} \quad \overline{d \, b^1 \, e \, d} \quad \times \quad \overline{g} : \overline{b^1 d} \quad \overline{g} \quad : \overline{b b^1 e^1}$$

ποταμῶν ῥοθίων πᾶσαι ὑμνούντων δ' ἡμῶν

$$\overline{a \, a} \quad \overline{g \, a} e^1 \quad : \overline{g \, a} \overline{g} \, \overline{g} e \quad : \overline{d \, e} \quad \times \quad \overline{e \overline{g} \, g} \quad \overline{g \, b^1 \, b}$$

(π)ατέρα χ' υἱὸν χ' ἅγιον πνεῦμα πᾶσαι δυνάμεις

$$\overline{b \, b \, b} \quad \overline{b d} \quad \overline{b} \quad e: \overline{e e^1 b^1} \quad \overline{e d \, d b^1}$$

ἐπιφωνούντων ἀμήν, ἀμήν·

The notes are nos. 6, (7), 8, 12, 13, (14), 15, 16, in the Hypo-
Lydian scale, together with ∩, the note or sign just mentioned,
here transcribed as X. There are some dashes above the notes
and curves below them, the curves connecting the notes belonging
to a single syllable and the dash generally denoting that the
syllable is long. There are also many dots; but their meaning
is not clear. The notes themselves give the little intervals of
b–b^1 and e–e^1 of about an eighth part of a tone, no others less
than tones, ratio 9 to 8, but then two intervals of ratios 8 to 7
and 7 to 6 in a–b^1–d, making 231 and 267 respectively at the
rate of 200 to a mean semitone. And they also give largei
intervals, fourths, fifths, &c., up to a sixth, g–e, intermixed
with the small intervals.

In the song of Seikelos half the intervals are tones or semitones, and the other half are larger, the largest being a fourth;
and there is nothing smaller than a semitone. But in the
fragment of Euripides there are quarters and eighths of tones,
a–a^1, e–e^1, as in the hymn to Nemesis and in the Delphic hymns
and in some of the foregoing fragments; and the old Greek
music lost its character when small intervals went out of use.
Broadly speaking, its characteristic was excessive use of the
very smallest intervals and a free use of the largest intervals
without any proportionate use of intervals of intermediate size.
And it contrasted them abruptly: after a dozen or twenty
notes of nearly equal pitch, the next note might be several

tones away. Yet that style may have been well adapted to the instruments they used: it would sound well with harps or lyres, hautboys or flutes, though it would not suit a modern orchestra.

All musical instruments were known as organs; and what we call an organ was known as the hydraulic organ, or hydraulis. The instrument is described in detail by Vitruvius and Philo, and was essentially the same thing as a modern organ blown by water power. It was invented at Alexandria about 220 or 240 B. C., but the true water-organ was another invention of the same man Ctesibius. In this the water itself produced a musical note in passing through a narrow orifice. There is nothing about water in the story of how Ctesibius came to make the so-called water-organ. He wanted to hang a barber's mirror so that it would stay at the right height: he hung it on a cord which went over a pulley in the middle of the ceiling and over another in the corner of the room, and down into a tube where it carried a counterpoising weight: when this counterpoise went down the tube, it drove the air out and thus produced a note. His organ was merely an enlargement of a very ancient instrument, Pan's Pipes; but with sheaves of great bronze pipes a player could control vast waves of sound. It delighted Nero and other Emperors like him, such as Heliogabalus, and some of Nero's last moments were devoted to improvements in the instrument.[1]

The organ would drown most other instruments unless their power was increased; and about A. D. 350 Ammianus speaks of a lyre as big as a cart with an awning, xiv. 6. 18. The lyre was normally a little instrument that could be carried in one hand. The first lyre was made of the shell of a tortoise fitted with reeds and wrapped round with cow-hide, and it had seven

---

[1] Hero, *Pneumatica*, 66; Vitruvius, ix. 9. 2-4, x. 13. 1-6; Athenaeus, iv. 75. 174 A–E; also xi. 13. 497 D, for the true water-organ, λιγὺν ἦχον σαλπίζει, κρουνοῦ πρὸς ῥύσιν οἰγομένον. (It was in the reign of Euergetes I, not II—the abbreviation β stands for 'king' as well as 'second'.) Suetonius, *Nero*, 41; Lampridius, *Heliogabalus*, 32; Claudian, *De consulatu Fl. Mallii Theodori*, in A. D. 399. In line 317 he calls the organ pipes 'seges aena'. Plato, *Republic*, iii. 399 C, D, for the word 'organ'.

sheep-guts stretched out to a cross-bar between two arms or horns; and the lyre of later times recalled the legendary make. In the Homeric hymn to Hermes the instrument is called a 'lyra', a 'phorminx', and a 'citharis', as if these names were interchangeable; but the last two names were used in later times for a wood or metal instrument of less fantastic shape and having many more strings. There was a greater difference between the two wind instruments that were in common use. The 'syrinx' or 'fistula' was a pipe like a flute, whereas the 'aulos' or 'tibia' was a pipe with a reed in the mouthpiece, like a hautboy, and it usually was played in pairs. The two mouthpieces were fixed into the 'phorbeia', a sort of bandage that went over the player's mouth and round the back of his head, taking off the weight of the pipes and leaving both hands free for fingering the notes. A man could thus play more than one note at a time.[1]

Instruments and voices were not invariably in unison; otherwise there would not have been two separate letterings for them. And the Greeks would not have talked so much about the concords of the Fourth and Fifth if they had never sounded them together. But apparently they thought so much of melody that they did not care to sound two notes at once, and were content to get their concords by sounding the two notes in quick succession. In their Music of the Spheres there should have been a vast concord, as the heavenly bodies moved in circles and the notes would never change: hence the explanation (mentioned by Aristotle, *De Coelo*, ii. 9) that we really hear this music, but do not notice it as it is always going on. But after Kepler had discovered that the planets go round in ellipses he worked out all the scales that they can play, *Harmonicê Mundi* v. 4-9. In gazing at nocturnal skies musicians should remember that Saturn is playing a major third and Jupiter a minor third with its lowest note an octave above Saturn's highest.

---

[1] There are good articles (by Théodore Reinach) on the instruments Tibia, Syrinx, Lyra, in the *Dictionnaire des Antiquités* edited by Daremberg and Saglio, III. 1437, IV. 1596, V. 300.

Writing at Alexandria in A. D. 400 or thereabouts, Olympiodorus speaks of the decay of music.   There were, he says,
survivals of arithmetic and geometry and astronomy, but none
of music; and he quotes a line of Homer, ' we only hear reports
of it and know nothing of it ourselves '.   But if there was decay
just then, there was revival afterwards; at any rate his follower
Proclus knew all about the lengths of string required for the
notes.[1]   Boetius dealt with the whole subject in his *De Musica*,
a tersely written treatise of over 40,000 words.   He discusses
the theories of Pythagoras, Aristoxenus, Ptolemy, and the others,
and covers the whole ground.   And he always uses the Greek
names for the notes, and gives the Greek lettering for them in
both notations, iv. 3.   The only change he mentions is that
Albinus had translated the names of the notes into Latin, putting ' medias ' for ' mesas ', and so on, i. 26.   Boetius died in
A. D. 524 and Cassiodorus in A. D. 575.   He wrote a similar book,
and likewise quotes the standard authors, Euclid, Alypius, &c.
And, like Boetius, he gives the fifteen scales just as they are
given by the earlier writers.

Apparently the ancient lettering was still in use when Pope
Adrian (A. D. 772–95) sent musicians to Charlemagne.   One of
these musicians 'signified the notes by letters of the alphabet
either upright or inverted or forward or backward ', and this
cannot well be anything except the old notation with letters of
the alphabet in various postures.[2]

The old notation was confused by Hucbald.   (He died in
A. D. 930, aged ninety, and thus was born about thirty years
after Charlemagne's death.)   Boetius (*De Musica*, iv. 3) had
given the Lydian scale with both the letterings, and Hucbald
reduced it to a single lettering, using the letters for voices with
some of the notes and the letters for instruments with others:

[1] Olympiodorus in the scholia to Aristotle, p. 16, ed. Brandis.   He received
Proclus at Alexandria in A. D. 426.   The ratios are discussed by Proclus, *in
Timaeum*, a work he had completed by A. D. 437.   The quotation is from the
Iliad, ii. 486.

[2] Eckehard, *De vasibus Sancti Galli*, p. 174, ' literas alphabeti significativas
notulis quibus visum est aut susum aut iusum aut ante aut retro assignari

not, apparently, on any fixed principle, but merely from caprice. And he did not understand what all the letters were. The first note of his scale was ⊢, and Boetius and all his predecessors had described it as a T lying down, but Hucbald took it for the left half of an H standing up. In manuscripts this half H signified an aspirate (*daseia*), and he spoke of it as such ; and his notation was therefore called Daseian. This is in his treatise *De Musica*, but there is quite another system in the treatise *Musica Encheiriadis* that is commonly ascribed to him, but probably is by Oddo, who was somewhat younger : died in A. D. 942 aged sixty-four.[1]

In the old notation the letter Sigma was written as C, not Σ, and it had various postures, C ∪ Ɔ and also Ꙅ୦୦3. Hucbald (or Oddo) seems to have taken these for C and S respectively, as he mentions those letters in the *Encheiriadis* (pp. 153, 174) in connexion with his half H or 'daseia'. He says that one note had a daseia capped by a sloping S (*inclinum*), another was capped by a C turned over (*versum*), and another by a C on its back (*supinum*) or a half C (*dimidium*). These were the signs ᛦ, ᚠ, ᚡ, and they were put in various postures. In this way he could have made an excellent scale with ꓄, ꓶ, ꓩ for *a*, *a*[1], *c*, ᛏ ᚠ ᚡ for *d*, *d*[1], *f*, ᚦ ᚱ ᚱ for *g*, *g*[1], *a*[2], ꓒ, ꓒ, ꓒ for *a*, *a*[1], *c*, and ᒷ, ᒃ, ᒃ for *d*, *d*[1], *f*. There would thus be the same three signs for the first three notes in each of the five fourths, and the posture of the signs would show which fourth they were in. The final note in three of the fourths was the same as the first note in the next fourth, *d g d*, and in one it was the same as the third note in the next, *c*. In the other fourth the final note

excogitavit'. Here 'ante' and 'retro' are equivalent to 'rectum' and 'conversum', and 'iusum' (inversum) to 'supinum' in Boetius, *De Musica*, iv. 3. This was the fourth Eckehard of St. Gall, in Switzerland. He goes on to say that it was all explained by Notker in a letter to Lantpert. This letter is extant—printed in Gerbert, *Scriptores Ecclesiastici de Musica*, vol. i, pp. 95, 96—but it is only an exercise in alliteration by somebody who did not know. Thus '*A*, ut *a*ltius elevetur *a*dmonet'. '*C*, ut *c*ito vel *c*eleriter dicatur *c*ertificat.' '*D*, ut *d*eprimatur *d*emonstrat.' And so on. This letter cannot have been written by such a man as Notker.

[1] These treatises are printed in Gerbert, *l.c.*, pp. 103-229.

was *g̱*, and with a reversed daseia ꟼ for that note and a plain
daseia Ⱶ for *g* at the beginning of the scale, the system would
have been complete. But he muddled it. He introduced a
sloping / (*inclinum*) and an / with a line through it (*perfixum*),
and also an N and a reversed N (*versum*), and made up
four fourths Ꜣ ꜣ N Ꜣ and Ꞙ Ꞙ / Ꞙ and ꞁ ꞁ И ꞁ and Ⱡ Ⱡ X Ⱡ,
but separated them by tones so that the final note of one
should not be the same as the first note of the next. He
thus made them answer to *g a b c*, and *d e f g* and *a b c d* and
e f g a with two signs left over to be used as *b c*. And these
fourths do not correspond with the fourths in the scale.

This notation was for the form of music adopted by the
Church. There were eight scales, or rather pairs of scales,
called Authentical and Plagial respectively. The first pair
(scales 1 and 2) ended with Ꞙ and could go down as far as Ꜣ, but
while the Authentical could go up as far as Ⱡ, the Plagial could
not go up beyond ꞁ. The second pair (scales 3 and 4) ended a
tone higher at Ꞙ, and had ꜣ and Ⱡ and ꞁ as their limits. The third
pair (scales 5 and 6) ended a semitone higher at / with N and
X and И as limits ; and the fourth pair ended a tone higher at
Ꞙ with ꜣ and Ⱡ and ꞁ as limits, as before. There were perfect fifths
between Ꞙ and ꜣ and ꞁ and Ⱡ, and between Ꞙ and ꜣ and ꞁ and Ⱡ :
also between Ꞙ and ꜣ and ꞁ, but not between ꞁ and Ⱡ, and
between / and И and X, but not between / and N. These
defective fifths, *b–f* and *b–f*, were each made up of two major
tones and two leimmas, and thus were only 588, whereas a
perfect fifth is 702 if an octave is 1200. There was also a
defective fourth, *f–b*, consisting of three major tones or 612, so
that this fourth was bigger than those fifths. When music was
in unison those intervals could be avoided, but not when
instruments and voices had to keep a fifth apart.

The old Greek music was normally in unison or with notes an
octave apart, as when men and boys were singing together.
And then came Diaphonia, not meaning Discord (the old sense
of the term), but only that the notes were not in unison. It was

also known as Organum, meaning 'instrument', not necessarily
the kind of instrument we call an organ.   The instrument
accompanied the voice, following its rise and fall, but always
kept a fifth above it or a fifth below.   If there were two voices
an octave apart, the instrument that kept a fifth from one of
them would be a fourth from the other.   And there might be
two instruments : if the voices sang *a* and *a*, the instrument
would either play *d* and *d* or else play *e* and *e*; and a lower
instrument might play *d*, if it was a fifth below the lower voice,
and the scale went down far enough to take it in.

Two specimens of this notation may be transcribed from the *Encheiriadis*, p. 214. They belong to scales 1 and 2, the upper being
from the first Authentical and the lower from the first Plagial.

fga   *a*   *ab*   *a aga*   *gf ga aaa*   *aaagf*   *gd*
Gloria et nunc et semper et in secula seculorum, Amen.
cd   *fe· fg*   *g fgfe*   *fd*   *df*   *fff*   *ffefe*   *cd*

This is a little like the old Greek music in repeating the same
note several times and then moving to the adjoining note and
back again or moving an entire fourth.   But there the likeness
ends.   This music had only seven notes in an octave, whereas
the Greek had twenty-one ; and these seven notes gave nothing
but tones and semitones, not quarter-tones or any of the other
curious intervals in those complicated scales.   That scale of
seven notes was the old Pythagorean scale set out by Euclid—
see above, p. 13—consisting of five major tones of 204 each,
a–b, c–d, d–e,f–g, g–a, and two leimmas of 90 each, *b–c, e–f*;
and Hucbald takes care to say (p. 109) that these intervals were
not precisely halves of tones, though frequently described as
semitones.   In his own notation the four finals Ⱶ, Ⅎ, Ⲓ, Ⅎ are written
as F, C, P, M, and he identifies them with notes (4) to (7) of the
Lydian scale: which is impossible, as there was only a quarter
tone between C and P, and he needs half a tone between.   No
doubt he pitched upon the Lydian scale for comparison, because
Boetius sets out that scale and does not set out any of the

others, although he says he will, *De Musica*, iv. 3 ; and probably Boetius began with the Lydian scale because it comes first in Alypius. But really no comparison is possible with Lydian or Phrygian or Dorian or any others of those scales. These musicians were full of the technicalities of music a thousand years before their time, and used terms denoting things which had gone out of use for quite five hundred years ; and they confused themselves with all this useless learning. They had only a very simple scale, and could have done much more by giving their whole minds to that than by fussing over information which they could not apply. And history now repeats itself. People concern themselves with sharps and flats and keys and scales and resolutions and modulations and all the other features of a system which they have discarded. They have instruments with nothing but equal semitones from one end to the other ; and instead of taking full advantage of the change, they lose themselves in the intricacies of music which those instruments cannot perform.

BIBLIOGRAPHY.

TEXTS. Ptolemy, *Harmonica*, ed. Wallis, Oxford, 1682. Aristoxenus, ed. Marquard, Berlin, 1868, ed. Macran, Oxford, 1902. Aristeides Quintilianus, ed. Albert Jahn, Berlin, 1882. Anonymus, *Scriptio de Musica*, ed. Bellermann, Berlin, 1841. Cleonis, Nicomachus, Bacchius, Gaudentius, Alypius, all in one volume as *Musici Scriptores Graeci*, ed. Karl Jahn, Leipzig, 1895. Boetius, *Musica*, ed. Friedlein, Leipzig, 1867. The later writers, Aurelian, Remigius, Hucbald, Oddo, &c., in vol. i of *Scriptores Ecclesiastici de Musica*, ed. Martin Gerbert, St. Blasien, 1784.

The music from Delphi was published first (and best) in the *Bulletin de Correspondance Hellénique*, vol. xvii (1893), plates 21, 21 *bis*, 22, vol. xviii (1894), plates 12, 12 *bis*, all from photographs. The music from Tralles, *ibid.*, vol. vii (1883), and better in vol. xviii (1894), plate 13. Karl Jahn printed some of the Delphic music in his *Mus. Scrip. Graec.* before the whole of it was found, and made large mistakes, corrected in a supplement in 1899.

Readers of the above article will learn with deep regret that the author died soon after finishing his essay, and before he had finally corrected the proofs.

His loss will be mourned by many through the whole world of letters, but by none more sincerely than by those who, like him, have known the lure of musical scholarship.

II

THE MUSIC OF THE HEBREWS

By the Rev. W. O. E. Oesterley, D.D.

I. THE GENERAL CHARACTER OF ANCIENT HEBREW AND ORIENTAL MUSIC

There is abundant evidence showing the love which the ancient Hebrews had for music, vocal as well as instrumental, secular as well as religious ; for it is clear from many passages in the Old Testament that music played a very important part in the social life and during the religious observances of the people. But as to the character of their music, the manner of singing, the kind of melodies, their structure and compass, the Old Testament gives extremely little information. If we had to rely on the Bible alone for our knowledge of the character of ancient Hebrew music we should not get very far. But from what is known of the music of cultured and semi-cultured peoples, of Egyptian and Assyrian music, and above all of the vocal and instrumental music of the Arabs (which will need special attention), we are able to draw certain inferences regarding ancient Hebrew music ; and in some respects these inferences are supported by the *data* given in the Old Testament.

Thus music was believed to be of divine origin ; the Egyptians held that their holiest melodies came originally from Isis ; the Assyrians believed that musical tones first emanated from the planets. According to an ancient tradition the Hebrews likewise believed that music came from the heavenly spheres, for at the creation of the world ' the morning stars sang together, and all the sons of God (i. e. the angels) shouted for joy' (Job xxxviii. 7). Evidently vocal music preceded

F

instrumental. According to another tradition, man first learned instrumental music when in the nomadic stage, for in Gen. iv. 20–22 Jubal, ' the father of all such as handle the harp and pipe ', is mentioned together with Jabal, ' the father of all such as dwell in tents and have cattle ', and Tubal-cain, ' the forger of every cutting instrument of copper and iron ', i. e. the smith ; these constituted the three classes among nomads. Other reminiscences of the music of the Hebrews in the nomadic stage occur in Exod. xv. 1 ff., 20, 21 ; Num. xxi. 17, 18.

Again, from the analogy of other peoples we are justified in believing that in Hebrew music the rhythmical element was regarded as of greater importance than the melodic. That this was, and is, the case among uncultured peoples is abundantly illustrated by the examples, gathered from very diverse countries, given by Ambros in his *Geschichte der Musik*, div. ii, pp. 538 ff. (1887) ; and see also Forkel, *Allgemeine Geschichte der Musik*, i. (1788).

From these it is seen that rhythm is the important thing in song, not melody ; the following examples will show this :

This Soudanese melody is repeated over and over again.[1] Two Jesuit missionaries working in Abyssinia many years ago took down two melodies of the simplest kind which well illustrate the rhythmical element :

These, too, were repeated many times.[2] For its very marked rhythmical character the following Senegalese melody[3] is also worth recording :

[1] Ambros, *op. cit.*, p. 546.
[2] Forkel, *op. cit.*, i. 94.   [3] Ambros, *op. cit.*, p. 546.
A large number of similar illustrations are given in these two works.

That great stress was laid on rhythm by the ancient Egyptians, whose cultural influence on the Hebrews is well known,. is to be gathered from the fact that some of their musical instruments were used for this sole purpose.[1] The same applies to the Assyrians, who also influenced the Hebrews in various ways, though at a somewhat later period (eighth and seventh centuries B. C.); thus, on one of the sculptures which adorned the palace of Sennacherib,[2] which was situated near the present village of Kuyunjik, women are represented singing and clapping their hands at the same time, the latter being obviously done to mark the rhythm of the song.

But in estimating the character of ancient Hebrew music there can be no doubt that the music of the Arabs is our most important source of information. Both in Arabia and in parts of Syria the Arabs are still in the nomadic stage; and all authorities are agreed that the nomadic Arabs of to-day are essentially what their forefathers have been for millenniums; and among the Arabs in general customs and manners are still retained which go back to a high antiquity.[3] Some of their musical instruments still in use are very primitive, and it is exceedingly probable that the same is the case with their singing and many of their melodies. Their close racial affinity with the Hebrews makes the evidence from this source the more valuable. Benzinger, who is able to speak of the music of present-day Arabs from first-hand knowledge, maintains that we must picture ancient Hebrew music to ourselves as being

[1] For an interesting account of Ancient Egyptian musical instruments, together with illustrations taken from inscriptions, see Sachs, ' Altägyptische Musikinstrumente ', in *Der Alte Orient*, xxi. 3. 4 (1920).

[2] He came to the Assyrian throne in 705 B.C.

[3] See e.g. Conder, *Tent Work in Palestine*, p. 332 (1889) ; Curtiss, *Primitive Semitic Religion To-day*, passim (1902).

very similar in character to that of modern Arabs.[1] It is, however, necessary to point out in passing that two types of music are to be distinguished among the modern Arabs, a primitive and a more developed type. There can be no doubt that among some classes of Arabs there has been considerable development; this is seen, apart from other indications, in the fact that the medieval Arabs employed musical notation, and in certain of the more modern Arabic music a heptatonic scale is used. A curious mingling of the ancient and modern is seen in the fact that singing is often accompanied by the old-world *derebukkeh*, a kind of tom-tom, and the chord-producing *kamanjeh*, or guitar. It is, of course, only the ancient type of music of which we are now thinking.

One of the main characteristics of Arab music is that rhythmical accentuation is the most important element. ' For the proper estimation of both ancient Hebrew and modern oriental music ', says Benzinger, ' one must realize above all things that with both rhythm plays an exceedingly important *rôle* at the cost of the melody.'[2] The rhythmical element is still the dominant one in Arab folk-songs which are sung at the present day ; and there can be little doubt that these folk-songs, at any rate in their musical structure, go back to a great anti-quity. It is well known that in early forms of song two accompanying actions usually assisted in marking the rhythm, namely, the beating of a drum (sometimes merely hand-clapping) and dancing. This is still done by the Bedouin Arabs ;[3] it is interesting, therefore, to find that in what may certainly be regarded as a reminiscence of what obtained among the Hebrews while still in the nomadic stage, these two accompanying actions are mentioned in connexion with song. After the ' Song of

[1] See his article ' Musik' in Hauck's *Realencyklopädie für protestantische Theologie und Kirche* (3rd edition).

[2] *Op. cit.*, xiii. 599.

[3] Dalman, *Palästinischer Diwan*, pp. 254 f. (1901) ; J. E. Harrison, *Ancient Art and Ritual*, p. 31 (1913); Oesterley, *The Sacred Dance*, pp. 6 ff. (1923).

Moses' in Exod. xv. 1–18, we read in verse 20: *And Miriam the prophetess, the sister of Aaron, took a timbrel in her hand; and all the women went out after her with timbrels and with dances.* The song they sang occurs in the following verse. The Hebrew word for 'timbrel' is *tôph*, probably the most primitive musical instrument among the Hebrews; a better rendering would be 'hand-drum', i. e. a tom-tom.

Where rhythmical accentuation plays this leading part melody is subordinated; this is the case with Arab music, and we may be certain that the same applies to ancient Hebrew song, which will have been more in the nature of rhythmic declamation than what we understand by melody. In any case, judging from Arab analogy, the melody must have been very short, not more than two or three bars, often repeated, with a compass of four or five notes. Harmony is, of course, unknown, both in Arab and Hebrew music. The Arabs sing mostly in the minor mode; and their song is generally of a plaintive character; this may be also postulated of ancient Hebrew song. In speaking of oriental music generally, Niebuhr says: 'The melodies of all orientals are solemn and simple ... when several instruments and voices play or sing together, it is always done in unison.'[1]

Another important fact to be noted about the music of the Arabs is that all tones are played or sung out of tune to our ears; but it is certain that their playing and singing out of tune is not due to what we call a 'bad ear', because their mode of playing and singing is 'constant'. The Arabs maintain, moreover, that it is the Europeans, not they, who play and sing out of tune. Further, their intervals are different from ours, which they regard as unmusical; they use the third of a tone, and even quarter-tones.[2] 'Arabian theorists', writes Dr. C. S.

---

[1] See his *Reisebeschreibung nach Arabien und andern umliegenden Ländern,* i. 175 ff. (1774) ; Lane, *An Account of the Manners and Customs of the modern Egyptians,* ii. 60 ff. (1871) ; Thomson, *The Land and the Book* (Lebanon, Damascus, and beyond Jordan), pp. 392 f. (1886).

[2] Benzinger, *op. cit.,* xiii. 599 ; Forkel, *op. cit.,* i. 126.

Myers,[1] 'included quarter-tones in the scales which they constructed, and it has been stated that in Syria a scale occurs
consisting of equally tempered quarter-tones. The various
quarter- and third-tone scales described by Arabian and other
writers are probably always general scales; they are rarely, if
ever, particular or instrumental scales. When quarter-tone
intervals occur in any piece of Arab music the notes concerned
are only grace notes, or play an otherwise unimportant part
in the melody.'

Antiphonal singing is very popular among the Arabs;[2] as
we shall see, the Hebrews were fond of this both in their secular
and sacred music. Two traits in the singing of the Arabs are
peculiarly distasteful: one is their fondness of a nasal twang;
it is an interesting fact that this is sometimes to be heard in
the intoning of the prayers by the Cantor in modern synagogues. The other is the habit of Arab women of producing
vibration when singing by means of shaking the hand under
the chin. How ancient this custom is can be seen from one
of Sennacherib's inscriptions, on which a woman is depicted
singing with her hand at her throat for the purpose just mentioned; the action is constantly to be seen at the present day
among Persian as well as Arabian women.

These few details regarding the music of the Arabs may with
a high degree of probability be taken as indicating the character
of ancient Hebrew music.

II. MUSICAL INSTRUMENTS AMONG THE HEBREWS

Before speaking of the place occupied by music in the social
and religious life of the Hebrews, according to the evidence of
the Old Testament, a few words may be said about their

---

[1] In *Anthropological Essays*, 'The Ethnological Study of Music', p. 245
(1907). See also Kiesewetter, *Die Musik der Araber nach Originalquellen
dargestellt*, pp. 18 ff. and Appendix (1842).

[2] Benzinger in the article referred to.

musical instruments. The most primitive were instruments of percussion. The *Tóph*, or 'drum ',[1] has already been mentioned. Sachs has shown, from the evidence of the monuments, that this instrument was borrowed by the Egyptians from the Semites during the 16th–15th century B. C.; before that time it was unknown in Egypt.[2] Owing to this fact we are able to see from Egyptian inscriptions exactly what the primitive *Tóph* looked like, and the manner of playing it. What was probably the earliest type corresponded with the modern tambourine; in shape it was either round or square, the framework being of wood, though sometimes of metal. Another type was the 'calabash' drum, the skin or membrane being fastened on to what looked like a calabash. It was held up in one hand and struck either with the back of the other or with the fingers. In the earliest times it appears to have been used by women rather than by men (cp. Exod. xv. 20 ; Judges xi. 34 ; 1 Sam. xviii. 6) ; on an Egyptian inscription [3] it is also women who are beating it. On a bas-relief from the palace of Ashur-bani-pal (he ascended the Assyrian throne in 668 B. C.) it is a man who is depicted playing it, and the drum, in shape like the modern one, is attached to his body, and he is beating it with both hands.[4] In another case a drum, also round in shape, stands on the ground and is almost of the height of the man who is beating it.[5]

Among the Hebrews the drum accompanied dancing and secular songs, but was not used in the Temple, though it was played during religious processions (see 1 Sam. x. 5 ; 2 Sam. vi. 5 ; 1 Chron. xiii. 8 ; Ps. lxviii. 25 (26 in Heb.).

The *Şelṣelim* ('cymbals') are mentioned in connexion with the drum in 2 Sam. vi. 5 ; 1 Chron. xiii. 8 ; Ps. cl. 5, and else-

---

[1] Rendered τύμπανον in the Septuagint. [2] *Op. cit.*, pp. 5 f.
[3] Perrot et Chipiez, *Histoire de l'Art dans l'Antiquité*, i. 701 (1882).
[4] Jeremias, *Das alte Testament im Lichte des alten Orients*, p. 337 (1904).
[5] Koldewey, *The Excavations at Babylon*, pp. 284 ff. (1914), gives illustrations of Babylonian terra-cotta figures of musicians, chiefly women, from very early times to the Greek period ; the instruments represented are the double flute, panpipe, lute, harp, and tambourine.

where. Similar to it were the M^eṣiltáim; both words come
from the same Hebrew root, but there must have been some
difference between the two since they are often mentioned
together. That they were used in the Temple music is clear
from 1 Chron. xv. 19, xvi. 5. On the Assyrian inscription
referred to above, a man is seen playing them; he holds them
vertically, not horizontally.

The M^ena‘an‘im, a word coming from the root meaning ‘to
shake’, must have corresponded to the Egyptian Sistrum, an
example of which is to be seen in the museum in Bologna;[1] it
consists of a small stirrup-shaped metal frame with several
loose metal bars, and makes a clanging noise when shaken;
originally it had metal rings attached to the bars. Among the
Egyptians it was used at the worship of the goddess Hathor by
women to drive away evil spirits. In the only passage in which
the word occurs in the Old Testament (2 Sam. vi. 6) it is
mentioned as being used in a religious procession.

The only other instrument of percussion was the Shálíshím,
likewise mentioned only once (1 Sam. xviii. 6); its meaning is
quite uncertain. The Septuagint renders it ‘cymbals’, but
this can hardly be right, as the Hebrew word clearly implies
that it was an instrument formed of ‘three’ things. It has
been thought by some authorities that it was a triangle with
rings attached, which was shaken; but, as Nowack points out,
there is no evidence of the existence of a three-cornered instrument of this kind in antiquity; for ‘the Trigonon, which
originated in Syria, was a stringed instrument’.[2] It is perhaps
best to think of it as a Sistrum of the kind in use among the
Egyptians just referred to.

Among wind instruments the most important was the flute
or pipe, called Ḥálíl, which means literally a scooped-out reed;
it is also called N^eḥílah, from the same root. This, too, was
used in religious processions, but not during the Temple

---

[1] An illustration of it is given in Sachs, op. cit., p. 17.
[2] Lehrbuch der Hebräischen Archäologie, i. 273 (1894).

service until much later times. Originally the *Ḥâlîl* produced only one note; but in course of time, by boring holes in the reed, it was made to give forth several notes. In later days flutes were made of wood, and ultimately of metal and even ivory. On both Egyptian[1] and Assyrian[2] inscriptions men and women are represented playing the double flute. While used on various occasions, weddings, banquets, processions, and as an accompaniment to dancing and singing, it was regarded as especially appropriate at funerals, and as a sign of mourning[3] (see e. g. Jer. xlviii. 36).

Another old-world wind instrument was the *Shôphâr*, 'ram's horn'; another name for it was *Ḳeren*, 'horn' (cp. Exod. xix. 13; Joshua vi. 4, 5). It is probable that in early days the *Ḥ^aṣôṣ^erah*, 'trumpet', was identical with the *Shôphâr*; after the Exile they became differentiated. Three ways of sounding the *Shôphâr* are indicated in the Old Testament: one expresses a short trumpet sound, the same word being used for the clapping of the hands; another implies a long drawn-out note, the word is also used of prolonging anything; and the third means a noisy trumpet-bray, the shouting of a multitude being expressed by the same word.

The *Shôphâr* is the only instrument which is still used in synagogues on special occasions.[4] Four *Shôphâr* calls are used among the Ashkenazic Jews; they illustrate what has just been said about the expressions used in the Old Testament; assuming the instrument to be pitched in the scale of G, the calls would be as follows:[5]

---

[1] Champollion, *op. cit.*, i. plate 175.

[2] Jeremias, *op. cit.*, p. 337; Nowack, *op. cit.*, i. 276. An illustration taken from a palace in Kuyunjik; see also Benzinger, *Hebräische Archäologie*, p. 275 (1894).

[3] An illustration is given by Steindorff, *Grab des Ti*, plate 60 (1913); Perrot et Chipiez, *op. cit.*, i. 701.

[4] This applies only to orthodox synagogues; the Reform Jews use an organ or harmonium.

[5] *Jewish Encyclopaedia*, ix. 305 (1905); excellent illustrations of its various shapes are given on pp. 302 f.

These traditional calls have been used from time immemorial. The shape of a trumpet (*Ḥᵃṣôṣᵉrah*) in the more modern sense of the word can be seen on a coin of the time of Bar-Kochba [1] (A. D. 132).

Among the Egyptians the trumpet was not a favourite; it does not appear on inscriptions until the time of the New Empire (about 1580 B. C. onwards).[2]

The '*Ûgâb* (Gen. iv. 21; Ps. cl. 4) was probably a primitive form of bagpipe; no representations of it seem to have been preserved on either Egyptian or Assyrian inscriptions.

Finally, we have the string instruments. The general name for these is *Nᵉgînôth*; the verb *naggēn* means 'to play a stringed instrument' (see 1 Sam. xvi. 16 f., 28 : xviii. 10 ; 2 Kings iii. 15; Ps. xxxiii. 3, and many other passages). Apart from the late Book of Daniel (165 B. c.) only two stringed instruments are mentioned in the Old Testament ; but they played a very important part in the music of the Hebrews. The older and most widely used, and therefore no doubt the simpler, was the *Kinnôr*, translated 'lyre'; [3] the other was the *Nebel*, 'harp'.[4] The former is mentioned in connexion with popular festivities; both were much used in the Temple worship. The *Kinnôr* was evidently the smaller, as it was played while walking or dancing (1 Sam. x. 5; 2 Sam. vi. 5). Doubtless it varied in shape, but an early example of it, used by the Bedouin,

---

[1] See Madden, *Coins of the Jews*, ii. 238 (1881).

[2] Sachs, *op. cit.*, p. 9.

[3] In the Septuagint it is usually rendered κίνυρα or κιθάρα.

[4] The Septuagint either simply graecizes the Hebrew word, νάβλα and νάβλιον, or renders it ψαλτήριον.

occurs on an Egyptian inscription of the Twelfth Dynasty (*circa* 2000 B. C.), and shows that it consisted of an oblong piece of wood, part of which was cut into a square frame across which at least eight strings were strung; it was played with the fingers of the left hand, while in the right hand the player holds a *plectrum*; as he seems to be using both hands [1] the instrument must have been attached to his body; he is walking in procession.[2] A somewhat similar instrument appears on Assyrian inscriptions of the time of Ashur-bani-pal; it is being played during the religious ceremony of pouring out a drink-offering by the king over lions which he has killed.[3] On Egyptian inscriptions we have the same type of lyre, though more ornate in shape; and a three-stringed, boat-shaped instrument carried on the shoulder is also depicted. They are played by women.[4] In much later times the *Kinnôr*, as represented on Jewish coins, appears in the shape of a cup, and has either three or six strings.[5]

The *Nebel* was a much larger instrument. The player either sat on the ground or on a low stool with the harp before him; on some Egyptian inscriptions he is represented standing. Some very ancient inscriptions give us a good idea of what this instrument looked like. One belonging to the time of the Sumerian king Gudea (*circa* 2600 B. c.) depicts Semitic musicians; in the case of most of them it is difficult to see what they are playing; but the one playing the harp is distinct enough; he is sitting on a stool with his instrument before him; it is of a rather primitive shape, but has eleven strings.[6]

---

[1] But it is of course possible, though improbable, that he is pressing the fingers of the left hand on the strings to vary the note.

[2] Riehm, *Handwörterbuch des Biblischen Altertums*, i. 328 (1884). See for other examples Perrot et Chipiez, *op. cit.*, i. 794 ff., 845.

[3] See the illustrations in Jeremias, *op. cit.*, pp. 269–70. On another Assyrian inscription of the same period the instrument is plainly seen attached to the body of the player, see Nowack, *op. cit.*, i. 267.

[4] Champollion, *op. cit.*, ii; plate 175.

[5] Madden, *op. cit.*, ii. 234 ff., for the former; Ambros, *op. cit.*, pp. 151 ff.

[6] Hommel, *Geschichte Babyloniens und Assyriens*, p. 243 (1885).

The other is an Egyptian one, belonging to a time before 1600 B. C.; the player is kneeling before his instrument, which is in the shape of a large bow and seems to have ten or eleven strings.[1]

The Hebrew *Nebel* is likely enough to have been similar to one of these, or, with changing fashion, to have resembled each in different periods. Nowack [2] believes, no doubt rightly, that the *Nebel* is to be identified with the *Sanṭir*, an ancient kind of harp still used by the Arabs.

The Hebrews, according to 1 Kings x. 11, 12, made their musical instruments of the wood of the 'almug-tree', i.e. sandal-wood. But the passage in question refers to the requirements of the king; it is probable that ordinary folk contented themselves with instruments made of less costly wood. The strings (*Minnîm*, cp. Ps. cl. 4) were made of gut, sometimes probably also of twisted cord; [3] metal strings were unknown. Stringed instruments were played with the fingers, less frequently with a *plectrum*; the bow was unknown in antiquity.

The musical instruments of the Hebrews thus consisted of the drum, cymbals, sistrum, flute or pipe, and trumpet; a primitive kind of bagpipe, and the lyre and harp.[4] The flute produced several notes; for, judging from Egyptian forms of the instrument, it had from three to seven finger-holes,[5] and the stringed instruments had from three to twelve notes (possibly more); but, so far as can be judged from the inscriptions depicting early stringed instruments, it is improbable that the fingers were pressed on the strings to produce different notes.

The question naturally arises as to what the intervals were; and here we have nothing to guide us excepting what we know

---

[1] Sachs, *op. cit.*, p. 23.   [2] *Op. cit.*, i. 275.   [3] Nowack, *op. cit.*, i. 273.

[4] The *Sabbᵉka, Kitharis*, and *Pᵉsantērin*, mentioned in the Book of Daniel, were different kinds of lyre; they belong to later times; the same is true of the *mashrôḳitha*, a kind of mouth-organ (Dan. iii. 5 ff.), and the *sûmpônya*, a bagpipe (Dan. iii. 5. 15).

[5] See the illustrations in Sachs, *op. cit.*, p. 21.

of the character of oriental music generally, and especially of that of the Arabs. The use of the third of a tone and even of the quarter-tone suggests the possibility of these having been the intervals between the strings, at all events on the larger instruments. In this case there would have been but few full tones; but this would accord with what we have already seen reason to believe, viz. that ancient melodies were extremely simple, not having a compass of more than three or four tones.

Another problem which confronts us, and which can only be partially answered, is that of the manner of instrumental accompaniment. That this was their only function is well known, the human voice being always the most important in music, whether secular or religious, among the Hebrews. The fact that particular stress is laid on the unison of voices and instruments (2 Chron. v. 13) presumably implies that this was not always the case, and that, therefore, the instrumental accompaniment was not always in unison. But whatever other form the accompaniment may have taken it is impossible to say owing to want of evidence.

III. SONG AMONG THE HEBREWS

The expression 'instruments of song' (*K^elê shîr*), which occurs a number of times in the Old Testament (e. g. 1 Chron. xv. 16, xvi. 42, and elsewhere), clearly indicates that musical instruments were simply used for accompanying song. The song was, therefore, quite indepen^r.ent of the accompaniment, and was undoubtedly sung far more often without it than with it.

Among the various kinds of song among the Israelites the earliest were *Folk-songs*. Though these are included under secular music, which in the pre-exilic period was more prominent than sacred music, it must be remembered that a sacred vein runs through many of them owing to popular religious beliefs, especially in the earlier times.

Probably the earliest of these preserved in the Old Testament is that occurring in Num. xxi. 17–18 : 'Then sang Israel this song,

> Spring up, O Well; sing ye unto it,
> To the well which the princes digged,
> Which the nobles of the people delved,
> With the wand, and with their staves.'

The ancient nomadic Arabs, in the same way, used to dance round a well and sing to it;[1] they offered an act of homage thereby to the spirit inhabiting the well, as they thought. In modern times the Bedouin sing snatches of song while drawing water for their flocks from the well.[2]

Although there must have been many popular harvest-songs none have been preserved in the Old Testament. On an ancient Egyptian inscription, however, which may well serve as a parallel, oxen are represented treading out the corn (cp. Deut. xxv. 4) and the following words occur :

> Thresh, ye oxen,
> Thresh the sheaves ;
> Thresh for your owner,
> Thresh for yourselves.

The Old Testament gives several references to vintage-songs, from which it is evident that they were numerous (see Judges ix. 27, xxi. 21; Isa. v. 1, xxvii. 2, and elsewhere). The first line of a vintage-song is quoted in Isa. lxv. 8 :

> . . . As the new wine is found in the cluster and one saith,
> 'Destroy it not, for a blessing is in it,' so will I do . . .

The words 'Destroy it not . . .' are clearly a quotation; in the Hebrew the words are markedly rhythmic (see further on this folk-song, p. 49). Another vintage-song is quoted in Joel

---

[1] Goldziher, *Abhandlungen zur Arabischen Philologie*, i. 58 (1896).
[2] Seeken, *Reisen*, ii. 223 (1854).

iv. 13 (iii. 13 in the English versions), where the Hebrew is
again rhythmical :

> Put in the sickle, for the vintage is ripe ;
> Come, tread, for the winepress is full,
> The vats overflow.

The prophet boldly quotes this popular folk-song for the
purpose of adapting it to a prophecy of woe.

Another song sung by the people, though not a folk-song in
the ordinary sense, is worth a passing reference.   In writing
about the music of the Egyptians, Herodotus (Book ii. 79)
says : 'They have, among other strange pieces, a song which is
sung in Phoenicia, Cyprus, and elsewhere, but which goes by a different name in each case.   It corresponds (συμφέρεται) to that
which the Greeks sing under the name *Linos*.   I marvel, concerning many things in Egypt, and I also wonder how it was
that they got hold of the song of *Linos*.   Yet, as it seems to
me, they have been accustomed to use it from time immemorial.
Linos is called *Maneros* (*Menes*) in the Egyptian language, and
was, as they tell, the only son of the first king of Egypt, and
his early death was mourned in dirges.'   Now, Herodotus is
here referring to a legend which was widespread among the
peoples of antiquity ; for the *Linos* dirge was the 'mourning'
for Adonis, Tammuz, Attis, Osiris, Lisyerses, which was known
and sung in Syria, Babylonia, and Phrygia, as well as in Egypt
and Greece.[1]   *Linos*, or *Linus*, is a shortened form of *Ailinus* and
this in reality is the cry *Ai lanu* ('woe to us'), which the
Phoenicians uttered when they mourned for *Adôn* ('Lord') or
Adonis.   That the Hebrews observed this annual mourning at
which they sang the '*Linos*-dirge' is shown in the Old Testament, see Isa. xvii. 10, 11 ; Ezek. viii. 14 ; Zech. xii. 10 ; and
there is little doubt but that it underlies the story of Jephthah's
daughter in Judges xi. 34–40.

A different type of song among the Hebrews was that which

[1] For full details see G. J. Frazer, *The Golden Bough : Spirits of the Corn
and the Wild*, i. 216 ff., 257 ff. (1912).

commemorated a victory of some signal deliverance from danger. Quite short, of this type, are those preserved in Exod. xv. 21, the 'Song of Miriam', and in 1 Sam. xviii. 7 (repeated in 1 Sam. xxi. 11, and xxix 5) when the women sang:—

> Saul hath slain his thousands,
> And David his ten thousands.

These were sung antiphonally ; the word used makes this certain, and we know from many other passages that the Hebrews loved antiphonal singing, see e. g. 1 Chron. xvii. 36 ; Jer. xxxiii. 11 ; Ezra iii. 11 ; Ps. lxxxviii (title), cvi. 48 ; cxviii. 1–4 ; cxxxvi ; cp. also Rev. iv. 8 ff., v. 9 ff., vii. 10 ff., xix. 1 ff.[1]

More elaborate are the very ancient 'Song of Deborah' (Judges v. 1–31) and the 'Song of Moses' (Exod. xv. 1–18). These, and others like them, partake of a religious character because a battle, being believed to be sanctioned by the national God, was a sacred act. All those referred to, as well as many others (mainly incorporated in the Psalms), have the rhythmic element already spoken of, and are markedly different from prose.

There can be little doubt that the beginning of a new era in the development of religious music among the Hebrews must be connected with the name of David. Although the attribution to him of so many psalms and their music cannot be regarded as historical, yet the fact that tradition assigns the origin of so much of the nation's religious music to him may reasonably be believed to rest on some foundation. On this Benzinger pointedly remarks : 'The *rôle* which singing and music played in the second Temple, and the place taken by singers and musicians in the *personnel* of the Temple, is only comprehensible on the supposition that music had a definite place in Temple worship *before* the Exile. And when tradition traces all this back to David, and makes him the real founder of the Temple music, it is not mere phantasy which has spun itself out of the early indications of David's proficiency in musical art.

---

[1] See further, Graetz in *Monatschrift für die Literatur und Wissenschaft des Judenthums*, p. 179 (1879).

It is in the nature of things highly probable that the king, who clearly took great delight in music, and who had at his court his men and women singers, his musicians and dancers, should have employed these in worship as well.' [1]

An interesting point, especially in view of the practice in later centuries of the Synagogue, is the fact that the Hebrews took over the melodies of popular folk-songs for use in the Temple worship. For example, in the titles of Ps. lvii, lviii, lix, lxxv, it is directed that each of these psalms is to be sung to the tune of *'Al-tashḥîth*, which means 'Destroy it not'; this, as we have seen, was the opening word of the first line of a popular vintage song, which is quoted in Isa. lxv. 8 (see above, p. 46); it was so well known that it could be referred to by its opening word in the titles of the psalms mentioned. Another example is Ps. lvi, which, according to the title, is to be sung to the tune of 'The dove of the far-off saints'.[2] Perhaps there is a reference to this song in Ps. lv. 6, 7: 'O that I had wings like a dove; then would I fly away and be at rest. . . .' Once more, Ps. xxii was sung to the tune of the song known as *'Ayyeleth ha-shaḥar*, 'The hind of the morning'. And there are various other instances.

The expression *'Al ha-shᵉmînîth*, 'On the eighth', which occurs in the titles of some of the psalms, has often been taken to mean that the melody was sung an octave lower; and the expression *'Al 'Ălāmôth*, 'After the manner of maidens', has been explained to mean that the melody was to be sung an octave higher. In both cases the explanation is very precarious because it assumes that the expression means an octave as we understand it; that does not necessarily follow; it is not known what the ancient Hebrew scale comprised.[3] The expressions mentioned are susceptible of different explanations.

---

[1] *Op. cit.*, p. 598.
[2] Reading with the Septuagint rendering τῶν ἁγίων for the Hebrew אֵלֶם (' silently '), which is corrupt.
[3] Benzinger thinks it must remain an open question whether the Hebrews had any idea of a scale or not.

H

As illustrating the increased importance of music in the Temple worship we have the musical accompaniment during the offering of sacrifices; this was not the case in earlier times. There is an Assyrian parallel to this, as seen on an inscription of the time of Ashur-bani-pal (see above, p. 39). Whether this was in vogue in pre-exilic times or not cannot be said with certainty. But there is no doubt that after the return from the exile, music gained continuously in importance in the Temple worship, see Ezra ii. 41; iii. 10 ff.; vi. 8 ff.; vii. 20 ff.; Neh. vii. 44; xi. 22 f.; xii. 28, 37 ff., 47; xiii. 10, and many passages in the books of the Chronicles.

It was during the post-exilic period that most of the psalms were composed, and we can judge from the structure of many of them that the melodies to which they were sung were very short; probably it served for only half a verse, and was repeated throughout the psalm. Another point to be noted is that the number of words varies greatly in each half-verse; to this the notes of the melody had to adapt themselves; but we do not know on what principle this was done. The accents are no guide here as they are of much later date, and only serve for reciting purposes and for regulating the cantillation, i. e. they indicate the rhythm and the undulations of the voice which depend upon the rhythm.

During the Greek period it seems certain that the taste for secular music increased (see Ecclus. xxxii. 3-6; xl. 20-21). The probability is that Jewish music was influenced by that of the Greeks since this influence was exercised in every other direction; but it must be confessed that we have no definite evidence of this in the musical sphere until the time of Josephus, who ascribes the introduction of Greek songs with instrumental accompaniment among the Jews to Herod the Great.[1]

---

[1] *Antiq.* xv. viii. 1; he was born in A. D. 37.

IV. THE MUSIC OF THE SYNAGOGUE

In dealing with the music of the Synagogue, the first question which naturally suggests itself is as to whether any traces of the Temple music are to be discerned in it. The opinions of authorities on the subject differ. Benzinger, for example, maintains that we have no example of an ancient Hebrew melody, but that all the extant synagogue music is of post-Christian origin.[1] Breslaur says he is unable to find any support for the contention that the origin of synagogal music is to be sought in the time of the Temple.[2] He says : 'Our old melodies have not emanated from the Jewish spirit, and therefore they do not bear any specifically Jewish impress. That many of them have been borrowed from other cults and from foreign music has already been emphasized by noted scholars.'[3] Others hold similar views. On the other hand, there are those who believe that a few examples of Jewish melodies dating from pre-Christian times are extant. De Sola, for example, gives the melody to the 'Song of Moses',[4] and refers to an ancient Spanish work which claims that this was the very melody sung by Miriam ; while this is not, of course, to be taken seriously, the claim shows that in the Middle Ages the melody was regarded as of extreme antiquity. It may, at any rate, be regarded as having descended from some originally much simpler melody. The Sephardic Jews, among whom it is sung, have retained in other directions some very old liturgical elements. The melody is as follows : [5]

---

[1] In the article already referred to.

[2] *Sind originale Synagogen und Volks-Melodien bei den Juden geschichtlich nachweisbar?* p. 58 (1898).

[3] *Op. cit.*, p. 63.

Exod. xv. 1–18; called *Shirath ha-Yam*, 'the Song of the Sea'.

The Ancient Melodies of the Spanish and Portuguese Jews, no. 12 (1857).

the altar, and so participated in both services ', so that the system and mode of singing in the Temple was adopted as the earliest synagogal music.[1] The conclusion to which one is forced in view of these considerations is, therefore, that these melodies are the elaborated descendants of far simpler themes which underwent development in the course of some centuries. We may well believe that the original kernel is contained in each; but what the original form of the kernel was can no more be determined. In any case, since the instrumental music was, as already pointed out, merely accompaniment, the voices could sing their part quite independently of the instruments; it followed, therefore, that when, with the destruction of the Temple (A. D. 70), instrumental music in worship ceased, its absence did not affect the mode and system of singing.

After the destruction of the Temple, music of all kinds, whether sacred or secular, was discouraged by the Jewish authorities as unfitting in such times of sadness for all Jews. But this met with great opposition on the part of the people; and although officially there was a general prohibition of music which continued into the Middle Ages, it was in the main a dead letter and grew less forcible and effective; indeed, some authorities themselves abrogated the prohibition.[2]

The earliest definite indication which we have of the character of Jewish music after the destruction of the Temple is the evidence of Josephus, already referred to, that Greek songs with instrumental accompaniment were introduced among the Jews by Herod the Great. The reference is presumably to secular music; but religious music would certainly have been affected too; for throughout their history, from the time of the Exile at least, right up to the present day, the Jews have never been afraid of adapting the music of the outside world

---

[1] The evidence occurs twice in the Babylonian Talmud, in the tractates *'Arakhin*, 11 *b* and *Sukka* 53 *a*. See further F. L. Cohen's article in the *Jewish Encyclopaedia*, ix. 120 *a* (1905).

[2] See Abrahams, *Jewish Life in the Middle Ages*, pp. 253 f. (1896); Löw, *Lebensalter in der jüdischen Literatur*, p. 311 (1875).

to the purposes of worship. We have seen that this was the case in the times of the Temple,[1] when psalms were sung to the tunes of popular folk-songs; and we shall see that the same kind of thing was done later. So that we may well believe that Greek music exercised some influence on the synagogal music. And this is borne out by what is said by Clement of Alexandria (born about the middle of the second century A. D.), who compares the manner of singing in the Temple with the Dorian mode;[2] this, of course, refers to the synagogal music of his day; he takes it for granted that this followed the Temple usage.

Ambrose, when he introduced the antiphonal singing of the Psalms in Milan, speaks of this as being 'after the manner of the East'; no doubt he is referring to the manner of the Eastern Church, and there can be little doubt that this was based ultimately on Jewish usage. We have seen that in the worship of the Temple the Psalms were sung antiphonally. Rabbinical information regarding musical instruments, while based mainly on biblical *data*, is expressed in a way which shows that their ideas are 'saturated with the Greek spirit'. Among the instruments mentioned are silver trumpets, zithers, harps (the Greek word *kithros* is used), cymbals, and flutes; and the representations of harps on ancient coins show similarity with the Greek *lyra*.[3] These points—and many other details could be adduced—show that Greek influences affected the music of the Synagogue as well as Jewish music generally.

But if Jewish music was influenced by Greek music, it is, on the other hand, in the highest degree probable that the music of the Synagogue influenced that of the early Church. 'The forms of the liturgical chant,' says Hadow,[4] 'on which our Church music was largely founded, probably came, in the first instance, from Jewish sources.' But it is a question as to

[1] See p. 49 above.   [2] *Paedagogus*, ii. 4.
[3] Krauss, *Talmudische Archäologie*, iii. 83 (1912); the information given in the Talmud refers to times prior to 500 A. D.   [4] *Op. cit.*, p. 51.

what synagogal musical form really lay behind 'these liturgical forms'. Hadow, together with most writers who refer to the subject, believes it to have been the chants to which the Psalms were sung in the Synagogue; and the probabilities of the case point to this. But it seems certain that this was not the only Jewish source.[1] One of the things which has played an important part in the history of Jewish music has been the method of reciting Scripture, which from early times took the form of a kind of 'musical declamation'. It is true that the Psalms, as well as the prayers, were recited in a similar manner; but insufficient stress has been laid on the chanting mode of reading Scripture, which, as Cohen suggests, influenced the composition of chants in the Church. He says that 'the earliest reference to the definite modulation of the Scripture occurs in the Babylonian Talmud (*M^egilla*, 32 *a*), where Rabbi Johanan deprecates the indifference of such as "read (the text) without tunefulness".' The use of the term *n^e'imah* ('tunefulness') shows that a melody definite enough to cause a pleasant impression was already attached to the scriptural reading, and that it had long passed the stage of syllabic plainsong.[2]

Written musical notes were, of course, not used; they were unknown to the Jews until about the seventeenth century A. D. It is held by some that the Hebrew poetical accents signified musical notation; but this is very doubtful. These accents, added to the Hebrew text at the earliest in the eighth century A.D., were only meant to regulate the rhythm and the modulation of the voice; they did not indicate the notes of a melody.[3]

A considerable development of synagogal music arose with the

---

[1] See Fleischer, *Neumen-Studien*, ii, pp. 16 ff. (1897).

[2] See Cohen's article on 'Cantillation' in the *Jewish Encyclopaedia* iii. 537 *a* and his article on 'Music', ix. 121 *b* ff., where references are given to illustrations. And see further the same writer's 'Ancient Musical Traditions of the Synagogue', in *Proceedings of the Musical Association*, xix (1893). A good example, among many, of the method of cantillation will be found in Naumbourg, *Chants religieux des Israélites* . . ., p. 231, no. 185 (1847).

[3] See further the article in Riehm's *Handwörterbuch*, ii, 1945, referred to above.

introduction of *Piyyuṭim* into the services ; this probably began
about the seventh century A. D., and greatly increased during
the succeeding centuries. These were sacred songs which received this name because they were composed by a *payyeṭan*,
a word adapted from the Greek ποιητής ('poet'). They were
sung to fixed melodies, which were composed either by the
writer himself or by the *Ḥazzân* ('precentor') of a Synagogue.
The melodies were often adaptations of tunes from the outside
world ; sometimes the tune itself was appropriated. One source
of these is, in all probability, to be found in the poems and songs
of the Troubadours and Minnesingers ; but their earliest sources
were Moorish Spanish melodies. With the Mohammedan ascendancy in Spain, from the seventh century onwards, Jewish
settlements greatly increased in that country ; for toleration
under the Moors offered the Jews a welcome refuge from
Christian persecution.

Alfasi, towards the end of the eleventh century, deplores the
introduction of foreign melodies in the synagogal services.
During the same century Abraham Ibn Ezra speaks of the
same subject, but does not seem to object to the practice. In
later days Simon ben Zemach Duran (fourteenth century)
remarks on the fact that a number of synagogal melodies are
adapted from Moorish songs ; and he approves of these Arabian
tunes because, as he says, they are so beautiful.[1] The love of
music among the Jews was energetically fostered by its scientific
study ; in the twelfth century in Arabian Spain, music was
part of the ordinary course of study among them. They were
therefore in a position to appreciate what they heard.[2] How
strong the influence of this music was upon the Jews is seen
from the fact that it is observable even at the present day.
Ambros says that he has found among the Spanish and Italian
Jews the same type of song as that sung among the Arabs,

---

[1] In his Commentary on *Pirḳe Abôth*, and in his *Mâgēn Abôth*, p. 526;
cp. Breslaur, *op. cit.*, p. 63.

[2] Cp. Abrahams, *op. cit.*, p. 365.

whose octave is divided into seventeen thirds of a tone.[1]   De
Sola has also noticed that the melodies of the Sephardic Jews
are a conglomeration of old Moorish and Spanish melodies,
which date, as he believes, from the time of the Moorish
ascendancy in Spain.[2]   Many Spanish rituals have the title
over some of the prayers 'in Arabian melody'.

But there are yet other influences whereby synagogal melodies
have been affected.   Breslaur, who has made a special study
of the subject, says that the augmented intervals, characteristic
of so many of the present-day synagogal melodies, are similar
to those occurring in Hungarian melodies, most of which are
written in the following form of the scale of C minor :

Several of the twelve Perso-Arabian scales are constructed in
a way similar to this scale.[3]   Elsewhere he gives reasons for
believing that the influence of Slav music, or that of the
gipsies,[4] is to be discerned in the 'coloratur' which occurs so
much in the synagogal music, and which was originally due to
the attempt to imitate passages played on the violin.[5]

In whatever country the Jews settled they adapted the
national airs for use in their religious services.   Just as in
Spain Moorish tunes were taken over, so in France the tunes
of the Troubadours were borrowed ; in the East oriental and
Turkish melodies were utilized, and so on.   Hence, apart from
some fundamental traditional material of Jewish origin and
development, the variety of synagogal music among the Jews
living in different countries.   Portuguese Jews, for example,
have music in their Synagogues which differs from that of

---

[1] *Op. cit.*, i. 432.
[2] *Op. cit.*, Introduction.   [3] *Op. cit.*, pp. 10 ff.
[4] The gipsy scale consists of quarter-tones.
[5] *Op. cit.*, pp. 48 f.   On the subject generally see Ferencz Liszt, *Des
Bohémiens et de leur musique en Hongrie* (1881).

French and Italian Jews; Polish Jews have other melodies not
known among English and German Jews.¹ In the distant past
the Hebrews, as already pointed out, sang some of their psalms
to the tunes of popular folk-songs; just in the same way the
Jews in later ages borrowed the tunes of the folk-songs belonging to countries in which they settled down; to some of these
they sang psalms, to others the sacred poems composed by the
Payyetânim. An example of the former is the following melody,
to which the *Hallel* (Psalm cxvii) is sung by the Sephardic
Jews:²

The next illustration is the medieval melody to the prayer
called *'Alēnu* ('It is our duty'); the prayer itself is one of the
most ancient pieces in the Jewish Liturgy; the form of the
medieval melody here given is simpler than that usually sung
in the Synagogues:³

¹ See further Breslaur, *op. cit.*, pp. 64 ff.
² Aguilar and De Sola, *op. cit.*, no. 42.
³ It is taken from the *Jewish Encyclopaedia*, i. 339.

One of the outstanding ancient melodies of the Synagogue is that to which *Kol Nidrē* ('All vows') is sung. In its original form it must have been much simpler than it appears at the present day with its endless varieties; 'it must obviously date from the early medieval period, anterior to the eleventh century, when the practice and theory of the singing school of St. Gall, by which such typical passages were evolved, influenced all music in those French and German lands where the melody of *Kol Nidrē* took shape.'[1] It consists of an introductory intonation sung on *Ali*; then follows the theme which was the original basis of *Kol Nidrē*; this is repeated in various forms several times; the final part takes on a somewhat different form from the rest. The melody has been frequently published with accompaniment.[2] It will suffice if we give here the melody only. To cite the whole of it would take up too much space; but the following extracts contain the most important parts:

Introductory theme.

---

[1] *Jewish Encyclopaedia*, vii. 543 *b*.

[2] Marksohn und Wolf, *op. cit.*, no. 7; Breslaur, *op. cit.*, pp. 43 ff. It is also published by Moritz Deutsch, *Col Nidre, Text und Melodie nach der Tradition* (undated) and in the *Jewish Encyclopaedia*, vii. 544 f.

Opening theme.

Central theme.

This last theme is repeated several times in varying forms. Breslaur shows the extraordinary similarity between the opening bars of the Introductory theme with the first five bars of Beethoven's C♯ minor string quartette (Op. 131), section 6 in the *Adagio quasi un poco Andante*.[1]

The very few illustrations which are all that can be given here cannot, of course, give a real idea of the large variety and character of the music which the synagogues of many different countries have used through the centuries. But we may quote the words of one whose wide knowledge of synagogal melodies is perhaps unrivalled; speaking generally, and without reference to exceptions, he notes that they are mostly in the minor key, 'with melodic turns which our music does not know. They seem to point either to ancient times or to the national music of the peoples of eastern Europe, Slav or Magyar, and even to oriental nations. Further, there is a mixture of a simple cantillation character with elaborate passages adorned with *coloratur*. Yet they exhibit an affecting (*herzergreifend*) expression of deep feeling often rising to poignant emotion.'[2]

---

[1] *Op. cit.*, p. 35.   [2] Quoted by Breslaur, *op. cit.*, p. 1.

V. SECULAR MUSIC AMONG THE JEWS

Finally, a few indications may be given of the *rôle* of music in ordinary everyday life of the Jews outside of the Synagogue; for although no actual copies of any music, either vocal or instrumental, have come down to us from the Middle Ages, there are plenty of references in various medieval records of the fondness for music which the Jews had, and of the different occasions on which they were accustomed to enjoy it.

Of its performance at banquets we have evidence from very early times; it will be sufficient to quote the words of Ben-Sira (written about 180 B.C.), for they show an appreciation for music and a respect for the musician's art which is distinctly interesting. In speaking of proper behaviour during a banquet, he says, among other things :

Speak, O Elder, for this liketh thee,
Yet let it be with discerning discretion,—and hinder not the
    singing.
When the music beginneth, pour not forth talk,
And display not thy wisdom when it is not wanted.
As a signet of cornelian in a golden necklace,[1]
So is good music at a banquet of wine.
A setting of gold and an emerald signet
Is the strain of music at a pleasant carouse.[2]

Whether at this early period Jewish music was already influenced by that of the Greeks cannot be said with certainty, owing to want of evidence; but we are told in the Jerusalem Talmud (*Sotah* vii. 2) that the songs sung after festive meals were in the Greek manner, for the Greek language was best adapted to song ; and this must refer to the early centuries of Christianity, at the latest. It is said of Elisha ben Abujah,

---

[1] The meaning of this line in the original is a little uncertain, but presumably the 'signet' is the musician, while the 'golden necklace' is the circle of appreciative listeners.

[2] Ben-Sira is the author of the book called *Ecclesiasticus* in the Apocrypha; the quotation is from xxxii. 3-6, and is translated from the Hebrew, not from the Greek version of it.

who lived at the end of the first century A. D., that he always sang Greek songs (Babylonian Talmud, *Ḥagigah* 15 *b*).[1] In later centuries the evidence becomes fuller, and the words of many table-songs are available; they show a strange mixture of the religious and worldly elements; they were at once serious and jocular, prayers and merry glees. 'On Friday evenings,' Abrahams tells us, 'in the winter, the family would remain for hours round the table singing these curious but beautiful hymns . . . the favourite Jewish wine songs were merry, but they contained not one syllable of licentiousness.' Many of them were set to Arabian tunes.[2] Strangely enough, Jewish professional musicians were often employed to play and sing at Christian banquets.[3]

At wedding festivities music naturally figured prominently. In the period following the fall of the Jewish State (A. D. 70) music on these occasions ceased, according to the Mishnah (*Sotah* ix. 11); but it is doubtful whether this lasted for long (see above, p. 54). We are told, at any rate, in another Mishnah tractate (*Kethuboth* ii. 1) that during the bridal procession songs were sung in honour of the bride, and that these gave the name of ὑμέναια (הינומא) to the wedding festival; another mark of Greek influence; the singing during the procession was accompanied by the playing of flutes, harps, zithers, castanets, and cymbals.[4] In later centuries we read of Jewish professional musicians providing the music at weddings; but if the ceremony was arranged for on a Sabbath, Christian musicians were employed. Mohammedan musicians are also mentioned in this connexion during the Middle Ages. On the other hand, records tell us that by the end of the sixteenth century several communities possessed Jewish orchestras which were hired by Christians.[5]

The part played by women in the performance of music, both vocal and instrumental, religious and secular, is full of interest.

[1] Krauss, *op. cit.*, p. 79.   [2] Abrahams, *op. cit.*, pp. 133 ff.
[3] Abrahams, *op. cit.*, p. 197.   [4] Krauss, *op. cit.*, iii. 81 ff.
[5] Abrahams, *op. cit.*, passim.

We have seen how prominently they appear in this respect among the Egyptians and Assyrians; but in these cases they were probably not free women. One cannot say with certainty what the position of the women singers was who are mentioned in Neh. xii. 27, 1 Chron. xv. 16.[1] In the Mishnah (*Kelim* xv. 6, xxiv. 14) reference is made to the 'harps of women singers'; these were presumably different from the harps of the sons of Levi used in the Sanctuary; and it is probable that 'the harps of the women singers' were used for secular song. We hear of women joining in choruses with men (this is fourth-century A. D. evidence)[2] in secular music; but the women were not allowed to sing solos! *Ensemble* singing, in which men begin and the women join in, is also mentioned in the Babylonian Talmud (*Sotah* 48 *a*).[3] F. L. Cohen mentions the very interesting inscription on a tombstone in the old Jewish cemetery at Worms, dated 1275, which runs : 'This monument was erected in honour of the pious maiden Urania, whose beautiful singing and great liturgical knowledge were so well known. She used to act as Precentor in the women's chapel of the Worms synagogue.'[4]

There are, obviously, many details with which it is not possible to deal in a single essay ; we therefore add a bibliography, which, while making no pretension to be exhaustive, will be found to contain works in which a great deal of information can be obtained. Some of the books and articles in the list have been referred to in the preceding essay, but lack of space made it impossible to take them all into consideration.

For the earlier periods :

AMBROS, *Geschichte der Musik*, vols. i, ii (1887).
BENZINGER, *Hebräische Archäologie*, pp. 271–8 (1894).
——, Article on 'Music' in Hauck's *Real-encyclopädie für die Protestantische Theologie und Kirche*, xiii. 585–603 (1903).

---

[1] Eccles. ii. 8 points clearly to female slaves.
[2] Löw, *op. cit.*, p. 309.   [3] Krauss, *op. cit.*, iii. 76.
[4] 'The Rise and Development of Synagogue Music,' in *Papers read at the Anglo-Jewish Historical Exhibition*, p. 84 (1887).

FORKEL, *Allgemeine Geschichte der Musik*, vol. i (1788).

GRESSMANN, ' Musik und Musikinstrumente im A. T.', in *Religionsgeschicht-liche Versuche*, Bd. ii, Heft i (1903).

KIESEWETTER, *Die Musik der Araber nach Originalquellen dargestellt* (1842).

NOWACK, *Lehrbuch der Hebräischen Archäologie*, i. 270–9 (1894).

PERROT et CHIPIEZ, *Histoire de l'Art dans l'Antiquité*, vols. i, ii (1884).

REIHM, Article on ' Musik' in *Handwörterbuch des Biblischen Altertums*, ii. 1029–45 (1884).

SAALSCHÜTZ, *Geschichte und Würdigung der Musik bei den alten Hebräern* (1829).

SACHS, ' Altägyptische Musikinstrumente', in *Der Alte Orient* (1920).

STAINER, *Music of the Bible* (1871).

For the later periods :

ACKERMANN, ' Der synagogale Gesang in seiner historischen Entwickelung ', in Winter und Wünsche, *Jüdische Litteratur*, vol. iii (1894).

AGUILAR and DE SOLA, *The Ancient Melodies of the Liturgy of the Spanish and Portuguese Jews* (1857).

BRESLAUR, *Sind originale Synagogen und Volks-Melodien bei den Juden geschichtlich nachweisbar ?* (1898).

COHEN, F. L., ' The Rise and Development of Synagogue Music ', in *Papers read at the Anglo-Jewish Historical Exhibition* (1887).

——, ' Ancient Musical Traditions of the Synagogue', in *Proceedings of the Musical Association*, xix (1893).

——, Articles in the *Jewish Encyclopaedia*, esp. ' Cantillation ', iii. 437 ff. and ' Synagogal Music ', ix. 119 ff.

——, ' Le Plain Chant de la Synagogue ', in *Revue du Chant Grégorien* (1899).

——, Preface to Pauer's *Traditional Hebrew Melodies* (1896).

DELITZSCH, *Physiologie und Musik* (1868).

DUKES, *Zur Kenntniss der neu-hebräischen religiösen Poesie* (1842).

GÜDEMANN, *Das jüdische Unterrichtswesen* (1873).

KAISER and SPARGER, *A Collection of the Principal Melodies of tl ᵓ Synagogue* (1893).

LISZT, Ferencz, *Des Bohémiens et de leur musique en Hongrie* (1881).

MARKSOHN und WOLF, *Auswahl alt. Hebr. Syn. Melodien* (1875).

NAUMBOURG, *Chants religieux des Israélites, contenant la liturgie complète de la Synagogue des temps les plus reculés jusqu'à nos jours* (1847 . . .).

——, *Recueil de Chants Religieux* (1874).

SINGER, *Die Tonarten des traditionellen Synagogengesanges* (1886).

ZUNZ, *Synagogal-Poesieen* (1884).

III

NOTATION

THE GROWTH OF A SYSTEM

By Sylvia Townsend Warner

THE function of musical notation falls into two main divisions: the expression of relationship in pitch, or *interval*; the expression of relationship in time, or *measure*. It is fortunate, both for those who teach the history of European notation and for those who learn it, that these two main divisions were developed in different epochs and can, therefore, be treated independently.

The first elements of pitch-notation were two strokes, one rising to the right, and the other falling from the left. These signify respectively the rising and falling intonation of the voice. They were not invented for music, but borrowed from the rhetoricians or public speakers, who had definite rules for the conduct of the speaking or reciting voice, and used these two strokes as indicators or reminders above written-out speeches or passages for recitation. The rising and falling strokes could also be joined together to show that a single syllable was to carry both a rising and falling inflexion. A similar effect of the voice is indicated by italicizing for emphasis: 'I shall *not* do it.'

These signs ╱ ╲ and ╱╲ are familiar to most people under their names of the acute, the grave, and the circumflex accent. They are probably of Byzantine origin, and Gevaert supposes that they were first used in connexion with Church music about 680.[1] Thus used to illustrate the singing, as opposed

---

[1] I am informed by Mr. Arthur Waley that a corresponding device of rising and falling strokes was used to regulate the intonation of the reciting voice in the Japanese Nō plays—a curious instance of similar conditions independently adopting similar methods.

to the reciting voice, these strokes no longer represent processes but states: that is to say, the acute accent stands, not
for a rising inflexion but for a degree of the scale higher than
that which preceded it; the grave accent for one lower than the
preceding.

As the reciting inflexions developed into the system of plain
chant, the element of melody asserted itself in the growing
importance of *melismata*, i. e. passages of several notes to one
syllable. The circumflex accent is, of course, a rudimentary
example of this, and other more complex melodic figures were
expressed by various arrangements of the rising and falling
strokes until by the ninth century these arrangements had
established themselves in the system of *neumes*. Each neume
had its name, and there were rules for their phrasing or
accentuation. But the neumatic system had no rules of exact
time-measurement, nor needed any, since the rhythmic basis of
plainsong was the rhythm of well-spoken prose.

In the following table of the principal neumes the reader will
observe that the grave accent has changed from a long, thin
stroke to a short, thick one, except in such neumes as the clivis
(circumflex accent), or the porrectus, where it joins the acute
accent. Any one who takes a broad-nibbed pen and makes a
few upward and downward strokes will see how this change
came about. The difference is commemorated in the neumatic
terms for these two elementary figures: Virga and Punctum.

FIG. 1.

The two elements:

/ , virga or acute accent, marking a relatively high sound;

` , punctum or grave accent, marking a relatively low sound;
combined in the principal neumes thus:

(1) Clivis ∧	i. e.	up, down.
(2) Podatus ∨	„	down, up.
(3) Porrectus ∧∨	„	up, down, up.

(4) Torculus Ⱳ   i. e. down, up, down.

(5) Climacus Ⱥ.   „   up, down, down.

(6) Scandicus ⟋   „   down, down, up.

(7) Porrectus flexus Ɱ   „   up, down, up, down.

(8) Torculus resupinus Ⱳ „   down, up, down, up.

These neumes could also be combined among themselves, as in the podatus subpunctis, in which the descending strokes of (5) may be added in any number to the rising figure of (2). Refinements of phrasing were further expressed by the semi-ornamental figures such as the ancus, quilisma, and strophicus, which indicated delicate shadings of accentuation and intonation; and by the Romanian letters (whose *locus classicus* is the Einsiedeln Antiphonary, known to have been written before 996), a very comprehensive system of supplying 'expression marks' by initial letters.

The next illustration shows a fragment of plainsong in neumatic notation.

FIG. 2.

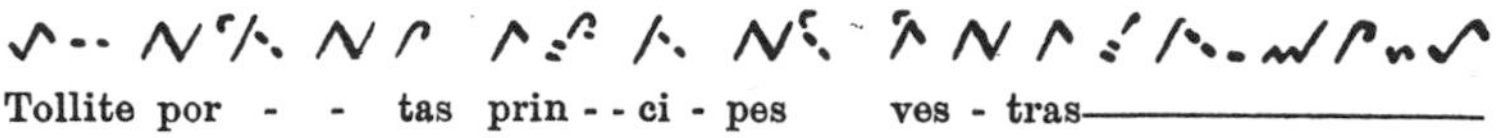

Tollite por - - tas prin - - ci - pes   ves - tras————

The neumes in order are: torculus, punctum, punctum, porrectus, climacus (the c before the climacus is one of the Romanian letters; it stands for celeriter, its modern equivalent would be *leggiero* rather than *poco accel.*), porrectus, cephalicus (the 'liquescent' form of clivis, by which the second note takes on the character of a grace note: its occurrence here 'probably indicates only a slight reduplication of the note for the right pronunciation of the r'[1] of *portas*), clivis, scandicus (in a modified form affected by the ancus in order to effect a delicate liaison with the climacus which follows it), porrectus subpunctis, clivis (both with the celeriter), porrectus, clivis, scandicus, climacus, quilisma (a shake or turn sung between two notes, a

---

[1] *Elements of Plainsong*, Plainsong and Mediaeval Music Society.

minor third apart, light in itself but slightly lengthening their duration by, as it were, hesitating between them), clivis, pressus (a note whose accentual value is enhanced by shortening the note immediately preceding it), torculus. This is merely a recital of the neumes. There is more to notice. The first and last syllable of *principes* each contain five notes, but in the first case these are broken up by the use of two neumes into groups of two and three, in the second case the five are grouped together in one compound neume, and the celeriter over the join ensures that there shall be no gap there. By this device the sweep and continuity of the phrase is guarded, but where, before the final torculus, it is desirable to show that the phrase is, as it were, coming to earth, the pressus is introduced, whose extra accent and duration gives the same steadying values as a retard, though by subtler means.

This is a short passage, and by no means an elaborate one. Yet this analysis shows how sensitive the neumatic notation was, how supple, how expressive, and how explicit; for this last quality certainly cannot be denied to a notation which tells the singer how to roll his r's. There is only one thing which it does not tell (for it has been pointed out that in noting plainsong there is no need for mensural definition), yet this one omission renders it incomprehensible to modern readers. It tells of notes rising and falling, but it does not define a single interval of those rises and falls: unless we know the melody it notes we can only translate it by conjecture. This fact, so painful to us, troubled nobody in the neumatic period. The plainsong melodies were learnt by ear, and singers were presumed to know them by heart; all that was required of notation was that it should remind the singer of his repertory and show him how to sing it.

The definition of intervals, in other words the change from evocation to statement, is the first step towards notation as we know it. This is generally supposed to be due to the rise of organum. The first impulse was to throw-back to the alpha-

betical system. This had been the Greek method of notation,
and a tradition of it had been lingering on, preserved, as traditions are, by the theorists, while the practical musicians had
been developing their neumatic system. In the matter of exact
definition of intervals a letter system can claim the merit of
being unimpeachably watertight; but it is cumbrous, a very
grave disadvantage; and it is completely inexpressive, a graver
disadvantage still, since a melody, however accurately defined
by alphabetic means, does not look like a melody.   In
the following example the first 'distinction' of the passage
already given in neumes is given in the Dasia-notation, a
letter system of the tenth–eleventh century, based on Greek
precedent.[1]

Fig. 3.

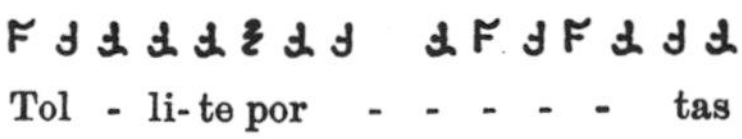

Tol - li- te por - - - - - tas

Putting himself in the place of a contemporary musician,
accustomed to the finesse of the neumatic system, and con-
temptuously aware that the Dasia-system could show no accentual distinctions, made no difference between the ancus and
climacus, grouped no phrases, and was incapable of rolling an *r*,
the reader will sympathize with that unscientific frame of
mind which clung to neumes and rejected the unmitigated
accuracy of pure alphabetical methods.

But the attempt to define intervals had been made, and, by
admitting an inadequacy in the neumatic system, musicians had
entailed on themselves the task of finding some means of
remedying that inadequacy. The tenth century saw many
experiments. Besides the alphabetical system, such as the
Dasia-notation, which is based, like tonic sol-fa, on the principle
of fixed symbols for the degrees of the scale, there was another
letter system by which the intervals themselves were described

---

[1] The letters were differentiated forms of the Greek aspirate sign ⊦.

by alphabetical equivalents : each interval was given a certain
sign, and dots above or below indicated whether the intervals
were in an upward or downward direction.

Fig. 4.

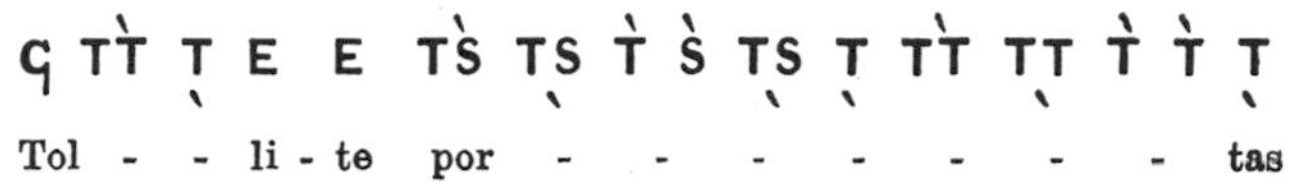

ç T̀T̀ T E E T̀S̀ TS T̀ S̀ TS T T̀T̀ TT T̀ T̀ T

Tol - - li - te por - - - - - - - tas

Odo of Clugny (early eleventh century) propounded a compromise system whereby alphabetical signs were placed above
the neumes (Montpellier Antiphonary); this seems a good
working compromise, but it is wasteful, obliging the singer to
read two notations at once.

The solution was not arrived at until two new expedients had
been independently experimented with, and at last, and
seemingly almost at hazard, combined. The first of these expedients was the use of horizontal lines, each representing a
degree of the scale and defined by alphabetic and interval signs.
On these the words of the plain chant were written. This
adumbration of the stave should have been an exciting discovery (although the fact that the melody was represented by
words vitiated it for the purpose of representing melismata);
but the value of these lines was not recognized ; they were only
used as leading-strings for beginners, who were expected, as soon
as they had learnt the alphabetical signs, to do without the
lines and to sing from a notation like Fig. 3.

The second expedient was the one usually known by the
Solesmes title of ' Notation à points superposés '. In this the
appeal to the eye was made by spacing the ' points ' (punctums,
heads of virgas, and extremities of neumes) at definite degrees
of highness and lowness. As a guide in writing a line was
scratched with a dry pen across the page. This line, from being
a guide to the scribe, was developed into being a guide to the
singer, to whom it indicated a degree of the scale. Presently it

was inked in; and when another line was drawn above it, representing another degree of the scale a fixed distance above the first, and the neumes grouped upon and between these, the framework of the stave was finally established.

These lines were at first of different colours. The addition of clefs was a simple matter, since the alphabetical-cum-horizontal line system had made them a familiar idea. To begin with, all the letters from *a* to *g* were made use of, and changes of clef were frequent. But F and C, the common equivalents of the original two lines, asserted themselves. The coloration of the lines was recognized as a redundant assertion of what was already established by the clef, and the twelfth century saw the four-line one-colour stave with the F or C clef which is used for plainsong at this day.

Perhaps the greatest merit of the stave thus achieved is the fact that it employs the spaces between the lines. The alphabetical stave did not do this; and if the 'notation by points' had not adhered to the method of grouping between lines implicit in its early form of grouping between the intervals of the fifth, the whole progress of notation might have been hampered by a stave either too wide to be comfortably traversed by the eye, or too narrow to express a melody without frequent changes of clef. Yet the risk of this must have been a near thing, for the novel merit of the linear system would naturally induce a tendency to disregard aught save lines. It seems possible to the writer that it was the neumes themselves which saved us from the exclusively linear stave: separate points could be dotted about on lines easily enough; but (unless the lines were very close together, which involves hard writing and hard reading) a three- or four-note neume straddling from line to line would look ungainly and would be awkward to inscribe.

The reader is now given the fragment of plainsong on a stave and in the square notation which developed from emphasizing 'points'.

FIG. 5.

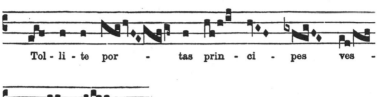

Tol - li - te por - tas prin - ci - pes ves -

tras

It will be observed that the Romanian letters are gone. There will be no more 'expression marks' till the seventeenth century, though the sixteenth century had a very capable and interesting technique for indicating phrasing. But there is a new-comer, the ♭. The signs for our ♭ and ♮ were, like the clefs, supplied by the alphabetic school of notation. Their forms were originally the Roman and Gothic B: b and ♮; their names, B molle and B durum,[1] derive from the hexachordal system of Guido of Arezzo, but the use of these two forms to distinguish the two varieties of B dates from the earlier alphabetical experiments. B molle was used in stave notation both as an accidental and in the signature, in which position it is sometimes counted as a clef. But as the clef ♭ was taken to be invariable, and as the accidental ♭ only affected the note it stood before, it will be seen that there was little call for the services of the ♮, which remained proper to the alphabetic notation. The ♯ (crux, diesis), original form ✗, came into use later. It is said to have been invented by Josquin de Prés (1450–1521), and to owe its form to a ♮ crossed out (hence the name, B cancellatum; both these statements may be received with the piety due to legends). ♭ and ♯ were used to correct each other; a ♭ following a sharpened note restored that note to its original pitch; a ♯ following a flattened

[1] B durum is the B of the Hexachord called Natural, preserved in our English term.

L

note performed the same function, and also sharpened or raised
a note flattened by signature. C♯, F♯, or (in the sixteenth-
century music) G♯ might also be corrected alphabetically, i. e.
by the corresponding letters, but this is rare. A recollection
of the modal system will show that B♭ was germane to tonality,
whereas the ♯ was not (cf. *musica ficta*, false music); this
explains why there were no ♯ signatures, even when the trans-
posed modes had licensed signatures of ♭ and ♭♭.

It has been stated already that the first elements of pitch
notation were the rising and falling strokes of the rhetorical
intonation. There is a comfortable symmetry in the fact that
these same strokes, the Adam and the Eve of notation, having
in the course of five centuries changed their shapes from ╱ and
╲ to ▜ and ▪ (put on flesh, one might say), became the first
elements in the definition of measure.

It must be premised that the novelty of measured music was
merely the novelty of something in a new place. There was
nothing new about periodic rhythm; no one, I imagine, supposes that the golden age of plainsong was accompanied by
a complete atrophy of the impulse to dance, or that church
bells were rung with a devout avoidance of keeping time. Nor
need we assume that periodic rhythm was looked on as being
something necessarily rather vulgar, rather low-class. Scholars
and Churchmen might avoid regular scansion in Church music,
but they studied and practised it in the poetic metres; and
when the exigencies of the exciting new art of polyphony made
it necessary to contrive some method of regularizing both the
composition and the notation of scanned music, it was to the
poetic metres that they turned.

Why this scanned music should in practice have been almost
exclusively developed in the triple measure is a question for
a committee of psychologists, philologists, and prosodists, with
perhaps, if the old legend be venerated, a theologian thrown in.
For the notationer it is sufficient to say that it was so. The
elements of the new music were a long and a short in the propor-

tion 2-1; the forms in which these elements were combined were the six rhythmic modes, and virga and punctum start on their new career under the names of the long and the breve.

Though the long and the breve would have been sufficient in themselves to represent the simple metres of the rhythmic modes, and though the long by increasing its value into the large, and the breve by dividing into the semibreve with its further division into the minim, spanned a mensural scale equivalent to our scale from semibreve to semiquaver, these good gifts were not fully appreciated and the system of early mensural notation is darkened by a redundancy of material. This is due to the continued employment of the compound neumes, new-fitted with mensural values thus:

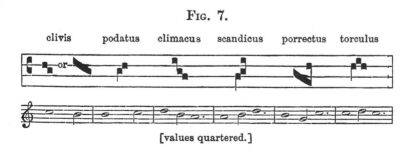

Fig. 6.

[values quartered.]

It will be seen that these represent ∪ — metres, iambic and the iambic anapaest of the rhythmic modes. The following table shows how the same neumes were altered to express the — ∪ metres, trochaic and dactylic:

Fig. 7.

[values quartered.]

It will be seen that the alteration is in their tails, the descending ligatures becoming improperly tailless, the ascending receiving tails. This exchange is commemorated in the terms 'cum proprietate' for the iambic group, 'sine proprietate' for the trochaic (the tail, of course, equals the virga, the ascending stroke for the higher sound).

With this new significance applied to its neumes, the example *Tollite portas* would become a tune in iambic anapaestic measure, thus :

FIG. 8.

(The breves of the original have been turned into longs to preserve the scansion of the rhythmic mode. It must be understood that this translation is purely hypothetical. The plainsong melody is kept in the examples for convenience of illustration. Actually the rhythmic modes were not imposed upon plainsong except in such polyphonic constructions as the motet.)

If it be desired to reverse this tune from anapaest to dactyl, all that is needed is to change the ligatures from 'cum proprietate' to 'sine proprietate'; the insertion of a preliminary threefold long, however, would be necessary to express the dactylic scansion.

It will be noticed that in Fig. 8 the penultimate notes have reverted from cephalicus to clivis. This also is demanded by observance of the mode. It will also be noticed that if the modes be strictly observed the melody will become strictly jog-trot. In actual composition this jog-trot quality was obliterated, first, by the licence called mixing the modes (i. e. by interpolating a foot of a different metre); secondly, by altering the note values, either by compounding them, ◼ ♩ becoming ♩ •, or by dissolving them, the long becoming two breves, ♩ ◼ to ◼ ◼ ◼, the breve turning to an iambic or trochaic two-semibreve group,

■ to ●■ or ■● .[1]

The chief sign for indicating these changes is the plica. The plica has four forms.

FIG. 9.

[values quartered.]

The first two, in which the longer tail is on the right, dissolve the long into two breves. These represent two-thirds of a triple measure. The last two, in which the longer tail is on the left, dissolve the breve into a trochee ; these represent one-third of a triple measure. The body of the plica is properly one square note, the direction of the second note following the direction of the tails ; if the tails ascend, the second note is one degree higher ; if the tails descend, one degree lower. In the descending-tail plicas, however, the body of the note is commonly slightly oblique, slanting down to the right. The plica is peculiar to the early stages of measured notation (twelfth-fourteenth centuries).

The next figure illustrates the iambic dissolution of the breve.

FIG. 10.

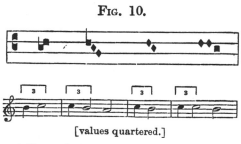

[values quartered.]

[1] The triplet bracket is of course editorial.

The one tail ascending on the left marks the well-known ligature 'cum opposita proprietate'. This ligature had a long career, persisting into the seventeenth century. The fact that its two notes immediately preceded by an ascending tail equalled two semibreves (the iambic scansion was ironed out in the course of time, and the semibreves made even) made it very useful during the later stages of polyphony, when the semibreve had supplanted, first the long, and afterwards the breve, in their function as the normal note of medium duration.

The development of the semibreve is also seen in the tailless form of the figure. In plainsong notation the lozenge-shaped note is a scribal convention, having the same (non-mensural) value as the square note. Here it is a semibreve, opposed to the square breve.

In the management of the note-values of the early mensural system there were two potential causes of misunderstanding :

(1) The ambiguity of the long.

(2) The ambiguity of the brevis recta and brevis altera.

Except in the first mode, which consisted of three perfect (threefold) longs, the long was imperfect (twofold), and the measure was completed on one side or the other by a breve. But should perfect longs be introduced by mixing the modes there was no means of distinguishing them from those that were imperfect. This was awkward ; but the ambiguity of the breve was more confusing still. In the compound modes, anapaestic and dactylic, the ∪ ∪ of the poetic metres had been recognized by their notation as two breves. Since the rhythmic modes duplicated the value of the second of these breves it was necessary to sing the second breve for the space of an imperfect long, a parallel change to the iambic scansion of the two semi-breves in Fig. 10. This change was known as the change from brevis recta (the true breve) to brevis altera (the altered breve).

Theoretically the proper values of the perfect or imperfect long and the breve recta or altera were determined by position, that is, by their relation to the measure ; and in the earlier stages this was not as difficult as it may sound, for two reasons: that the music followed fairly closely a metrical text;[1] that the end of each line of the text was indicated by the pausa, a line across half the stave, which, like our bar-line, showed the close of a measure. But this bar-line was as much textual as musical; in later settings of prose texts it only showed the end of a clause or paragraph, and with the growing tendency to extended word-setting and melismatic passages upon one syllable it only occurred at such infrequent intervals as to be equivalent to our double-bar, and consequently of very little help in defining values of variable long and alterable breve. Some other sign for defining time-values was needed; and two such adjuncts to notation were evolved: the point of perfection, or dot; coloration of notes.

It was a rule that the pausa line indicated a rest, either a breve rest, completing the previous measure, or a complete measure of silence. It would appear that this pausa line was sometimes used simply to define time-values, for Walter of Odington speaks of the confusion between the sign of division which defines grouping, and the pausa which indicates the rest proper to the 'hoquetus' (a method of breaking the flow of tone by rests, analogous to the 'soupir' of seventeenth- and eighteenth-century use, but systematically applied, sound and silence being alternately distributed between two voices). It would be better, he says, to keep the pausa (the line half across the stave) for the indication of a rest, and to use for the sign of division a small circle. Actually the sign of division has the form of a dot. This is familiar to us in the dot after a note which indicates its triple value, either by scheme or by augmentation. Thus employed to confirm the perfection of a note, or to indicate its augmentation in a duple-value scheme, the dot was placed on a level with the note to which it referred. But for the purposes

---

[1] Prose texts, such as that of the Mass were still sung in plainsong. In fact it may generally be said of the early measured music that it was a secular development and, even when setting devotional texts, extra-liturgical.

of defining a measure it was placed usually above the stave,
always above the lie of the notes.   When on a level with the
note it could be used inconsistently to the measure ; as we should
say, tying a note across the bar-line or across the beat.   But,
with one later exception, the dot in the higher position always
coincided with the measure.

FIG. 11.

The above hypothetical rendering of *Tollite portas* is designed
to show the various uses of the dot.   The first occurrence shows
that the long and semibreve make up a measure, therefore the
imperfect long must be enlarged by one quarter.[1]   The second
and third dots placed before the two apparently equal breves, by
showing the completion of the preceding group, indicate that the
second breve must be converted from brevis recta to brevis
altera ; in this use the dot is called the dot of alteration.   The
fourth dot shows that the second breve is not to be altered, since
it is the short of an iambus following the short of a trochee.
Thus interpolated between a change of foot the dot is called the
dot of division.   Note the plica, and the pausa line, implying a
rest.   It must be realized that this example is improbably over-
crowded with rhythmic changes in order to illustrate the dots in
short compass.

In course of time the long and breve of the rhythmic modes

---

[1] This use of the dot, which may be called the dot of fractional augmentation, is subsequent to the dots of alteration and division.

yielded to the breve and semibreve of perfect Time, the semi-breve and minim of the greater Prolation; but their values were defined by the dot exactly as the values of long and breve had been. And in the sixteenth century we find this sign invested with an additional function, and used (still in the higher position) as a phrase-mark to articulate the rhythmic modelling of the individual part. Thus used it coincides no longer with the close of a measure, it has become extra-mensural, a mark of punctuation instead of a sign of scansion. This extra-mensural use of the dot in no way interfered with its use for mensural definition; it was employed sometimes with one sense, sometimes with the other, just as a capital letter in the notation of verse is employed both for form (at the beginning of a line) or for sense (in the course of it).

It has been said earlier that in the beginnings of the stave colour was experimented with as a means of marking the relative pitch of the different guide-lines. Later this principle of definition by colour was applied to relative values. At first all notes were 'full', that is, inked in. Ordinarily they were black, but if it was desired to indicate that they were to receive a different value to the value they would appear to bear 'by position', they were coloured red. This statement by Philip of Vitry (first half of fourteenth century) suggests that the alternative colours had no fixed association with the alternative values; a change from black to red might mean either a change from apparent perfect to actual imperfect, or vice versa. In the triple measure system perfect whole-values were less common than imperfect ones; and as the prevailing ink was black ink, it seems reasonable to suppose that the red colour became thus associated with per-fection, threefold value of long or breve. On the other hand, the abandonment of the old method of filling in the body of notes for the speedier method which merely outlines them (= for ▪ : this development invalidated the earlier permission that a 'void', i. e. outlined or white note, might represent a red one if red ink were lacking) may have given rise to a convention that either reddening or blackening the body of the note indicated a diminution of its value. This would account for Morley's rather unexpected statement that a red note loses a fourth part of its value: a statement which smacks rather of theory than of practice (for the usual effect of reddening a note is to perfect it), unless it is a complicated way of indicating perfection of the order next below ; i. e. a duple breve by losing one-fourth would equal a semibreve perfected by the addition of one-third.

There is no such doubt about black notation, the common form of coloured notation during the fifteenth–sixteenth centuries, whose significance is always on the less side. Blackening was used in the triple measure to indicate the imperfection (duple value) of longs, breves, and semibreves, or to indicate the duple accentuation of a passage of such notes, when by the measure they might be scanned with a triple accentuation.

FIG. 12.

[values quartered.]

This last appearance of *Tollite portas* shows the later date by the time-signature, the five-line stave, and the ousting of long and breve by breve and semibreve. This example shows (with one exception) the 'lesser significance' of black notation, referring not to the lessened value of the notes but to the lesser value of the scheme (duple) by which they should be accented. This accounts for the blackened minims, which are blackened merely for accentuation, the value of the minim still being intrinsically duple. The exception mentioned above is the last occurrence of the blackening, where the sign 3-2 indicates the proportion of sesquialtra. The first two notes of the example have the dot after them, but this use of the dot is practically redundant, since the blackening at this point would be understood as marking the completion of a previous measure.

Black notation was also used for noting the Proportions, when it was preceded by the proportional signature to distinguish in what sense it was used. Here the rule of the significance being on the less side is exemplified by the fact that the blackened notes lose value proportionately to the ratio between the imposed proportional scheme and the true mensural basis. That is to say, if the proportion is 3-2 (three false semibreves to two authentic) each semibreve in the proportional part loses one-third of its ostensible value ; if the proportion is 4-3, one-fourth of its value. Here again the rule of blackening for a lesser significance holds good. The same idea is preserved in our notation of the imposed triplet, $\overset{3}{\sqcap\!\sqcap\!\sqcap}$ = $\sqcap\!\sqcap$. 3-2, 4-3, &c., are proportions of the more inequality, i. e. the imposed scheme is the greater. In proportions of the less inequality, 2-3, 3-4, &c., the 'lesser significance' of black notation would appear to render it unsuitable for expressing the augmented nature of the imposed scheme. But the difficulty was attacked thus. A time-signature retorted, that is, turned backward, meant that note-values were diminished by one-half. The unretortable signatures were given the same significance by a stroke through them (ꓛ, ꓛ or ⌀, ⌀). Thus in the proportions of the less inequality augmented semibreves were sometimes represented by black breves preceded by a retorted or stroked signature. If the retorted signatures were stroked and the unretortable crossed (ꓛ and ⊕) the augmented semibreves might be written as longs, for these signatures have the effect of diminishing values to one-quarter.

These sophisticated refinements, which will seem to the reader, according to his temperament, either agreeably ingenious or merely diabolical, show to what richness and flexibility notation had attained in its journey from the two strokes of the seventh century.   Analysis reveals that a certain amount of the richness was due to hoarding.   Non-proportional black notation and the use of the dot supplement each other to the point of redundancy. The complicated structure in which Time was reared above the crumbling Modes, Prolation above Time, and the whole crowned and festooned with Proportions, resulted in a swarm of time-signatures.   Expedients, reasonable and needful in their day, such as the change from brevis recta to brevis altera, were preserved as sanctified nuisances when there was no need for them, and their reason had very likely been forgotten.   Indeed, at the beginning of the sixteenth century there was a risk that notationers would be entangled in the net which they had woven.   It was the vitality of the music that saved the method of recording it.   That music was aiming at a richer texture achieved by simpler means, and as the artificialities of composition were discarded, notation too became more straightforward and economical.

THE SIGNIFICANCE OF MUSICAL INSTRUMENTS IN THE EVOLUTION OF MUSIC

By Kathleen Schlesinger

A HISTORY of the evolution of musical instruments from the earliest ages to the end of the fourteenth century should help to elucidate many obscure and difficult points in the history and theory of music, and to promote a more intimate understanding of the social and religious life of the people with whom music was so closely connected. Musical instruments remain as the embodiment of the aspirations and ideas of countless generations; they are the depositories of innumerable progressive experiments forming the earliest beginnings of the empirical science of music.

In the brief survey here projected, of material that would easily fill a volume to itself, it will be necessary to assume on the part of the reader-student a certain modicum of knowledge of the various families of musical instruments in use at the present day, and more especially of the inter-relationship of structural features with the acoustic principles and natural laws to which these instruments owe the production of sound, their scale, and the qualities of their distinctive tone. This inter-relationship of structural features and natural laws becomes apparent as the guiding principle in the evolution of the instruments, upon which reliance may safely be placed. It will, indeed, be found almost invariably that when an instrument dies out, instead of progressing in evolution, the cause may be traced either to its being a hybrid or to the transgression of a natural law in the combination of structural features. In

the process of elimination of all that sins against the laws of
proportion and true harmony, of the unfit and ill-mated, evolution is often slow, but always uncompromising where Truth
and Beauty are at stake, and nowhere is this more apparent
than in the history of musical instruments.   As an example of
unrelenting nemesis may be cited the rebab—later rebec—an
instrument played with the bow, whereas natural law, by virtue
of the construction and shaping of the sound-chest of the instrument, demands that the strings should be plucked; it
deserved the epithet bestowed upon it in the fourteenth
century, '*el ravè gritador*'[1] (the shrill rebab), and its fate in
Europe.

In the course of evolution music and musical instruments, after
a lengthy reign in the individual experience of man, pass by way
of virtuosity and theoretical speculation into the realms of Art
and Science.   If the nature of the experience into which the
musicians of the ancient world entered through music is to
be realized, many of our preconceived notions will have to be
abandoned.   The early musicians of Greece, Egypt, Chaldea,
&c., were not at all times intent upon the mere design which
the plucked strings of their kitharas, harps, or psalteries, or
the long-drawn notes of their reed-pipes, wove rhythmically
into melodies.   As the finger plucked the string, or the performer's breath thrilled through the tiny mouthpiece into the
reed-pipe, a mass-chord of harmonic overtones rang out,
followed by the natural polyphony[2] due to the play of
harmonics in varying rhythms and intensities, which continues
until the energy imparted to the string has become completely
exhausted.

[1] *Precursors of the Violin Family*, by Kathleen Schlesinger, 1910, Reeves,
pp. 242–4 sqq.; *Encycl. Brit.*, s.v. Rebab, p. 948 a.   See also Rebec,
pp. 949–50.   In this chapter (*E. B.*) in the text may be understood as a
reference to the present author's work in the *Encyclopædia*, under the heading in question, where further facts bearing on the subject will be found.

[2] Strange as this may sound to some musicians and scientists, it is an actual
fact, as yet unrecorded in works on acoustics, but observed by the writer
and by many others accustomed to listening for overtones.

A number of musical notes sounding simultaneously coalesce into a compound sound-wave for transmission through the air, and it is in that form that the above-mentioned mass-chord reaches the ear. The ear, like the chemist with his compounds, possesses the faculty of instantly decomposing the most complex forms of sound-waves,[1] which impinge upon the drum of the ear, into their simplest components, known as pendular or simple vibrations, and of reporting them in this form to the mind.

It is here that the awareness and alertness of the individual steps in. What is usually miscalled *an ear for music* is not perhaps due to a special development of the delicate mechanism of the ear so much as to an interest and delight in music, which leads the owner to direct his attention with a varying degree of intensity in concentration upon the musical factors reported by the ear, and to call into play his faculties of memory and co-ordination and his aesthetic judgement. This new explanation of the musical experience of the ancients (for which the present writer is entirely responsible), established upon many well-authenticated data, upon countless experiments, furnishes the only satisfactory explanation of many puzzling scenes and incidents connected with music in antiquity. The delight of poet, musician, and prophet at being able to enter at will the realm of musical or mystical experience by merely plucking a string, or singing a few long-sustained notes, can be well imagined. 'Bring me a minstrel,' said Elisha when asked to prophesy, and when the minstrel played, the words of wisdom came (2 Kings iii. 15). Elisha did not call for a *skilful* musician, or for any special kind of music. Many such incidents are related in the Bible, as, for example, when Saul came to prophesy (1 Sam. x); when the Psalmist says: 'I will open my dark saying upon the kinnor' (i. e. kithara, mis-

[1] For a clear exposition of these phenomena students may consult *Musical Acoustics, or the Phenomena of Sound as connected with Music*, by John

translated harp). The most striking testimony of all, however, to the power of this melodic design of the harmonic overtones, in the creation of which man all unconsciously participates, is the account (2 Chron. v) of the effect of the music of the 120 priests, standing with their trumpets beside the altar, on the day of the induction of the Ark of the Covenant into Solomon's new Temple: 'It came to pass, as the trumpeters and singers were AS ONE, TO MAKE ONE SOUND to be heard . . . that the glory of the Lord filled the Temple . . .'

These were the trumpets of beaten silver, made by divine command (Num. x. 2) and played, 120 strong, in unison, the singers reinforcing the unison with their many voices.

It must not be forgotten that, since it is the quality of the concentrated attention which is the dominant factor in the phenomenon of hearing, the play of harmonics does not make prophets of us all, that it has fallen unheeded upon many ears, and that chords or a rapid succession of notes suffices to reduce the harmonic polyphony to a blur, which man's critical faculty tends to tolerate, so soon as his desire for a musical experience changes into a desire for taking an active part himself in the making of music.

The numerous bas-reliefs and frescoes of the Ancients representing, in musical scenes, various instruments played simultaneously, harps of different sizes and shapes, kitharas, tambouras, double-pipes and flutes, drums and cymbals, &c., have puzzled many generations of music-historians from the apparent implication of a kind of polyphony or harmony. If the musicians, however, were only providing a number of notes in unison or octaves, or even in fifths or fourths, but varied in timbre, i. e. in the composition of their mass-chords, the result would be an impressive and greatly enriched accompaniment of harmonic overtones, a natural harmony sounding above the melody and independent of theoretical knowledge. This faculty of the ear had not become entirely dimmed in the seventeenth century, for Mersenne, I believe, speaks of 'the three notes' of a string (i. e. the fundamental with its fifth and sixth overtones), and Tartini, a century later, still writes in the same terms.

Those, then, are the conditions under which music and musical instruments developed through the ages. Pursuing the guiding lines thus laid down, we should expect to find firmly established as favourites those instruments in which harmonic overtones occur in greatest profusion and possess the most insistent power of propagation through the air. And so it is. Paramount among the instruments in this respect are: (1) those having plucked strings, honoured by all nations as the favourites of the gods, as inspiring and exalting the soul of man; (2) the reed-blown pipes, leading to a more intimate musical experience which may become devotional or Dionysiac, according to the individual; (3) the trumpet (*E. B.*), in which the higher harmonics are developed in ever closer proximity and with the utmost propulsive power. Many passages in the Bible and in the Talmud show how dominating was the influence of this instrument among the Semitic races, and how sharp was the line of demarcation between the ritual and military uses of the trumpet. The voice of God was likened to the sound of the trumpet (Ps. xlvii. 5, &c.).

Investigation into the origins of musical instruments bring these before us under three different aspects (the first two being mentioned as a suggestion for study):

(1) Each as an instrument *per se*, considered iu regard to structural features, sound production, compass, quality of tone, devices, &c.

(2) In regard to historical development, distribution, and uses social, religious, and military.

(3) In relation to their influence on the practice and theory of music, on the building up of musical systems, such as the melodic, modal, and tonal; the polyphonic; the harmonic, both diatonic and chromatic.

In this third aspect we find that the instruments fall into

three important categories : (*a*) the *law-givers*, (*b*) the *recorders*, (*c*) the servants of man.

Every law-giver is also a recorder, but every recorder is not a law-giver.

The first category comprises instruments which embody a natural law in such a manner that when exploited by man, according to his natural instinct for proportion, the instrument *imposes upon him absolutely and inevitably a definite scale or sequence of intervals*, of which he had no preconceived notion.

The law-givers consist of certain wind instruments which are also recorders.

(*a*) The simplest example of law-giver is the pan-pipe or syrinx, consisting of several lengths of reed bound together, each member of which has a single note proper to itself by virtue of its length and of the diameter of its bore.   Man's innate sense of proportion prompts him almost invariably to cut each reed half as long again as the last (or one-third shorter); the pipes thus stand in the hemiolic ratio and form a sequence of perfect fifths.

In a syrinx of five pipes the result is the *pentatonic scale* composed, when starting from C, of the fifths C, G, D, A, E, or when grouped in the same octave according to length, C, D, E, G, A ; for a syrinx of seven pipes C, G, D, A, E, B, F♯, or the diatonic octave C, D, E, F♯, G, A, B ; while a syrinx of twelve pipes, cut according to the same proportions, produces the whole-tone scale, with its two forms, known to the ancient Chinese as the Scale of Heaven, C, D, E, F♯, G♯, A♯, and the Scale of Earth, C♯, D♯, E♯, G, A, B.

This applies to open pipes ; pipes closed at one end sound an octave lower, length for length, subject to a certain slight compensation in respect of the diameter of the bore.   The sound is produced by blowing across the top of the pipe, and not into it ; a method conducing to a tone almost lacking in harmonics.   The syrinx with its series of graduated pipes, when mechanically blown by bellows, supplied the idea of the organ.

The single reed or bamboo having lateral finger-holes and blown across the end like the pan-pipe, although probably representing the next step in evolution, and being likewise a law-giver, by virtue of the modality of its lateral borings, belongs to both (*a*) and (*b*).

The reed-blown pipe with lateral finger-holes, universal favourite in all ages and climes, is the most important of the law-givers, for it gave music the MODES ; it is extremely doubtful whether man would have discovered these unaided. They follow the trail of the reed-blown pipes in all civilizations of the world's history. It is from the modes that our major and minor scales are derived. It has long been supposed that scales either grew up gradually, and more or less fortuitously, from such simple units as a note accompanied by its fifth above and below, or, as already shown, from a cycle of perfect fifths. These hypotheses presuppose a conscious building up, guided by an inborn feeling for consonance, and carried out by means of primitive musical instruments ; such a hypothetical genesis of the scale is unsatis-factory, for it points to a mental development in advance of the actual state of arts, crafts, and sciences, or else accounts for the scale much too late in the development of music. The reed-blown pipe taught man the modes by purely mechanical means before he had formed any conception of the meaning of scale or interval. It is from Greek sources that most of our information concerning the *aulos* or reed-blown pipe is derived. It was the aulos that provided the foundation and idea upon which the modal system of ancient Greece was based. A set of seven pipes of the same length, but each having its own scheme of spacing in the boring of the finger-holes is sufficient to produce the seven ancient modes ; while a set of seven pipes, all having the same scheme of spacing but disposed on pipes of graduated lengths, produces what are known as the *species.*

In considering the aulos as the origin of the modes, it is impossible to make abstraction of the mouthpiece; it must always be included. The earliest form of mouthpiece was a double-reed vibrator, dear to the heart of every country child as the *squeaker*, and made from a shoot of fresh green wheat or oat, slightly flattened by pressure at a cut end, or later from the last green joint of the river reed before the flower.   Played by even breath-pressure, it produces differences of pitch in accordance with the length of the vibrating air column, at each of the holes uncovered by the fingers; increase of breath-pressure produces a slight increase in the dynamic intensity, but does not influence, control, or impede the pitch of the notes *unless the muscles of the glottis are relaxed or contracted*, for this is the unsuspected secret of the blowing of these pipes, which has not been taken into account by scientists.   A later type of mouthpiece, also known in the country-side, is the beating-reed of oat- or wheat-straw with a natural knot left at one end, from which a fine tongue from 1 to 1½ in. in length is raised by the insertion of a sharp blade; the base of the tongue is away from the knot, contrary to the practice of the Arabs in the mouthpiece of Arghool or Zummarah, which admits of little manipulation or persuasion on account of the direction of the cut.

The elasticity of the tongue of the beating-reed is a factor that makes for beauty of tone; the narrower the width of the tongue, the deeper the note given by the little straw, which frequently is as low as Cello C, a fact that will come as a surprise to many.   The pitch given by the mouthpiece alone may vary by as much as an octave or more, according to the player, and the notes rise as the result of an increase of breath proportional to the tightening of the muscles of the glottis, and fall as the muscles are relaxed and the breath-pressure becomes less.

The pipe with beating-reed mouthpiece is less inevitable as law-giver; it is the instrument of the artist, virtuoso, and *improvisatore* who has mastered the modes.   Through the adoption of this mouthpiece, the aulos passes into the second category from the point of view of practical and theoretical music; as a record, its value, through measurements, remains unimpaired.

These two types of mouthpieces used at different periods on the aulos have exercised a subtle far-reaching influence on the development of music. Regarded retrospectively through the ages, these two simple devices gave rise to the two well-known families of wood-wind instruments :

The aulos with double-reed mouthpiece to the oboe family.

The aulos with beating-reed mouthpiece to the clarinet family.

The behaviour of these two mouthpieces under various conditions stimulated the faculties of observation, analysis, and deduction, and laid the foundation of the speculative science of acoustics on a sound basis of empirical practical knowledge, and modern science has not made any great advance in this field. The acoustic explanation of some of the problems arising out of the behaviour of the aulos is still lacking ; for instance, the curious effect on the pitch of the aulos produced by the drawing apart of a pair of pipes while they are being played, and of bringing them again alongside. Aristoxenus [1] refers to this expedient, but without offering any explanation of the phenomenon, which occurs likewise when the pair or a single pipe is raised from a vertical to a horizontal position. As an example may be cited an actual experiment made by the present writer : a carefully measured facsimile of one of the Elgin pipes with six holes, belonging to the golden age of Art in Greece (c. 500 B. c., preserved in the British Museum), gives the notes of the ancient liturgical libation mode, the Spondeiakos Tropos (σπονδειακός τρόπος), a simple and austere form of the Dorian. Holding the pipe in a vertical position, the sequence produced by opening the finger-holes rang out from C = 64 v.p.s. ; when raised to the horizontal the pitch of the fundamental went up to F = 88 v.p.s., on which the sequence, true in intonation as before, was rendered with ease. The two positions of auletes on Greek vases and bas-reliefs thus signified *a change of key* ; and this was not the only means of obtaining that result on the pipes.

The little bulbs often seen near the mouthpiece on the aulos,

---

[1] *Harmonics*, Macran's edition, 1902, p. 196 : Clarendon Press.

one, two, or three in number, were fitted into the reed pipe to conceal the protruding straw of the mouthpiece, one or more being required according to the length of the latter; a longer straw mouthpiece in the same pipe would denote, not a change of key, but of modal species.

The sound is produced in all reed-blown pipes by blowing directly into the pipe through the mouthpiece. The piper who is able to distinguish harmonics, as he feels and hears the sound come in response to the propulsion of his breath through the tube, passes through an experience of an extraordinarily intimate nature when using the beating-reed mouthpiece of oat- or wheat-straw. The little mouthpiece is the sound producer, the pipe a mere resonator, and the piper the master of both.

Having bestowed upon the Greeks the proportional sequences known as modes (ἁρμονίαι) as a basis for the development of an art of music, the aulos passed from the first and second categories into the third, and from law-giver became the servant of the musician, who had by that time mastered what the aulos had to teach him. Technically, the change was brought about by the difference in the mouthpiece inserted into the reed. The significance of such a change is deep and interesting. Played with the double-reed mouthpiece, the aulos was the uncompromising law-giver, the creator and stern guardian of the modal scales: tested by the monochord the intervals are true to ratio. With the advent of the more wayward and artistic beating-reed, the tone of the instrument became resonant, deep, and full when the tongue was finely cut to the right proportions. Musicianship came into being, the aulos-player improvised his own music, he discovered the resources of his instrument and, by using these to the full, advanced his art by leaps and bounds. In the sixth century B.C. musical contests were instituted at all the solemn games and processions, restricted at first to performances of singers accompanied on the kithara, but at the eighth Pythian Games,[1] c. 550 B.C., the first contests for solo playing on

[1] Paus. x, 7, § 4 sqq. ; *E. B.*, s.v. Cithara.

Facsimile of the Elgin Aulos (British Museum)

PLATE I*a* (p. 94)

Reproduction of a Greek Kithara, by H. Kent, from a Greek
Vase, *c.* 500 B.C. (British Museum)

Photograph by Donald Macbeth

PLATE I*b* (p. 95)

both kithara and aulos were initiated. One of the principal features at the later Pythian Games was the ambitious composition for the aulos known as the *Nomos Pythicos*,[1] describing in five parts the victory of Apollo over the Python.

The progress of music brought in its train many improvements in aulos and kithara, upon which our theoretical knowledge of the state of music in different eras is largely based. There were various devices for increasing the compass, for producing enharmonic notes, for changing the key or pitch, while retaining the same mode, such as the one already mentioned in connexion with the Elgin pipe. The same result may be obtained with a beating-reed by shortening the tongue of the mouthpiece with the lip by $\frac{1}{3}$ or $\frac{1}{4}$, which amounts to the same thing while being less spectacular. Uncovering a hole by means of three graduated movements produced two new notes, occurring in pitch between those of the two finger-holes concerned. Cross-fingering was also probably used by Greek auletes, since it was a well-known device in antiquity. Bhārātā, the fifth-century Hindu author on the Drama, describes both practices in a chapter dealing with flutes. An increased compass makes further demands on the ingenuity of the pipe-maker, who had to find means of covering holes, in excess of the number of fingers, when not in use. Bands of silver or bronze, pierced with holes corresponding with those on the pipe, and made to revolve round it, opened or closed the holes at will. The fact that some of these bands have been found with holes differing in position and in diameter in the same band (*E. B.*, Aulos, Figs. 1 and 2) reveals the fact that successful efforts were being made to produce upon the aulos a plurality of modes, which recalls Plato's lament over the Panharmonious aulos on which all the modes could be played (*Rep.* 399 c). Professor J. L. Myres shows in the drawing of the bands that advantage has been taken of the acoustic principle that a hole of smaller diameter placed nearer the

---

[1] Strabo, ix, p. 421, and Kathleen Schlesinger, ' Researches into the Origin of the Organs of the Ancients ', *Int. Mus. Ges.* Sbd. II, 1901, ii, p. 177.

mouthpiece may be substituted for a larger one in the theoretical position. The present writer has found many instances of this on specimens of pipes found in the sarcophagi of ancient Egypt.

During the best classical period the aulos was a reed-pipe, and therefore had a cylindrical bore with the properties of a stopped pipe, overblowing harmonics given by the odd numbers of the series 3, 5, 7, &c., whereas a conical bore confers the properties of an open pipe and produces an octave instrument; it is not, however, safe to build too much upon an instrument apparently conical (especially in illustrations), for in short tubes with lateral holes the difference in internal diameter often does not amount to more than a *couple of millimetres*—the bell excepted, which does not affect the scale—and that is not sufficient to disturb either the sequence indicated by the holes, or the overblowing.

A Roman representation of a pair of oboes with slightly conical tubes opening out into a bell, and played by means of a double-reed mouthpiece clearly visible and differing little from the modern one, may be seen at the British Museum (in the Gem Room of the Graeco-Roman Department).

By the middle of the thirteenth century the true characteristics of both oboe and clarinet are to be distinguished in illuminated manuscripts, as, for instance, in the famous miniatures of the fifty-two musicians in the Cantigas de Santa Maria.[1]

The flute, whether blown across the end like the *nay* of the Egyptians, or from a side embouchure among Hindus and Chinese, did not enjoy the same universal popularity as the reed-blown pipe; probably owing to the paucity of harmonics in the composition of its timbre. The flute may, under certain conditions, be a law-giver, as, for instance, when the lowest hole is left uncovered as vent (exit) instead of the end of the pipe being used for the purpose. This expedient is rendered necessary by the influence of the diameter of the bore of the flute upon the length of the air-wave, thus calling for compensation when the

---

[1] Riaño, *Notes on Early Spanish Music*, Quaritch, 1887.

position of the first hole is being determined. The necessity for making this allowance is not self-evident, for it is only discovered when the scale formed by the finger-holes is found to be out of tune with the end note of the flute. Primitive flute-makers get over the difficulty by the expedient mentioned above, and the scale then begins with the first hole, which may be placed at any desired distance from the end ; the spacing for the finger-holes taking effect from the centre of the first hole next to the exit.

A complete set of fifteen modal flutes is described by Sārñgadeva [1] in the *Ratnākara*, a thirteenth-century Hindu treatise. The flute has always been found a useful instrument from the ease with which it overblows the octave and twelfth. At the end of the fourteenth century the transverse flute was beginning to be used in the West; it was made in one piece, had six finger-holes and no keys. Half-stopping and cross-fingering could be used for an occasional semitone, but the making of a flute was such a simple matter in those early days, that the flute-player could easily procure a set in different pitches.

Whereas each wind instrument that survives constitutes an incontrovertible record of pitch, scale, or mode, stringed instruments—with the exception of those provided with fretted necks—remain speechless as to their past use. When the vast number of species of instruments which have sprung from the use of a stretched spring is viewed retrospectively, the adoption of guiding lines based upon fundamental issues is felt to be necessary when classifying them. The influence of strings has been above all aesthetic; to them we owe our ideal of a beautiful tone. Therefore, that which bestows upon an instrument the elements which contribute to the realization of a beautiful tone-quality—sonority and depth, richness and variety—is its most precious possession and constitutes its characteristic feature.

---

[1] *Encycl. de la Mus.*, Paris, 1913, Fasc. 12 ; *Inde*, par Joanny Grosset, p. 353.

There is in stringed instruments one feature of great importance that goes far to compensate for the lost records of mode,
scale, and pitch; it forms the basis of classification.   That
feature is the sound-chest or resonance-box which is mainly
responsible for the quality of the tone.

All instruments with strings plucked, struck, or bowed may
be divided into two main classes :

(1) Those having a body or sound-chest of box-like structure,
with parallel back and belly, joined by ribs of equal width—the
best possible structure for both plucked and bowed strings.

(2) Those having a body shaped like a tortoise, a boat, or
half a pear, covered by a sound-board or belly of vellum,
serpent-skin, or thin wood glued over the cavity of the body
without the intermediary of ribs—a structure suitable for
plucked strings *only*.

The form imposed upon the volume of air, acting as resonator
within the sound-chest of a stringed instrument, by the structural
features of that container influences the acoustic properties of the
instrument and consequently the tone-quality of the musical
response to the impact on the strings.   The ingenuity of man
found means of modifying and improving the conditions thus
imposed ; by the discovery of (1) pitch pine as the best material
for the belly or sound-board in view of its function as resonator,
reinforcing passively the vibrations of the strings conveyed to
it through the bridge upon which these rest.   (2) The best
shape, material, and position for the bridge (to which was added
much later, in the violin, the sound-post) supporting the strings,
determining their vibrating length from the nut, or in primitive
instruments from the point of attachment to the tuning-pins,
and conveying the form of the sound-wave to the resonating
chamber within the sound-chest.   (3) Of the most suitable shape
and position of the sound-holes cut through the belly, through
which the complex sound-waves, definitely constituted by the
combination of all these factors, make their way to the ear.

The stringing of instruments gradually brings into being a

certain empirical balancing of the factors of length, density or thickness, and tension or weight of the string. Length is the simplest of the factors; tension the most subtle and the most important; it always has the last word. By virtue of its implications, the application of length to the problems involved by stringing actually divides instruments into two categories independently of the structure of the sound-chest: (1) those in which the strings, however numerous, are of equal length, as in the kithara and some psalteries; in instruments with necks, such as guitars, lutes, &c., and in the early fretted clavichords. (2) Those in which the strings are of graduated lengths, such as harps, psalteries and dulcimers, virginals, spinets, and harpsichords.

In the monochord and, to a certain degree, in fretted instruments both classes are equally represented; for its single string is to all intents and purposes either one or many strings of the same length in turn, all of which may be of the same or of different pitch, according to whether the use of the string is to be modal or tonal. The divisions on the rule or canon of the monochord, on the other hand, convert it by the use of movable bridges into a harp-like instrument having strings of different lengths.

The manner in which strings are set in vibration exercises a powerful influence upon the instrument as a whole, leading to the modification of some of the features and to the invention of various devices. Strings are set in vibration: (a) by plucking with finger or plectrum, (b) by striking by stick or mallet, (c) by the friction of bow or rosined wheel.

The corollary of (b), for example, is a strengthening of the structure of the sound-chest to enable it to resist the disruptive force of increased tension necessitated by the blow on a tense string, as in the dulcimer, which perforce becomes less and less portable as the number of strings increases.

The best-known archetypes of the two classes of stringed instruments are (1) the kithara and (2) the lyre of the Greeks,

Musicians playing the Guitar and Bagpipe. From a Hittite Slab
at Eyuk (c. 1000 B.C.)

Photograph presented by Prof. John Garstang

PLATE III (p. 101)

ment, played by means of a plectrum, is seen to have a box sound-chest with incurvations similar to those of the modern guitar and a long neck with frets. With the guitar-player is a player upon a bagpipe (*E. B.*) in the shape of a dog.

It is a strange circumstance that, although many instruments were known to the Greeks of Hellas, harp, barbiton, pandura, flute, psaltery, &c., three alone seem to have been found worthy of serious consideration and to have won their way into the practical music of ritual and social life, viz. the kithara, lyre, and aulos, and later on the organ (known as syrinx, organon, and hydraulos). To the aulos Greece owed, as we have seen, the inception and discovery of the modes or harmoniai (ἁρμονίαι) which were transferred by tuning to the kithara. The gradual addition above and below the central Dorian mode of one string at a time for the purpose of playing the other modes in species on the same kithara without retuning, produced, when the seven original strings had been increased to fifteen,[1] the double octave scale known as the Greater Complete System, for which the nomenclature belonging to the strings of the kithara was adopted.

Why, it may be asked, did the Greeks reject the harp and adopt the kithara? In both instruments the strings are plucked, both have a resonance-box, offer much the same facilities for the accompaniment of vocal music or for solo playing. There is one great but subtle difference between the instruments, viz. the principle of scaling; in the harp the degrees of pitch are obtained mainly by the proportional decrease in the length of the string, tension being maintained practically equal, whereby homogeneity in timbre results, to be varied slightly at will by the empiric selection of the point of impact in plucking the string. In the kithara all the strings are of the same length; the factors in the variation of pitch here are, therefore, the

---

[1] This genesis of the Greater Complete System is fully traced in a work by the present writer on *The Modes of Ancient Greece* in the light of her recent discovery, which is in course of preparation.

thickness or diameter of string, and the tension proportional to the length.[1]

The effect of this paramount use of tension is to vary the harmonic constituents of the tone of the different strings. It will be obvious that, to musicians endowed with the power of hearing the play of harmonic overtones, the scaling in use on the kithara produced a more subtle and varied accompaniment to the string note than that of the harp, which was the more sonorous.

It is evident that the Egyptians attached a special significance to this harp-scaling, for when they borrowed the kithara from the ancient Chaldeans they made the supports of the cross-bar of unequal length,[2] so that it was oblique to the base of the kithara, and the scaling of the strings became harp-like in consequence.

The origin of the lute is probably remote, since the tamboura, the smallest member of the family, figures on a bas-relief coeval with the above-mentioned from the palace of King Gudea (2700 B.C.). An Egyptian lute or barbiton[3] (*E. B.*) of the Greek post-Mycenaean period, with wide body and short neck, is shown on a little terra-cotta figure found by Prof. Sir W. Flinders Petrie in 1906, in the cemetery of Goshen, and now preserved in the Ashmolean Museum at Oxford. The numerous examples of members of the lute family in the ancient realms of the East, and later on all over Europe, testify to the wide popularity of the instrument. Obtained by the Arabs from Persia, and called by them *el-'ūd*, the lute became the popular national instrument. Owing to the rapid spread of scholastic learning from Greek and other sources in Islam from the eighth century, we are in possession of very full indications as to the tuning, fretting, and scale of the lute from the middle of the ninth

---

[1] Ptolemy and other Greek theorists understood something of the relative significance of these factors.

[2] *Precursors*, p. 435 ; C. Engel, *Music of the most Ancient Nations*, Reeves, p. 197.

[3] *Prec.*, Pl. XIII.

century. As the result of a recent inquiry into the treatises of
these Arabian theorists, some interesting data have come to
light which have an indirect but important bearing on the
nature and genesis of the Ecclesiastical modes as developed in
the Christian East, a subject which still invites research [1] and
speculation owing to the paucity of documents due to the
destruction of the libraries at Alexandria and elsewhere, and to
the rifling of monasteries later on by the Arabs. Until the
tenth century the lute possessed four strings tuned in fourths ;
four frets were fixed along the neck, named from the fingers by
which they were governed. These frets gave with the open
string five notes to the tetrachord, two of the notes being
alternatives; the intervals obtained thereby were tone, semitone or tone, the last fret on each string producing a perfect
fourth with the open string, and giving the same note as the
next open string higher. The theorists equated the sequences
thus obtained with the Greek system beginning with Proslambanomenos, and were able to play with ease not only in the Lydian
or Phrygian species, but also in the Dorian, and with change of
key. The Greek double-octave system as a whole, however,
did not lie well within this accordance of the lute in fourths,
which suggests that the equation was a purely theoretical one,
an hypothesis which is confirmed by statements of the theorists
themselves, and by the rapid increase of alternative notes
within the tetrachord up to nine frets ; this is an unmistakable
sign of modal activity, since the additional frets gave intervals
other than tones and semitones which belong to the real modes
of the ancients. There was another accordance in local use in
Syria and in Bagdad, introduced by Ishāk-al-Mausili (of Mosul),
767–850, who, according to al-Ispāhāni,[2] the celebrated tenth-
century chronicler, had come upon it during his intercourse
with the Christian monks. This new accordance consisted in

[1] See *Mélodies Liturgiques Syriennes*, par Dom Jeannin, O.S.B., 1924,
Paris (Leroux).
[2] See Kosegarten Alii Ispah, *Kitāb al-Aghāni*, Greifswald, 1840.

tuning the two highest strings first in fourths, and the two lower ones in octaves below these, which gave the two conjunct tetrachords on each pair of strings with the tone of disjunction between them, exactly as in the Greek scale. Ishāk learnt further, obviously from the same monastic source, to use the modal species, which he called in Arabic the *majra*, and these with the new accordance give the four Authentic and four Plagal Ecclesiastical modes. These species, when seated upon the framework of the Greater Complete System (through the frets of the lute) correspond in every particular with those given by Hucbald (840–930). Thus the indications concerning the technique of the lute from Arabian sources give a long-sought clue to the last stage in the development of the Greater Complete System of Ancient Greece, which came about in the Christian East and passed thence into Europe. The final stage was reached when, through the predominance of the Phrygian mode in Hellenic Asia, the Proslambanomenos, emerging from its subordinate position as added note outside the tetrachords, and later as tone of disjunction at the beginning of the *Hypo* species, now still later became the starting-point of the sequence of tetrachords, thus usurping the function of Hypatē Hypatōn, in consequence of the change of mode from Dorian to Phrygian—the Phrygian species beginning, as is well known, upon Lichanos Hypatōn. Those who are interested in this question may work this out for themselves [1] in the *majra of wosta*, i. e. using the second instead of the third fret, and compare the results with Hucbald's [2] statement of the four Authentics and the four Plagals.

In the hands of the Arabs the lute strongly favoured the tetrachordal system of mixed modes, more especially in the East, whereas in the west of Europe the Spanish lute tended towards a fretted major scale with Pythagorean intervals, which,

---

[1] Or they may consult the *Musical Standard*, Feb. 6 and 20 and March 20, 1926, in which the question is discussed in detail.

[2] *De Harm. Institutione, Gerbert. Scriptores*, vol. i, pp. 115 sqq.

however, according to Ramis de Pareia (quoted on p. 112), probably belonged more exclusively to the theory than to the practice
of music. As long as man was able to enjoy the harmonic accompaniment to the tones of the plucked string of harp, kithara,
or lute he was content. By varying the place of impact he was
able to change the composition of the mass-chord. When the
weaving of melodies became the goal of his desires, the number
of strings increased little by little, bringing in their train
expansion and changes in the musical system and a whole sheaf
of new problems for the instrument-maker.

It has been suggested that supplementary notes could be
obtained on kithara and harp by stopping the free string with
nail or knuckle, in order to avoid the inconvenience of constant
retuning. Such a practice, however, could only belong to a
period of decadence, for the higher note produced by stretching
the string, i. e. by increasing both length and tension until
sufficient rigidity is obtained for the string to yield a steady
note, is a gain at the expense of beauty and sonority of tone.
This expedient can, in any case, only succeed as to pitch near
the nut, where the rigidity of the string is naturally greatest.

The advent of the bow in Europe must be placed in the
ninth century, or even somewhat earlier. It came in all probability by way of the Christian East, since the first known illustration of a bow is to be found on the frescoed walls of the Greek
monastery of Baouït [1] (Bawit), in North Africa. On a mural
painting, assigned to the sixth or seventh century, Orpheus is
depicted bowing a pear-shaped instrument of the rebab or lute
family. It is difficult to take seriously Dr. Curt Sachs' [2] discovery in the Utrecht Psalter [3] of the earliest 'trustworthy'
record of a European fiddle played with what he calls a bow, but

---

[1] *Le monastère et la nécropole de Baouït*, by Jean Clédat, Caire, 1904;
E. B., s.v. Bow.

[2] *Handbuch d. Musikinstrumentenkunde*, Leipzig, 1920, p. 170-1, Fig. 51.

[3] *Precursors*, Kathleen Schlesinger, pp. 343-82, pl. VI (1), more specifically
pp. 347 and 374; Ps. cviii in our version.

what is very obviously a long sword in the original manuscript, of which a complete autotype facsimile exists at the British Museum. In the enlarged reproduction of part of the drawing given in Curt Sachs' book,[1] the draughtsman, meeting the wishes of the Professor more than half-way, has curtailed the sword by more than half its length, so that it is made to resemble the fiddle-bow. King David, moreover, is turned into

King David bearing harp, kithara, and long sword.
(*From the Autotype Facsimile of the Utrecht Psalter in the British Museum.*)

a *blind minstrel* in the text of the book, whereas the naïve artist of the Utrecht Psalter, mindful of the fact that he is illustrating a Psalm for a Psalter, has drawn David holding the two instruments, mentioned in verse 2, in his left, and the very long sword suggested by verse 13, 'through God we shall do valiantly', in his right hand; in another part of the picture, the artist, who had a strong sense of humour, has drawn King David preparing to swing a pair of shoes over Edom. The

[1] *Handbuch d. Musikinstrumentenkunde*, Leipzig, 1920, p. 170–1, Fig. 51.

Utrecht Psalter is probably the most famous and most copied
of early medieval pictorial manuscripts; the vicissitudes of the
original Codex (which belonged to the Cottonian Library)
have called forth many lengthy monographs from distinguished
experts of various nationalities. According to a consensus of
opinion, the actual Psalter emanated from the Carolingian
School of Rheims, at the beginning of the ninth century, but

The Kithara evolving into the Guitar with fretted neck.
(*From the Autotype Facsimile of the Utrecht Psalter in the British Museum.*)

the drawings illustrating each Psalm had been copied from an
older Greek or Syrian prototype, probably of the sixth century.
It is in this famous manuscript that the present writer found the
missing links in the evolution of the Kithara into Violin. Dr.
Curt Sachs acclaims the 'bowed lute' of the Utrecht Psalter
as the *fidula* mentioned by Ottfried von Weissenburg (800–870);
he has unfortunately pinned his faith to a faulty reproduction.

A long bow, used with a pear-shaped instrument, occurs on
a ninth-century ivory casket of Italo-Byzantine workmanship
in the Carrand collection at Florence, and in the tenth and

eleventh centuries the bow is found adapted to various instruments. The present writer has found nothing since the publication in 1910 of her work on the origin of the violin family [1] to modify the theory expounded therein.

A recent Scandinavian writer, Dr. Otto Andersson, has published an interesting monograph [2] on what he calls the *Northern Bowed-Harp*, which bears no resemblance to a harp, but seems akin to the Crwth or Crowd. Dr. Andersson suggests in this book, which contains much new and interesting material, a possible Northern origin for the bow, on evidence that seems scanty and indefinite to archaeologists accustomed to the abundance of monuments and data available in research over the rest of Europe and the ancient East. No definite, attested dates are given to show how early these instruments were played with the bow, and developed the nail technique, which is one of the chief characteristics of the instrument. This irregular technique was not open to the same objections in a bowed instrument as it was in one with plucked strings, as discussed above.

The advent of the bow, whether from the East via Byzantium, or via the Moors of Spain or from the North, was an event of capital significance to the destiny of Music.

The bow ushers in a new epoch in the development of Music. For the first time it became possible to produce on a string a sustained tone independent of changes of pitch, as in the voice, the music of reed-pipes (*E. B.*, s.v. Reed), and the organ.

All the earliest examples of bowed instruments are of the rebab type with vaulted backs.

The bow accomplished for stringed instruments what the little mouthpiece with beating-reed had done for the aulos ; it favoured the individual emotional expression in music ; the reign of the Solo was at hand.

As soon as they had been tuned, all instruments so far

---

[1] *Precursors.*

[2] *Stråkharpan*, Stockholm, 1923. An English translation is in the press. William Reeves, London.

considered, all pipes and flutes, kithara, lyre and rotta, psaltery, dulcimer, lutes, and keyboard instruments (*E. B.*), one and all possessed a fixed scale, which tends to develop finger-technique to the prejudice of musicianship.

In bowed instruments without frets, as also in the trumpet (and later in the sackbut or slide trumpet), horn, and tuba (*E. B.*), the instrumentalist was in a different category; he had to make his scale by ear, to preserve his intonation pure, and to keep his feeling for tonality or modality to the end of the melody. Since these instruments are unfettered, and possess unlimited freedom in their choice of scale, interval, and intonation, it follows that upon them it was possible to play at will the true modal scales, with their strange intervals, from which the key-board was debarred. There is documentary evidence of the survival of these scales up to the middle of the sixteenth century, and reed-blown pipes, flutes, and pan-pipes are still being made and used at the present day for the modal sequences which have been treasured and fostered by the Folk. It is not difficult to realize the fascination which the bowed instruments, rebecs, guitar-fiddles, vielles, exercised as soon as some of their resources were discovered.

The bowed instruments formed the link between the two streams of music, which were evolving side by side, but separated by an apparently impenetrable barrier. On the one hand, the Ecclesiastical modes, supported by the authority of the Church, and musically by the keyboard of the organ, formed the basis upon which the theory and practice of music were developing. In the country-side, on the other hand, the Folk played, sang, and danced to the music of pipes, rebecs, guitars, and vielles, without theory, notation, or records, to the music of the same modes that delighted and inspired the ancients, that gave rise to the cogitations and speculations of philosophers and writers innumerable. When instrumental music came into its own, the music of the modes had to be approximated to that of the keyboard and Church, as we may learn from the schemes for cross-fingering published by Martin Agricola in his *Musica Instrumentalis* (1528-9).

During the period under survey the trumpet and kindred instruments endured through many vicissitudes. The trumpet, indeed, has as yet been presented only as the silver ritual instrument of the Hebrews, the *ḥᵃṣōṣᵉrāh*. Special instructions are given in the Bible, and many more in the Talmud (Babylonian), for two very different musical effects to be obtained from the instrument: (1) blowing, the musical playing of long-drawn notes, sonorous and powerful, for use in the ritual of the Temple; (2) sounding the alarm, i. e. the flourish or fanfare, founded upon the 4th, 5th, 6th, and 7th overtones, which possesses a more military or secular significance. Two other instruments were frequently but erroneously translated trumpet, viz. the *keren* or cow-horn, and the *shophar* or ram's-horn, which was used at the siege of Jericho, and is still used at the present day in the Synagogue at the solemn festivals. In the Roman Empire the true trumpet was known as the *buccina* (*E. B.*); its tube, narrow and cylindrical, measuring 11 to 12 ft. in length, was wound into a circular form resembling a wide letter C; one end holding the mouthpiece and the other, passing over shoulder and head, opened out gradually into a bell. The late Victor Mahillon, of Brussels, made a facsimile of one of these buccinas, discovered in the ruins of Pompeii, and found that it was in G and gave almost the same harmonics as the French horn and trumpet. The keren has become the *cornua* of the Romans, bent in form of a crescent, and consisting of a conical metal tube widening gradually into a bell; the shophar resembled the Roman *lituus*.

From the eleventh to the fourteenth century the trumpet, as *busine*, was widely known and used all over Europe, but since the art of bending metal tubes was lost after the fall of the Roman Empire, the busine was made straight in sections, joined and strengthened by means of rings or circular bosses.

Towards the end of the fourteenth century the sections were made to telescope, and the bosses were used for drawing the tubes out or pushing them in; the busine had thus become a draw-trumpet or sackbut, which developed into the trombone.

The tuba had a conical bore of larger calibre than the cornua, and was long and straight. It is from these elements that the brass wind of our orchestra evolved through the Middle Ages, differentiated by the following characteristics:

(a) The shape of the bore, influencing the compass and scale, was narrow and cylindrical in the trumpet, facilitating the formation and production of high harmonics, up to the 16th (or even higher with a clarino mouthpiece), and therefore of a diatonic scale of an octave or more; in the horn (known as French horn at the end of the seventeenth century), a delicately elongated cone of slender proportions, which, while robbing the instrument of the lower half of the compass to which it was entitled by virtue of its length, gave it a diatonic scale; in the tuba the wide calibre facilitated the production of massive lower harmonics.

(b) The form of the mouthpiece (*E. B.*), influencing the quality of tone. In the trumpet, the shallow cup, leading by a sharp angle into the bore, produced the brilliant incisive quality characteristic of the instrument; the shallower the cup, the more easily are the higher harmonics produced; in the horn a moderate cup-shaped mouthpiece was at first in use, but the mellow richness of the French horn is due to the funnel-shaped mouthpiece gradually evolved for it during the Middle Ages. In the tuba and the hunting-horn (*cor de chasse*) the cup-mouthpiece was deep and wide, to facilitate the production of the fanfare, for which a tablature existed in the fourteenth century (*E. B.*, s.v. Horn).

To these instruments, all of which gave out by overblowing some section of the harmonic series, rich in true thirds and fifths, evolving Music owes some of her evident distaste for the ditone or Pythagorean third. There is, indeed, a strong probability that Ramis de Pareia,[1] writing in the fifteenth century, had made a discovery true not only in his own day, but in the preceding centuries also, when he asserted that the 5 : 4 major third was the one used in practice, whereas it figured in speculative theory as 81 : 64, the ditone of the Pythagoreans. This discrepancy between practice and theory in the use of intervals, which was likewise noticed by the Arabian theorists Al-Fārābi, Avicenna, and others regarding other intervals, probably explains the difficulty experienced by monks in teaching their pupils to sing to the monochord, upon which was enthroned the Pythagorean scale : the natural musical feeling rebelled against the unnatural interval.

The earliest record of the characteristic method of setting a string in vibration by striking it with a stick or small mallet is to be found on the Assyrian slabs from Koyunjik in the galleries of the British Museum. The dulcimer (the pisantir, psantērīn, or santir of the days of Nebuchadrezzar, translated psaltery in Daniel) seems to have been a favourite instrument with Assyrian monarchs, for it figures at many of their functions. There is no possible doubt that some of these instruments were dulcimers and not psalteries—as they would be if the strings were plucked by the fingers, or by sticks used as plectra—judging from the position in which the stick is held by some of the musicians, standing with hand clenched, and the stick balanced lightly between thumb and forefinger, ready to give the elastic wrist-blow which alone produces a fine round tone from the string. From this we may surmise that technique was in those early days directed by a feeling for quality. The inevitable corollary of striking the string is the demand for increased tension, since a slack string gives bad results, and as a consequence a corresponding reinforcing of the resonance-box likewise becomes necessary. Running its course through the

---

[1] *Musica Practica*, Bologna, 1482, reprint by Joh. Wolf, Leipzig, 1901, p. 98, note 3.

centuries, the evolving piano-hammer has brought in its train a formidable array of strain-resisting devices, for the aggregate tension of the strings of a modern grand pianoforte totals something like 33 tons.

Without attempting to follow the development of the dulcimer (*E. B.*) up to the fifteenth century, we may note that the scaling of the strings, in which traces of both the principles discussed above, viz. by equal length and by graduated length respectively characteristic of kithara and harp, may be observed. Some sound-chests closely follow the shape of the scaling, which is carried out by means of low wooden bridges.

The organ supplied the next step in the evolution of the pianoforte, viz. a balanced keyboard, first described as part of the hydraulic organ by Hero of Alexandria, in the second century B. C., and later by Vitruvius. These instruments were made by Byzantine craftsmen, and the keyboards were applied to both pneumatic and hydraulic organs, which were in use in the Roman Empire and the Christian East during the early centuries of our era. In the twelfth century the keyboard appeared on small portative organs with the compass of an octave or twelfth. Some ingenious and enterprising maker in the fourteenth century conceived the idea of applying the keyboard mechanism to the popular psalteries and dulcimers, together with a device for plucking or striking the string affixed to the lever of the key. When this device consisted of a jack furnished with a quill, the clavicembalo and harpsichord, the spinet or virginals, came into being. The tangent keys of the organistrum (*E. B.*) for stopping the strings at certain measured distances, according to the ratios of the intervals to be produced, no doubt supplied the idea of the tangent used for converting the dulcimer into a clavichord. In the keyboard instrument with plucked strings, the requisite vibrating lengths are determined by scaling; the actual place at which the string is plucked affects the quality but not the pitch of the note. In the clavichord, on the contrary, the strings are of

Q

approximately the same length, the tangent, as it rises with the key-lever, performing the double function of setting the string in vibration and of dividing the vibrating length by cleaving to the string and stopping it at the point of impact, until the key is released, when all vibration is instantly damped by a small strip of cloth interwoven among the strings. One string served for several tangents on the earliest fretted clavichords.

The keyboard with its predetermined fixed scale proved one of the chief factors in establishing the use of the Ecclesiastical modes on a firm basis in the liturgy. The keyboard also played a part in the development of musical notation evolved in the ninth century, and shown by Hucbald (840–930) to consist of the first seven letters of the Latin alphabet in recurrent sequence for each octave. These letters were by Hucbald equated at first with the nomenclature of the Greek scale of two octaves, and, to avoid possibility of error or misunderstanding, they were in addition evaluated by tone and semitone. From Hucbald also comes the information that in his day the organ, hydraulic as well as pneumatic, was tuned to our major scale, since he states that the semitones occurred in the tetrachord between the third and fourth degrees; this, according to him, was the favourite mode.

The keyboard, or series of sliders, was marked with the alphabet from the ninth century, or earlier still, and we hear that the remarkable organ installed in Winchester Cathedral [1] by Bishop Elphege (d. 951) had two manuals, each with its own alphabet.

England and Germany seem, after Byzantium and the Christian East (where Arabian craftsmen also had learnt from the Greeks to build organs), to have been foremost in organ-building from the ninth century. The balanced keyboard of the Alexandrians remained in use in the Roman Empire until the fifth century at least, if one may judge from the representa-

[1] R. C. Hope, *Mediæval Music*, 1894, pp. 66–9: *E. B.*, s.v. Organ; Part I, 'Hist. of Ancient Organ', by K. S.

tion of a pneumatic organ engraved on a brass plate in the church of St. Paul *extra muros* in Rome, which has fifteen keys and flue-pipes (*E. B.*). After the fall of the Empire the art of organ-building fell for a time into disuse, and sliders, drawn in and out to open and close the valves, replaced levered keys in the earliest organs of European origin. The practice of having three or more ranks of pipes to each key—as in the model of the Carthage hydraulic organ (*c.* A.D. 120)—with register keys or knobs, allowing of the different ranks being sounded separately or together (when three notes would sound simultaneously as each key was depressed), may probably have suggested the idea of the *organum*, the earliest known form of polyphonic music. The fact that when first described by a theorist (Hucbald) the melody was played with rigid accompaniment of parallel fifths and octaves, suggests an instrumental origin, which must have antedated the theoretical description. John Scotus Erigena (mid-ninth century), Greek scholar and philosopher, refers (as pointed out by Hugo Riemann [1]) to the singing in *organum*, in which the voices moved freely according to the rules for each tropos (or mode), rising and falling independently of each other, by intervals of different but harmonious proportions, from which it is obvious that it is not here a question of mere parallel singing in rigid fourths or fifths with the octave, but of an art-form already well known and developed, since Erigena refers to existing rules for singing in organum; the description, besides, occurs not in a theoretical treatise, but in his fine philosophical work, *De divisione naturae* (Bk. V), when the *organum* had already passed beyond the initial stage.

What European music owes to Greece is incalculable, and does not appear to have been fully realized at the present day. All the spade work was done by her; no other sources of theoretical knowledge were available at the beginning of our era; no other great nation of antiquity has left traces of a

---

[1] *Gesch. d. Musiktheorie*, Berlin, 1920, pp. 18 sqq.

musical system or notation committed to writing; our very notions of a scale, of the octave, of modes, species, and keys; of the diatonic, chromatic, and enharmonic genera, of intervals and their mathematical ratios, of notation and nomenclature, of the principles of melody-making, of metre and rhythm, of modulation, of our major and minor modes, our first notions of the acoustics of musical instruments—all are derived from Greece; it was she who laid the foundations of the art and science of music. If, therefore, this survey has been made largely through eyes steadily fixed upon Greece, it is because the writer feels that living, pregnant knowledge of these foundations, of these essentials, gained not only from literary sources, but also in some cases from recent practical experiments, is likely to conduce to a better understanding of the position of Western music at the dawn of the Middle Ages, and to a realization of the attitude of our budding theorists and musicians —an attitude of mingled reverential dependence and virile originality—from the eighth century onwards towards the legacy of Greece. And if the nations of the West developed their music, not so much individually as in common, along a new path, it is probably because their growing culture had a common origin in the Hellenic civilization, modified by a fresh stream of inspiration from the Greek Christian East.

Note 1 (page 100)

Two additional representations of these characteristic Sumerian kitharas, similar in all main structural features to the one in Salle Sarzec in the Louvre (illustrated above on p. 100), and having likewise a figure of a bull on the sound-box, are among the valuable finds brought back in 1928 by Mr. Leonard Woolley from the Royal Tombs at Ur ascribed to 3500 B.C. One kithara, played by a woman, figures on the lapis lazuli mosaic standard found in an inner chamber of the tomb; the second played with both hands by a donkey in grotesque scenes in mosaics inset in the chest of the large figure of a bull from the grave of Queen Shub-ab.

V

THEORETICAL WRITERS ON MUSIC
UP TO 1400

By the Rev. Dom Anselm Hughes, O.S.B., M.A.

The subject-matter of the early musical Theorists will be dealt with (after their own fashion) under separate headings, to the number of five, in rough correspondence with the five centuries under review. The writers of the tenth century are concerned chiefly with the exposition of Plainsong; in the eleventh the impetus of the Guidonian discovery turns their attention to the philosophy of the Scale and of the Modes; in the twelfth, mensurate notation follows on the Guidonian; in the thirteenth, an elaborate technique of rhythmical counterpoint is being constructed; while in the fourteenth we may say that all the preceding material is being worked over and manipulated, under the impetus of the *Ars Nova* movement, and its processes perfected, in preparation for the great advance associated with the names of Dunstable and Dufay. Alternatively, we may sum up the centuries in the following way: the tenth as Primitive, the eleventh as perfecting monodic notation, the twelfth as experimenting in polyphonic notation, the thirteenth as practising it, the fourteenth as beginning to compose (rather than to contrive) counterpoint.

But there is one factor which must be mentioned by way of preliminary, for its influence is felt all through these five centuries, and its understanding will enable us to enter more readily into the style and reasoning of the old theorists. This is what we may term the Mathematical Bias.

To be an expert in the theory of composition it is not necessary, strictly speaking, to possess great creative faculties;

but in these days we expect a great composer to be also master of the theory of his art. It would be invidious to mention living musicians, but in the very recent past the names of Sir Hubert Parry and Sir Charles Stanford spring to mind at once.

Yet it was not always so. This system of a nice balance between theorist and composer (or, more accurately, between technician and artist), wherein each musical individuality expresses himself by an emphasis to one side or the other, was disturbed (or perhaps aided) in the Middle Ages by an outside factor, Mathematics. Exactly why music was considered to have such close connexion with Mathematics by so many of its learned doctors is not obvious to us, though its position next after Geometry in the Quadrivium, or course of higher University studies, is suggestive; but their relationship, confined nowadays to Acoustics, was certainly very much closer in medieval times. And on the whole we may be thankful for it; though it necessitates a sharper distinction between theorist and composer in respect of their output, work, and practice (and perhaps in respect of their equipment also) than we are accustomed to, it yet helped to mould the new-born, plastic, formless art of polyphonic composition into a firm shape, probably saving Music from being unduly vague and capricious; giving us occasional hints as to some of the natural laws which may lie behind our aesthetic canons or conventions, and making Music to share with Architecture the leading position among the arts of medieval Europe.

THE TENTH CENTURY

OTGER OF ST. PONS	ix cent.
Aurelian of Réomé	*ix cent.*
Regino of Prum	(? –915).
REMIGIUS OF AUXERRE	ix cent. (late).
HUCBALD OF ST. AMAND	(840-930).
Odo of Clugny	*(879-942).*

Our period opens at a time when the official chant of the

Western Church had reached its final form : recensions and
codifications under Ambrose and Gregory, recognitions and
promulgations by Charlemagne, had brought the *Cantus
Ecclesiasticus* to its Golden Age, and it has been the avowed
aim of almost every modern plainchant restorer to reproduce
things as they were in the ninth century or even earlier. Our
writers, as we may naturally expect, have a tendency to be, in
respect of their age, modernists, and the temptation to speculate
is sometimes too strong for the conservatism which they know
to be their first duty. The zenith of Plainsong's course has been
reached ; and as it is reached it is passed, in accordance with a
universal law of human progress ; so that already before the
ninth century is out, the seeds of decadence are beginning to
sprout. The late Dom Gatard [1] traces two reasons for this : the
current of Graeco-Roman music with its metrical doctrines of
rhythm, and (in the following centuries) the growing art of
mensural and polyphonic composition. These new currents are
beginning to play havoc with the Theorists' science of Plainsong,
and with the exception of an occasional remark (obscure or
illuminating as the case may be) about the execution of some of
the ' grace-notes ' or ornamental forms of the single note (*virga*
or *punctum*) of Plainsong, such as the *strophicus, oriscus,
quilisma*, their chief value for us is confined to their *Tonalia*.

The *Tonale* is a list of Antiphons arranged in such a way
that it may be seen which ending of the appropriate psalm-tone
is to be sung when that Antiphon is used ; incidentally, of
course, it tells us in which mode the melody of that Antiphon is
written, as the Antiphons are all classified by their modes. An
examination of the *Tonalia* reveals the fact that the tenth-
century chanters had not such a fixity of modal doctrine as we
might expect. They had, however, a certain modal tradition ;
for instance, out of twenty Antiphons, nineteen times each
tonale will prescribe the same psalm-tone and ending ; but in
the case of the twentieth they may differ widely, sometimes with

[1] *Plainchant*, p. 45 (The Faith Press, 1921).

apparently no reason.   And so the theoretical writings tend to support the claim made in recent years that the Modal System is an arbitrary, ' Graeco-Roman ' thing imposed in later centuries upon a more elastic and primitive scale-system of the earlier Christian centuries.   *Tonalia* are found in other treatises later than those of Regino, Hucbald, and Odo ; such as Berno of Reichenau, John de Muris, Jerome of Moravia, Frutolf, Königshofen, Walter Odington, Aristotle, Petrus de Cruce, Johannes Gallicus, and Simon Tunstede.   In the case of the last nine (all of the twelfth to fourteenth centuries) it is not easy to see why *Tonalia* formed part of their compendium of musical information, as the spread of Antiphoners with the four-lined stave must have made them really unnecessary.   Possibly a kind of traditional conventionalism explains their inclusion.

Theoretical descriptions of the Organum, or current harmony-singing of the period appear for the first time in *Musica Enchiriadis,* formerly attributed to Hucbald, later to Hogerus, Otger, or Odo, a Provençal abbot.   The practice is also referred to by John Scotus Eriugena at an even earlier date, but without any theoretical discussion, and the name of Organum is hardly applicable to the Celtic singing which he describes, which should more probably be classed as primitive Gymel.   Remigius is a writer of some importance from the fact that he was the teacher both of Hucbald and of Odo of Clugny ; he is a clear exponent of the principles of rhythm, and his distinction between metre and rhythm is worth quoting, for it holds good for use to-day, if we remember the mathematical meaning of *ratio* :

Metrum est ratio cum modulatione ; rythmus vero est modulatio sine ratione, et per syllabarum discernitur numerum.

Metre is melody in mathematical measure ; while rhythm is melody without mathematical measure, determined by the number of the syllables.   (Gerbert, *Scriptores,* i. 23.)

His *Scholia Enchiriadis Musica,* as its name implies, is a commentary on the work ascribed to Otger.

THE ELEVENTH CENTURY

Berno of Reichenau   (? *–1048*).
Guido of Arezzo   (? –1050).
Hermannus Contractus (? *–1054*).
Anonymus, Ad Organum Faciendum.
Aribo Scholasticus   (? *–1078*).
John Cotto   (*c.* 1100).

Opinions differ as to what may truly be adjudged the most revolutionary advance in the science of Music. The eleventh century opens with one such advance; for the development of polyphony, strangely modern in its origins by comparison with the antiquity of the plastic arts, seems to have been waiting the time of Guido and his stave. Indeed, it is hard for us to conceive how musicians could have made progress until this step had been achieved. For until the Guidonian stave had come into use it was not possible to teach any melody and (*a fortiori* any harmony) except by rote ; nor was it possible to appeal with certainty to any authority save the aural or oral tradition of the elders (and cannot we imagine the deaf, stupid, and crotchety old man to whom sometimes appeal would have to lie ?). It was not possible for men to compose music in the ordinary way, save through the machinery of memory ; if a new melody was to be preserved it must forthwith be taught to a body of trained singers who would be able to remember it accurately and to reproduce it with the sole aid of the mnemonic neums *in campo aperto*. Nor was it possible to send music from place to place, except in the person of a skilled chanter ; and it is for this reason that we find such emphasis laid by our chroniclers upon such journeys as those of Petrus and Romanus to St. Gall and Metz, or James (the papal precentor) to York.

But now all this is changed. The development of the fixed stave, worked out in stages, first of the 'carefully-heighted' neums, then in red Fa-lines, with a yellow C-line added later, down to its final perfection by Guido, makes it possible (*a*) for music to be sung or played at sight, (*b*) for sure appeal to be made to authentic documents, (*c*) for music to be composed, sometimes 'for its own sake', and written down at once on parchment or paper, (*d*) for it to be sent to other places 'by post', as we should say. And now, also, it becomes more possible, and indeed relatively easy, for the 'speculator' or investigator to manipulate his materials in the quiet of his cell, to evolve descants and to note them down. *Notator* is the ordinary word for composer used in the valuable account of 'Anonymus IV' (see below, p. 128), and it means that the skilled musician appeared to his contemporaries not as a man 'expert in composition' so much as a 'writer-down of music'.

Rightly then do the later writers refer to 'Magister Guido'. And if they are a little over-anxious to lay at his door more discoveries than are in strict accordance with the historical facts (as also in the case of Franco), they may be pardoned to some extent, for they did at least realize the greatness of the man who gave them and us the stave. It matters little that Guido is not entitled to the sole honour of the whole invention; he was almost certainly its perfecter, and its zealous propagator.

And he was a prolific writer. Seven treatises are ascribed to him (five in Gerbert, vol. ii, and two in Coussemaker, vol. ii). His systematization of the Hexachords, which from now onwards replace the old Tetrachords derived from Greek music, and his device of teaching solmization by showing intervals on the finger-joints of the left hand, added to his fame in medieval times, but are of less interest or value to us now, as they have not lasted; though his mnemonic idea of the syllables *Ut re mi fa sol la*, by which the most unlearned singer might track the semitonic intervals by reference to a hymn-tune as well known then as 'St. Anne' is now, has developed with certain alterations into the Tonic Sol-fa of to-day.

Guido is one of the first writers after Otger and his commentator to mention Organum. More than a century has elapsed since the *Musica Enchiriadis*, and we find a different state of things, for Guido regards the fourth as the normal consonance, instead of the fifth. We have no means of testing whether this was a universal development at the opening of the eleventh century, or whether it was merely a local Italian fashion, which it may very well have been. At any rate, the Organum of the Fourth may perhaps be regarded as ephemeral, the chief importance of Guido's diaphonic writing being the increased use of oblique motion instead of similar. Theory as usual lags behind practice, for the contemporaneous Winchester Troper has contrary motion as well as oblique, though the former is not very frequent.

Much of our remaining information about eleventh-century part-singing is derived from the anonymous *Ad Organum Faciendum* (see Coussemaker, *Histoire de l'Harmonie au Moyen Âge*), where there is considerable sign of advance, not only in the use of contrary motion, but also in the crossing of parts. The author is a man of eminently practical turn of mind, and gives us actual directions how to compose, but his theorizing is weak, and his classification of methods a grievous example of cross-division. The date is towards the end of the eleventh century, and about the close appears the last of the writers before the dawn of mensurate notation—Johannes Cotto—who definitely advocates contrary motion. He says, 'Ubi in recta modulatione est elevatio, ibi in organica fiat depositio, et e converso'—' Where the original melody rises, let the organal voice fall, and conversely' (ch. xxiii). This agrees well with the contemporary specimen described by Dr. Bannister, from a Chartres manuscript, in the first volume of *Revue Grégorienne*, so that we may perhaps rate Cotto as being neither behind his times nor in advance, but (what is comparatively rare in the Theorists) on a level with them.

THE TWELFTH CENTURY

No writer of note can be definitely located in the twelfth century, which is comparatively bare in theoretical literature. Some small hints are gleaned from Guy of Chalis about the middle or third quarter of the century ; with him the contrary motion is the normal form, oblique being allowed for, but similar motion ignored. For the most part, musicians may have been content with exploring the practical possibilities of the new notation, whether plain or mensurate. And the details of the transition from the unmeasured Organum of the eleventh century to the mensurate polyphony of the twelfth are still obscure, owing mainly to the relative inaccessibility of the original sources. The scarce and costly printed collections of Gerbert (1784) and Coussemaker (1864–76) include probably the majority and the more important of the medieval manuscripts, but they are admittedly inaccurate, both in palaeography and in typography, the latter work especially so. An international Committee was formed in 1912 to go into the question of publishing a complete and critical Corpus Scriptorum : the project has been (1928) in abeyance for some years, but is not dead. A good idea of the work involved can be gathered from a glance at *Initia Tractatuum Musices,* by C. Vivell, O.S.B. (Graz, 1912), which tabulates nearly a hundred works under authors' names, and this number takes no count of the anonymous treatises, nor of the unprinted manuscripts, of which there may very well be an equal amount. In England alone Theinred, Torkesey, Gillebertus, John of Tewkesbury, John Wylde, and others still remain in manuscript.

Meanwhile, in this short summary we shall do well to overleap the days of Franco (or the two or three Francos, as the case may be), to whom is ascribed the invention of mensurate notation, and to inspect the system as we find it working and flourishing at the opening of the following century.

THE THIRTEENTH CENTURY

JOHN DE GARLAND	(FIRST QUARTER).
Peter of Picardy	(*c. 1250*).
(PSEUDO)[1] ARISTOTLE	(THIRD QUARTER).
Petrus de Cruce	(*c. 1220*)
ANONYMUS IV[2]	(THIRD QUARTER).
JEROME OF MORAVIA	(THIRD QUARTER).
WALTER ODINGTON	(close).

Writers are now prolific, and we have omitted fifteen or twenty names from the above list in order to confine our attention to those that seem the most useful. Our chief interest will now lie in the development of the art of Counterpoint—*Ars Antiqua* is the name given to it, to distinguish it from the *Ars Nova* of the following century. Its progress in the hands of the Theorists is highly interesting *per se*, though its attention is often turned to rhythmic problems rather than harmonic. Its value as an integral part of the history of music has been hitherto rated too highly by many writers; for our history of the art of composition should be built up on the music itself; we must go to the works of the composers rather than to those of the doctors, and where they differ we must try to deduce and re-write our history in accordance with such facts as survive for our examination, rather than from the theories (sometimes mere speculations) of the writers. True, with the exception of the Notre Dame manuscripts so exhaustively examined in the first edition of this History, we have not a very large amount of music extant for the years before, say, 1225, but there is at any rate something to go upon; and the middle and end of the

---

[1] Why 'Pseudo' is not clear. He never claimed to be the great Aristotle, so far as we know, nor did his transcribers claim it for him. His name was apparently Aristotle. If a man's name to-day is Moses, we do not find it necessary to call him Pseudo-Moses, to make sure that he is not taken for the Moses of the Bible.

[2] So called from the enumeration in Coussemaker, *Scriptores*, vol. i: also sometimes referred to as the Anonymous of Bury, or the Anonymous of the British Museum.

century is abundantly represented, even in English manuscripts, which are supposed to have been more thoroughly destroyed than the Continental.[1]

A further *caveat* must be added, in the form of a reminder that from this date onwards many of the existing manuscripts of the Theorists are not 'treatises' written by them, but students' note-books, containing matter taken down (accurately or otherwise) at lectures in Paris or Oxford or elsewhere. This applies probably to Garland's *Introductio* (Coussemaker, i. 157), to Anonymus IV (Coussemaker, i. 327)—whom I conjecture to have been a young monk of Bury St. Edmunds who was studying at Paris—and possibly to the various treatises beginning *Gaudent brevitate moderni*, which sounds almost like a kind of opening insult hurled at the heads of a not too patient class by its lecturer.[2] Alternatively, the five versions beginning with the *Gaudent* formula may be taken as different 'Abbreviations' or 'Expansions' of an original work ascribed to Franco. John Balloc (thirteenth century) wrote under the former title, Robert Handlo (1326) under the latter. Or again, all five may be varying editions of one and the same lecture, as delivered at different times, and formed on one conventional model.

Garland's other extant work, *De Musica Mensurabili* (Coussemaker, i. 175), is, however, one of the more important of the theoretical manuscripts. He divides Measured Music into Discantus, Copula, and Organum, but only deals with the first-named. He is nibbling at the idea of duple time, for the imperfect long is given. the honourable title of 'recta'; while the 'recta brevis', he tells us, is of the value of 'unum solum tempus'. But when we pass on eagerly to discover what the 'tempus' unit may be, and whether it also is normally divided by two instead of three, we meet with the explanation that a 'tempus' equals a 'recta brevis'. However, we forgive him

---

[1] Cf. *Proceedings of the Musical Association*, vol. li (1924–5), pp. 20–2.

[2] One 'Gaudent' MS. ends with what are, we fancy, the words of the student, not the lecturer, ' et de discantu haec dicta sufficiant. Amen.'

this vicious circle, for he spares us the far more vicious circles and parallelograms of the multitudinous diagrams which most of the theoreticians seem to find necessary as ornaments to their pages. In an expansion of Garland's teaching given under his name by Jerome of Moravia (see next page) a 'tempus' is actually defined as 'quod minimum in plenitudine vocis est'— i. e. the shortest note that can be fully uttered, as distinct from a grace-note. Garland also gives us the earliest account of Musica Ficta, but he is unfortunately far from clear, and the interpretation of his language (as given by Coussemaker) gives rise to discussion which space does not allow us even to summarize.

Rhythmic Modes 3, 4, and 5 (the dactylic, anapaestic, and molossic respectively) are described as 'ultra mensurabiles', the exact force of which is not clear, for though they differ from the simple iambic or trochaic modes in the normal value of the long, they are by no means without formidable rules of mensuration. Rules for rhythm, ligatures, and pauses follow. Garland is a very useful source for guidance in the task of deciphering the rhythm of Motet Tenors, one of the most difficult feats in the art of transcribing thirteenth-century music.

Aristotle's *De Musica* is fairly typical of a number of manuscripts of this period. He opens with a long preface in which Jove, Moses, and Tubal are pressed into service : the gamut, mutations, diagrams, a short note about Musica Ficta, and intervals follow, with solfeggi. An explanation of the Ecclesiastical Modes and a *Tonale* precede the section on Polyphonic music. And if we are not always sure at first sight what he means, we may take courage, for Aristotle's pupils were even denser than we are—they apparently needed these 'hexameters' to help them on their way:

> Ante vero longam, tria tempora longa fatetur ;
> si brevis addatur, duo tempora longa meretur.

(For verses like these at school, it would doubtless be said of the poet ' sex verbera dura meretur'.)

But his·explanation of the figure—

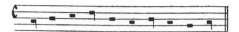

is gratefully clear. It is a rhythmic figure which, when occurring in actual Motets, often tempts the tyro to think ' duple time ', but it is to be taken as under, the breves being ' recta ' and ' altera ' in pairs, as he explains.

Rules for other formations which have caused difficulty in the past to transcribers—e. g. that of two longs separated by a series of four breves—are given succinctly : instructions for ligatures, pauses, rhythmic modes follow. Finally we notice that Aristotle gets very near to the simplification of the time system by which the 'tempus unum ' of the *recta brevis* is regarded as the unit, in place of the perfect *longa* from which all the theorists derive their note-values.

Aristotle's is so typical a treatise that it will be unnecessary in this brief description to give anything more than the leading special points of the next few writers.   Anonymus IV is note-worthy for giving us the names of eminent practitioners of the time, Léonin and Pérotin (both of Paris) being the two leaders; he refers also to Garland, but not by name.   And from clues afforded by his bibliographical remarks—if such they may be termed—the greater part of the repertoire of Notre Dame in the year 1220 or thereabouts can be pieced together, though it is now scattered all over Europe.   The so-called Medicean Antiphoner at Florence is the largest existing portion, but sections are also found—duplicating one another in part—at Bamberg, Madrid, Montpellier, Paris, Stuttgart, Wolfen-büttel, &c.

Jerome of Moravia throws further light on the ' unit of time ' to which we have referred, and we learn from him that one *tempus modernorum* is equal to one breve or three *tempora antiquorum*. His long mathematical section is naïvely headed *De quibusdam arithmeticis necessariis subtilitatibus* (!). A reference to an Arabic doctor (Al Farabius), Bell-founding, and Aesthetics of Enunciation are rarities occurring in his writing, and he provides an early instance of the use of the term *Cantus Firmus* (canto fermo). Perhaps of greater value than anything he says of himself is the fact that he adds to his work transcriptions of the twelfth-century *Discantus Positio Vulgaris*, which throws some light on an obscure period; with extracts from Garland, Franco (*Ars Cantus Mensurabilis*), and Peter of Picardy.

The close of the century brings us to the first of the great English theorists. Walter Odington, a monk of Evesham, who wrote about 1280, has been highly commended for his lucidity from the time of Burney onwards, and he marks a distinct advance in harmonic doctrine. For with him the intervals of the third and the sixths are not treated merely as passing formations on the way to the only true 'chords' (fifth or octave) but as being concords, though imperfect. In this he is influenced by the English or Celtic traditions of Gymel and Fauxbourdon, no doubt, but his theorizing is in touch with academic as well as with popular music. Like Garland, he is a writer who enlightens (instead of bewildering) the student of rhythm, and he illustrates his work by his own compositions. Of equal importance with his doctrine of the imperfect concords is his foreshadowing of the return to duple time which characterizes the fourteenth century.

THE FOURTEENTH CENTURY

MARCHETTUS OF PADUA	(*c.* 1310).
ROBERT HANDLO	(1326).
JOHN DE MURIS	(*c.* 1350).
PHILIP DE VITRY	(*ob.* 1365).
SIMON TUNSTEDE	(1351).
John de Grocheo	(XIV).

In this century the theorists become even more subordinate to the actual composers, headed by the prolific Machault. In the *Brevis Compilatio* of Marchettus of Padua we meet with the free use of the minim (under the complicated form of a semi-breve of the novenary or senary division) and even with the semiminim or crotchet (semibreve of the duodenary division). Marchettus was a pioneer who prepared the way for the *Ars Nova* of the middle of the century.

Robert Handlo, on the other hand, though he also knows of the minim, is essentially a conservative commentator on the rules of Franco, Garland, Petrus de Cruce, &c.

The learned John de Muris wrote a compendious treatise under the title of *Speculum Musice,* the length of which may be gauged from the fact that the last two books, which Cousse-maker wisely selected from the entire seven of the *Speculum,* occupy no less than 484 columns of the *Scriptores* (vol. ii); while six pages of the Introduction to that volume are taken up with the section-headings of Books I–V. De Muris was a great and renowned teacher, but he made little or no contribution to the progress of the art; a conservative, he tried to restrain the development of the *Ars Nova.* Probably he wrote, as an old man, towards 1350.

To Philip de Vitry is attributed the leadership of the new school of the fourteenth century whose work is known as *Ars Nova.* The name is derived from that of the first four short treatises attributed to him—*Ars Nova, Ars Contrapuncti, Ars Perfecta in Musica,* and *Liber Musicalium.*[1] Here we meet for the first time with coloured notation, and with binary rhythm as a fundamental form : minims and semiminims are taken as part of the ordinary normal state of things instead of being regarded as exceptional. Here, too, are those useful signs of prolation and perfection, the absence of which in the previous century has meant many hours of fruitless

---

[1] Couessmaker, *Scriptores,* vol. iii, pp. 13–46.

experiment in discovering the rhythm for modern transliteration—

$$\bigcirc \quad \mathsf{C} \quad \boxed{\text{ᵐ}} \quad \boxed{\text{ᵐ}} \quad \odot \quad \ominus$$

Vitry is undoubtedly a most important figure in the history of music, but his reputation rests on the valuation of his contemporaries rather than on his extant treatises, the authorship of which is not beyond question—Professor Wooldridge and others have expressed doubt as to whether he really wrote the four enumerated above.

Writing in 1351, not long after the *Ars Nova* had come into being, we can look to Simon Tunstede as codifier rather than as inventor. His treatise is exhaustive, occupying nearly 200 columns of Coussemaker's *Scriptores*, and it covers the ground fairly thoroughly. There are the usual geometrical figures, the Hand of Guido, monochord divisions, and so forth, with one special diagram of Simon's own, which looks for all the world like the plan of a model poultry-farm. But his style is quite pleasant to read, and stands out in this respect far above the generality of these treatises, and if what he says is not always strictly to the point, it is at least always clear what he means to say. His title is *De Quatuor Principalibus*, and it will be interesting to see what are to him the four obvious chief departments of musical study. These we find to be as under:

I. ' Music and its Parts.' (Partly philosophical.) Occupies eleven columns only.

II. ' Invention and its Proportions': i.e. the Science of Music; the division of the scale; the monochord; diatonic, chromatic and enharmonic genera. Reasons why the diatonic genus has ousted the others (the chromatic corrupts good manners, the enharmonic is tedious to listen to). Occupies twenty-five columns.

III. ' Planus Cantus et eius Modi.' The Gamut, tetrachords, mutations, intervals: the eight Ecclesiastical Modes, with a condensed *Tonale*. B molle in plainchant, plainchant technique.

In the colophon to this third section Plainsong is referred to as *Musica quae dicitur Continua,* which suggests that the *Basso Continuo,* first met with 200 years later in Italy, may have derived its name from the Plainsong Tenor of the Motet. Occupies seventy columns, including the poultry-farm.

IV. Mensurate Music.   Definitions from Franco, as of *Organum proprie ac communiter sumptum,* by now long out of date : Notation, Prolation, Composition, under the terms discantus, triplum, quadruplum, &c.   Occupies eighty-nine columns.

It is not easy to become thoroughly familiar with the works of the Theorists, for the only collections in print (those of Gerbert and Coussemaker) are costly and not very accurate.   It is greatly to be desired that some Maecenas will arise to enable scholars to give the world a satisfactory and inexpensive edition of the more important.   Until that time, the Treatises will almost certainly remain in their present semi-obscurity ; and they are worthy of a better fate.

VI

PLAINSONG

By the Right Rev. W. H. Frere, D.D., Lord Bishop
of Truro

I

The history of early medieval music in Europe is only very
partially known; and far less is known about the East than
about the West. It is clear that there was a very highly
developed art of monody in Italy, which reached its climax in
the sixth and seventh centuries; and that there was a revival
of musical interest and enterprise in the ninth century, which
was a real development of what had gone before. The later
development was evidently much affected by Byzantine influence; but there is, so far, no direct knowledge available of the
Greek music that exercised the influence in question.

Between these two periods there came one of decadence and
regression. On the heels of the new monody of the ninth and
tenth centuries came the beginnings of the development of
polyphony. With this we are not here concerned, except so
far as to say that, as polyphony and its companion, Measured
Music, arose and developed, so monody and plainchant receded;
indeed they were more or less steadily degraded until their
renaissance began only recently in the nineteenth century.

II

The material available for study is of two kinds, (*a*) the actual
music which has survived, and (*b*) the works of the theorists.
The latter are not very valuable for our purpose. There is
generally a wide gap between the composer or singer and the
theorist. In medieval times this was specially the case; for music,

as a development of mathematics or of the metrical art, had long
been considered a necessary ingredient in any polite education,
apart from what we should now call its 'musical' interests.
The theorists kept up a tradition that had its roots in Greek
music, and dated from the time of Aristotle and even from
earlier centuries.   This furnished them with one or two things
(especially the diatonic scale) which were of priceless value;
but also with a great deal of useless lumber, which had no real
bearing on the art of music as actually practised.   This learning
petered out with Boethius († 525) or Martianus Capella, who
was probably an earlier contemporary of Boethius; and musical
theory had no exponents between the sixth and the ninth
centuries.   Unfortunately some irrelevant or erroneous traditions
about Greek music, and a good deal of misleading nomenclature,
haunted the theorists when they began to write again; and
these have exercised a baneful influence on the study of medieval
music even down to the present day.

In dealing, therefore, with the living art of monodic music
between the fifth and the twelfth centuries, we will not here
concern ourselves with the theorists except in so far as they give
from time to time some information as to the actual practice of
their day.

The musical material available for study is of a restricted
kind.   There is no instrumental music available until the latest
part of the period; and very little in the way of secular music.
People must have danced, but there is no record of dance tunes:
folk must have sung, but their secular songs are lost.   The loss
of the dance tunes is particularly to be regretted.   Secular songs,
when they begin to appear, are found to be not unlike the
corresponding religious chants.   But dance music must have
been essentially unlike; for the essence of it is regular rhythm
and metre, while the chants which have been preserved are for
the most part set to prose texts and essentially 'plainchant',
i.e. free from regular metre.   When church metrical hymns
come into question we are in touch with something more like

the dance rhythm; but hymns form a small and a comparatively unimportant and late part of the great monodic music of the early Middle Ages.

It is church music alone that has survived. But while regretting this, we must remember that it was in church music that the great growth of the Art, which we desire to trace, in fact took place. In this sphere, as in others, the Church alone preserved the tradition of ancient art and learning through the chaos of barbarian conquests.

For the study of the Art of Music in the West there is a great body of church music available, extending from the fifth or sixth century onward. The music of the instrumentalists had vanished, perhaps under the frowns of the Church, but more likely under the pressure of the Goths, Huns, and Lombards. With this there vanished also the last living remains of the old Greek theory. But later on a new theory took its place as a practical proposition. When the theorists come before us again in the ninth century, and set to work to describe the existing music, not merely to hand on the disused tradition, it is clear that they are in possession of a new theory; and that it is also, as its terminology shows, Greek in origin. It is much debated how far an Eastern theory of the *Octoechos*, or system of eight modes, underlies this body of existing music. It seems probable that the earlier stages of Roman chant were anterior to it, and that, at a later stage, some conforming of practice to theory took place, without succeeding in reducing it all to conformity. But more than that cannot at present be safely said.

Equally it is not at present possible to trace this theory to its source. There is an even larger gap in the succession of Greek theorists than in that of the Latins. It extends from Gaudentius in the fourth century to Bryennius or Kukuzeles in the fourteenth. Moreover, there is no body of early medieval church chant for the East now extant and available, as there is for the West. Influence from Syrian or Arab sources probably came into play; in fact the *Octoechos* is very likely as much

Arab as Greek in origin. It is commonly attributed to St. John of Damascus, and he was the meeting-point of these two streams ; so the attribution has much in its favour. But here, again, no final verdict can yet be given.

It is therefore to the West that we turn, and to the music as it exists, investigating it in the hope that it may itself reveal the history of its origin and development. The ecclesiastical music has grown up with the services, which fall into two chief classes : (a) those of the Mass, or the altar services, and (b) those of Mattins, &c., or the choir services.

There are different collections of church music which arose in connexion with the different Rites, or Liturgical families. The Roman chant, the Milanese chant, the Mozarabic chant of Spain, the Gallican chant—these four represent the chief collections. They are unequally known to us. Down to the ninth century no method of recording the music was in general use. Alphabetic notation was only very slightly used, and mainly for teaching purposes ; and the system of accents was, so far, undeveloped and inadequate. The neums came into use, as a development of the system of accents, which the East had devised ; and when thus for the first time in the Middle Ages the Latin music was systematically written down, the Gallican chant had already for the most part disappeared before the invading Roman chant which the Carolingians introduced and imposed. Gallican music is therefore known only so far as parts of it made their way into the written tradition as a supplement to the Roman chant.

The Mozarabic chant of Spain survived long enough to be recorded in neums ; but then came the invasion of the Roman chant. Thereupon the traditional knowledge of the melodies, which was necessary in order to interpret the Spanish neums, was lost. Consequently little Mozarabic music has survived in an intelligible form, except such as came to terms with the Roman invader.

The Milanese music known as ' Ambrosian ' has survived, and

is still in use. It represents a collection of church music, allied
to the Roman chant but different from it. More will be said
about it shortly.

The Roman chant itself presents a somewhat complex
historical problem. It is clear that a great reform of the
existing music was taking place at Rome in the sixth century.
St. Gregory seems to have at least promulgated, if he did not
himself produce, a revised chant. It is this that has spread and
superseded local music, except at Milan. What this reform
effected we must consider shortly. But first a word is needed
as to the body of Gregorian music, its authenticity, its descent
to modern times, and its dispersion far and wide.

The revision belongs to the sixth century, but the musical
notation first begins in the ninth. There is a long gap in
between, of which some account must be given. The earliest
manuscripts to which we can turn contain the words only: they are
anterior to the existence of the notation in neums. But the
extant series of texts for the music bear witness to a single and
uniform tradition. Wherever the chant has penetrated, its
Roman origin is clear ; though there are found a good many
items which must have originated elsewhere than in the Roman
rite and have come into the Roman collection from outside.
The series of texts for the choir offices evidently contains much
that has been added later or locally ; but there is a solid nucleus
that is in general use, and represents the Roman collection to
which the later or local elements have been added. The accretions can be to a large extent discriminated from the rest.

In the series of texts for the altar services the additions are
far fewer, and the old nucleus has only in a very restricted
degree incorporated novelties. Here, too, the accretions can
easily be distinguished; and, when they are set aside, the nucleus
can be scrutinized and seen to be such as is consistent with the
time of St. Gregory.

Thus the words to be sung as found in manuscripts of the
ninth or tenth centuries belong partly to the Golden Age of the

T

Gregorian reform and partly to a Silver Age that succeeded it, in which, as it appears, the stream of progress has rather rapidly run dry.

III

On turning now to the books that have music, it becomes plain that they bear out and confirm this view. Not only the collection of words but the music, too, is (for the most part) uniform in the early manuscripts. The way of noting it may vary in different places, but this variation in the way of writing the melodies only makes more impressive the uniformity of the melodies themselves. A great collection of music has evidently been broadcasted from Rome, unwritten at first, but recorded later in different countries, where it is found identical, except for minor differences of notation, phrasing, interpretation, and the like.

This is the chief musical accomplishment of the early Middle Ages; it is well worth study, for it is still in widespread use after thirteen centuries. This permanence witnesses better than anything else to the fact that, in dealing with it, we are handling a masterpiece of musical craft.

The music also supports the distinction between a Golden and a Silver Age ; for the texts which seem to have come into the Roman collection after Gregory's time not only are few, but also have music of inferior workmanship.

We may now take up a copy of the *Graduale*, or the *Antiphonale*, or the very convenient *Liber Usualis* which contains the most frequented services with their music, and know a little what to expect.

As it arose out of the services themselves, this Gregorian music had to conform itself to certain liturgical requirements, which may thus be briefly summarized. There were four classes of-people who would sing it—the people, the choir, the chanters or cantors, and the soloists. In some cases one of these groups sang alone : the people, for example, sang their own part at the Mass—the invariable chants such as *Kyrie, Sanctus,* or *Agnus.*

It was the 'choir' that bore the main burden of psalmody in the Hour Services, being not usually a body of select voices, but the whole body of clergy or monks gathered in the stalls. But in other cases the groups alternated, the chanters or the soloists alternating with the choir, or, in rare cases, such as litanies, with the people. At the back of this variety of performance lay two fundamentally different conceptions of chant: (*a*) responsorial music was developed from the recitation of a psalm by a single voice, and the answer given in the form of a brief response by the rest; (*b*) antiphonal music grew out of melody, rather than out of recitation, and normally was performed by alternating bodies of voices. As time went on, each type of chant developed along lines of its own, in such a way that the two approximated one to another. But there remained always the root difference of conception, and it had not only a liturgical but also a musical significance.

All this will become clearer as we consider the classes of chant that make up the Gregorian music. We may leave out of account the simpler elements—the people's part, and the part of the officiants—which was mainly confined to simple inflexions. Among the more important classes of composition it is desirable to distinguish the following in the music of the Mass : Introit, Gradual, Tract, Alleluia, Offertory, and Communion. These six chants form a group which varies with every variation of the service. Of these the Introit and Communion belong clearly to the antiphonal class, the Gradual to the responsorial class. The two former have their origin in the antiphonal singing of a psalm, by alternating choirs, at the beginning and the end of the service; the latter in the more primitive custom of setting a single voice to recite a psalm between the Epistle and Gospel, while the choir has to answer each verse with a brief refrain.

By the time that the Gregorian mass music was systematized under Gregory, or at latest by the time from which our earliest manuscripts date, the Introit and Communion had been cut down

by the excision of psalm-verses; but probably the music of the
antiphon had been elaborated.   In any case, the antiphon, and
not the psalm, dominated the situation : it was repeated several
times with only a few psalm-verses intercalated.   By the ninth
or tenth century only a single psalm-verse and the *Gloria patri*
remained at the Introit ; and at the Communion no psalm-verse
at all survived.

The Gradual and the Offertory came to be the music of the
solo singers ; and, as the training at the papal choir-school
advanced, here again, but to a much higher degree, the music
was elaborated, and correspondingly the number of psalm-verses
was cut down.

It is important to get these distinctions clear, because each of
these four classes of chant, besides being in a different musical
form, acquired a style of its own as well. The Introit antiphon is
much more developed than the Communion antiphon, and has its
own distinctive methods and phrases.   Markedly different is the
musical style of the Gradual : even in its most elaborate forms
it can be recognized as having for its origin a recitation inter-
spersed with inflexions or cadences.   The clue to its meaning is
found in the reciting note ; whereas in antiphonal melody it is
the final (key) note which tells.

Still more distinctive is the Tract, an elaborate chant confined
to penitential services and intended for a single voice.   Most of
the Tracts of the year are derived from one or other of two
musical themes, one of which belongs to the Second Mode, and
the other to the Eighth. The chant is certainly ancient, though
it is highly elaborate.

The Alleluia, with its Verse, stands upon a different footing
from the rest.   For some reason, which it is not easy to deter-
mine, there was more composition going on in this class of chant
than in any other during the Silver Age.   It is also possible to
distinguish the earlier work from the later, because a different
method was followed with regard to the disposition of the three
elements of which the composition was made up, viz. the Alleluia

itself, the *Jubilus* following it, and the Verse. The later specimens show a more developed art of music than the earlier ones. It is the general custom in them that the end of the Verse should repeat the music of the Alleluia and its *Jubilus*; and so a distinctive piece of musical form is established.

The greater musical ability shows itself also in the internal development of the long *vocalises*. Phrases are often repeated, and repeated in a developed form which enhances their significance. In these and other ways more balance, more musical logic, and consequently more musical effect is obtained.

EXAMPLE I. AN ALLELUIA OF THE SECOND EPOCH

IV

Turning now from the Mass to the Hour Services we note the same principles prevailing, but the application of them is simpler. The responsorial chant is represented by a great collection of some eight or nine hundred ancient Responds, and the antiphonal chant by a great collection of Antiphons.

The music is here less elaborate. There is little, if any, music for the soloists; the 'choir', alternating with a few chanters chosen for the purpose from time to time, is responsible for all the music. Simplification in this sphere seems to go *pari passu* with elaboration in the other. For example, the tones for the psalmody are simpler in the Hour Services than those used at the Mass, and they become increasingly simplified as we watch them through the ninth and up to the eleventh centuries.

Here, too, the difference of style in different categories is preserved; not only the fundamental difference between responsorial music and antiphonal, but differences within those classes. The great Responds of Mattins differ from the smaller ones used at other Hours. The Antiphons of the Gospel canticles—*Magnificat* and *Benedictus*—differ from those of the psalms, in style as well as magnitude.

Having set out briefly these distinctions, we note the taste and artistic sense that they presuppose. For many centuries after the sixth the musical world saw nothing at all comparable to this fine distinction of styles. Is there, indeed, anything quite comparable to it yet?

V

We turn next to observe the main characteristics common in more or less degree to all this body of music. First it is 'plain' chant: the rhythms are all oratorical speech-rhythms not metrical or dance-rhythms. This implies an elasticity in singing which we are now trying to recover after a long servitude to regularity of beats and bars. The recitative of opera and oratorio has preserved in the interval between these early days and modern times some of the traditions of this freedom. It did so by leaving the voice almost unaccompanied.

Secondly, this music likewise is melody unhampered by either vocal or instrumental accompaniment. Pure monody of this sort develops certain characteristics which disappear or lose their significance under other conditions. Simple forms of monody, even when not of ecclesiastical origin, fall into the two types above described—recitation and melody. Children's singing games, for example, show this. But if more elaboration is required it necessarily takes the form of vocal ornamentation. The simple intonation that leads up to recitation on a reciting note, or the simple cadence that ends the recitation, must be expanded for glory and beauty into a series of groups of notes. It is the only way of enhancing the effect. As the occasion demands it, and as the singers become more proficient, such 'neums' or *vocalises* become more frequent and more difficult, till the most developed monody requires the skill of an able *coloratur* singer if it is to be adequately executed.

Then at such a stage a protest perhaps arises on behalf of the words, which are in danger of being obscured by the elaboration of the chant. In order to minimize this danger the *fioriture* are therefore kept to the last word of a phrase or the last few words ; or again to the opening of the phrase. Then the main part of the sentence remains quite intelligible. Beyond that there is a tendency to set the groups of notes on the lighter syllables. This plan seems at first sight paradoxical, but there is wisdom in it ; for in the middle of an elaborate chant and among groups of notes very rapidly sung, it is the words charged with few or single notes that stand out prominently. In decadent days this was forgotten. The chant had lost its flexibility : a group (say) of four notes instead of being roughly equated with a single heavy note was treated as being four times as long. Under such conditions it is not surprising that editors cut about the traditional chant, so that it was only known in a mangled form till the Benedictine revival in the last century.

Again, with regard to the all-important cadences, in monody it is to be observed that they are governed purely by melodic considerations, whereas in harmonized music they are constructed in deference to harmonic considerations. The leading note is, therefore, as unpopular in monody as it is popular in harmonized music; and the more modern forms of cadence, which aim at a full close, are avoided. The earlier harmonizations of the chant respected the melodic cadences, and set against them a congenial melodic counterpoint. But after the discovery of harmonic closes, and especially of the full close, this respect went by the board; and the cadences were not only mishandled but faked with *musica ficta* or an unblushing sharpening of the subtonic.

Such principles as these govern monody. However unfamiliar and strange they may sound to minds accustomed to think in duple or triple time, or to ears trained to the major and minor scales alone (with more or less of chromaticism) and accustomed to hear, or mentally to supply, harmonies accompanying a melody, they are, and must be, the essential principles of monody. The failure to recognize them has at various stages in the history led singers, accompanists, and editors to a maltreatment of Gregorian chant, from which it is only recently beginning to recover.

Thirdly, in classical plainsong much use is made of familiar themes, and themes are built up of individual formulas. This method of composition is not due to poverty of invention but to the nature of the case. For the purpose of daily worship repetition is valuable. An attractive antiphon melody, or Alleluia, will suit many similar texts, and its reappearance at intervals is welcome. Even in the case of a much more individual composition, such as a Gradual, the same is true. Consequently the best themes are constantly utilized. Great skill in exact and artistic adaptation of the theme to the words is a characteristic of the Golden Age, while clumsier handling betokens the period of decadence.

Individual formulas also recur over and over again. A good cadential formula will suit the end of many phrases or sections in a respond. Indeed many of the great Responds of Mattins are built up out of such materials. The composer's skill is shown in using the appropriate formula for each particular cadence, and in making the cadences balance, or contrast melodically with one another. Here also the decadence of the art is shown up in the compositions of later date. In the following respond a remarkable example is given of the use of common formulas and of well-planned musical rhyme:

EXAMPLE 2. A RESPOND

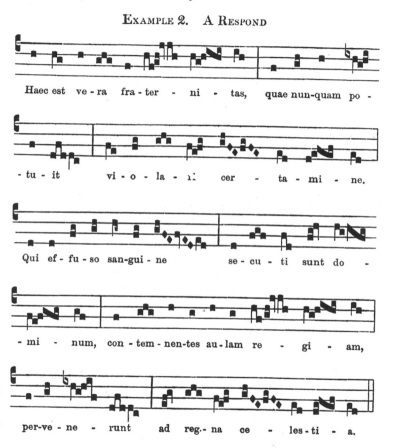

Haec est ve - ra fra - ter - ni - tas, quae nun-quam po -

- tu - it vi - o - la - ri cer - ta - mi - ne.

Qui ef - fu - so san-gui - ne se - cu - ti sunt do -

- mi - num, con - tem - nen-tes au - lam re - gi - am,

per-ve - ne - runt ad reg.- na ce - les-ti - a.

Another specimen is given below at Example 9.

But when distinctive music is required, it is forthcoming.

U

Many of the compositions are entirely individual and aptly calculated to bring out the meaning of the words.   Example 3

EXAMPLE 3

gives a graphic representation of the precious ointment falling down from the head of Aaron.   Example 4 by contrast is taken

EXAMPLE 4

from the opening of the Offertory of the Sunday after Ascension Day, and depicts the Ascension.

In the case of antiphons the method of composition is different.   These are not built up out of a series of more or less detachable sections, each of which is a piece of recitation with a cadence.   An antiphon theme is complete in itself.   It may be enlarged for a long text, or compressed for a short text, but its unity is preserved.   Naturally it falls into certain divisions, and each division is modified internally so as to fit the corresponding section of the words, but this modification does not destroy the unity of the whole.   The following specimen will make the matter clearer:

Example 5.   A Gregorian Antiphon-theme

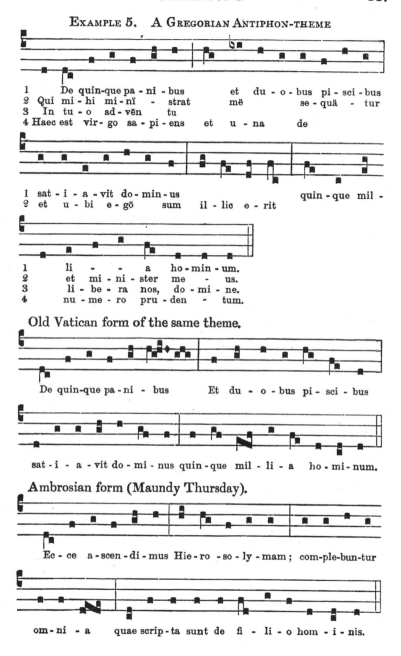

Old Vatican form of the same theme.

Ambrosian form (Maundy Thursday).

In these four specimens of the normal Gregorian form, the
first is fourfold; the second is extended to five clauses; and the
third and fourth are contracted to two and three clauses respectively. There follows the Vatican form of the antiphon; and
then comes an Ambrosian version of the same theme.

Fourthly, Gregorian music is modal. There is a good deal of
minute evidence which suggests that the old Roman chant may
have needed revision in order to bring it into line with the
eight-mode system, as has been mentioned above. For all
practical purposes, however, the collection, as we have it, must be
treated according to that system, even in places where it still is
found to be not strictly reducible to that pattern.

In this connexion further distinctions of style and composition
emerge into view. Each mode (and each *tonality* or pair of modes,
even more strictly) has its own melodic characteristics. Cadences,
phrases, and formulas which are appropriate to one are not appropriate to another. This fact was well recognized by the classical
composers, to whom the different modes were familiar as so many
dialects or languages, differing one from another. While
writing in one mode they would no more drop into another than,
in speaking English, we might drop into French. Failure in this
sense of modality is a pretty sure sign of the workmanship of the
Silver Age as contrasted with the Golden Age of the Gregorian
reform.

Fifthly, we may notice the sense of form and key relationship,
the development of themes, the use of imitation, and (within the
limitations of the modal system) the possibility of melodic contrast, that have become part of the composer's art. Form in
this music is mainly dictated by the words. Many of the texts
come from the psalter, and so a binary form is found in the
music, corresponding to the parallelism of the words. The
sentences constantly end with one or other of the prevailing
rhythms of the literary *cursus*. The music follows these; and thus
(particularly in the Responds of Mattins) cadences of 3, 4, or 5
syllables take shape accordingly, deriving their rhythmical

pattern from the *cursus* and their melodic character from the mode in which the composition lies.

Key relationship is of necessity determined melodically and not harmonically. The two scales that are chiefly contrasted are that of the final of the mode itself, and that of the note which lies a whole tone below the final. In the case of the First and Second modes, beginning from D, this expedient introduces a contrast between a minor and a major triad, which gave the composers much satisfaction.

In compositions which had a fairly extended compass, the structure of the diatonic scale and the position of the semi-tones in it pointed to the natural relationship existing between phrases which lay a fifth apart. But this adumbration of the coming relationship between tonic and dominant was for the present only faint.

The development of a given theme was a device which existed at first only in a rudimentary stage, but the Alleluias have shown us the advance in this respect that was being made. Imitation, on the contrary, was fairly fully developed. The art of composition depended a great deal on the clever hand-ling of familiar formulas. When such a formula was repeated at various points in the scale, not only were the key contrasts just mentioned brought into prominence, but a sort of musical rhyme was produced, which was very effective and very popular. See above, Example 2.

The principal form of melodic contrast that was available depended upon the use of the b♭ alternating with the b♮. This resource, limited as it may seem to those familiar with a chromatic scale, was used with very great effect.

EXAMPLE 6

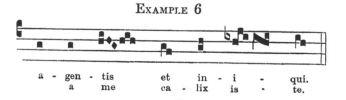

a - gen - tis   et in - i - qui.
   a   me   ca - lix is - te.

EXAMPLE 7

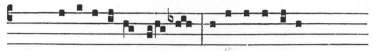

propterea per-se-cu-ti sunt me :   et in-tel-li-ge-re non potuerunt

It is thought by some that the music originally involved the use of quarter-tones in those places where in the diatonic scale the semitones normally stand ; and that this use only disappeared owing to the coming in of the Guidonian notation on four lines, which made no provision for quarter-tones. There is certainly some evidence that tells in that direction, but the point cannot be said to be proved.

Lastly, we cannot leave the consideration of the Gregorian music belonging to the Golden Age without noticing the extremely high standard of execution and musical sensibility that it demanded. The notation in neums preserved a tradition of delicate *nuances* in singing, which unfortunately disappeared when the neumatic notation was superseded by the staff notation. In singing the long trailing festoons of notes, it was essential to know, not only the exact grouping of them, but also such things as the slight variations of *tempo rubato*, the points of major and minor accent in a long and complex group, the place where a slight shake (*quilisma*) was desirable between two notes usually a minor third apart. All this the neums, and other signs utilized with them, recorded and notified. A group of three notes ascending might be treated as 2 + 1, or as 1 + 2, and the distinction was made accordingly by using two different neums. The long *roulades* would be (and indeed are) intolerable unless treated with all this refinement and skill. Groups of several repeated notes like a bird's call, or even the commonly found device of striking a note lightly and then repeating it with an accent in the middle of a group, presuppose and require the same vocal skill. Also the standard required in the pronunciation of the words is surprisingly high. This may be seen from the fact that when two consonants follow one another, the form of the neum is

modified in order to remind the singer to be careful.   Such are
some of the chief characteristics of classical plainsong.

VI

The hymn melodies stand in a separate class from the rest,
because they are set to metrical texts, and have, therefore,
a metrical character.   St. Ambrose in the fourth century wrote
his hymns to be sung, and in the century following the monks
gave a regular place in their services to hymns; but there is
no evidence to show what melodies were used in such early
days.   Later on the secular breviaries incorporated some
hymnody, and in the tenth century there is evidence of the
existence of a standard series of hymns and tunes, which, with
more or less of variety, was in general use, and remains still the
nucleus of existing Latin hymnody.

In the nature of the case the melodies were simple.   Ordinarily
no more than a single note, or a simple group of two or at most
three notes, was given to each syllable, in order that the metrical
movement might be preserved.   Such simple tunes as these were
easily modified, especially during the period in which they were
noted in neums.   So there is found to be less uniformity prevailing in the tradition here than elsewhere.   Indeed a considerable amount of refining and improving took place.   As a result
the melodies, particularly in their English forms, gained in
balance and artistic beauty.   The clauses were better balanced,
the closes at the end of the lines better contrasted, and some
attractive use was made of imitation and musical rhyme.   A
single instance must suffice.

EXAMPLE 8

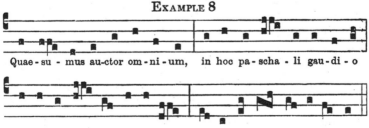

Quae-su - mus au-ctor om-ni-um,   in hoc pa-scha - li gau-di - o

ab om-ni mor - tis im-pe-tu   tu-um de-fen - de po-pu-lum.

VII

It may be possible, in some degree at any rate, to compare the reformed chant of the sixth century with the chant that it superseded. Certain manuscripts of St. Peter's at Rome seem to preserve it, though probably in a form which has been itself rather unskilfully elaborated. There are also other books surviving in Italy which perpetuate music that seems to have escaped, or lain outside of the Gregorian reform. The matter deserves, and awaits, fuller investigation, but meanwhile it may be said that this ' Old Vatican ' music shows a lack of the artistic sense which distinguishes the Gregorian music. It is very elaborate, but the elaboration is inartistic and meaningless. It often differs from the Gregorian just as the jungle differs from the Dutch garden. It is much less in accordance with the system of eight modes. Yet to a large extent it runs in its irregular way parallel to the Gregorian collection. Probably, therefore, it is a survival of the pre-Gregorian forms of chant. Alternatively it might be regarded as a unique deformation of the existing Gregorian chant. But one would be loath to charge the Basilica of St. Peter with such a crime; and in any case historical probability seems to point to the other alternative, viz. that it represents in some way pre-Gregorian music.

This conclusion is supported by an examination of the existing Ambrosian music. The Ambrosian rite has preserved a marked independence; and the music stands as aloof from Rome as does the text of the services. There is some common material—more in the words of the chants than in the music—but in any case not much. On the other hand the general characteristics of the music are similar : the two languages are akin.

But the Ambrosian music is in character more similar to the Old Vatican music of St. Peter's than to the Gregorian tradition. The jungle is here not quite so over-luxuriant and tangled, but

other characteristics show a backwardness in musical skill.   The
music is not so tidily fitted in to the modal systems, and in many
respects the modal sense is seen to be weaker.   There is much
less differentiation of style in the different categories of things to
be sung.   The psalmody, as shown by the use of the tones and
tone endings, is at a much more rudimentary stage than the
Gregorian psalmody : the same is shown by the nature of the
psalm verses of the Responds.   All seems to point to the conclusion that the Ambrosian music belongs to a stage of musical
culture that preceded, or at any rate did not profit by, the
Gregorian reform.

Some small opportunity of realizing the contrast has been given
already in the antiphons quoted at Example 5.   In Example 9
a respond is quoted as it figures in the three different forms—
Gregorian, Ambrosian, and Old Vatican.

EXAMPLE 9.   A RESPOND

The first line Gregorian, the second Ambrosian, and the third
Old Vatican

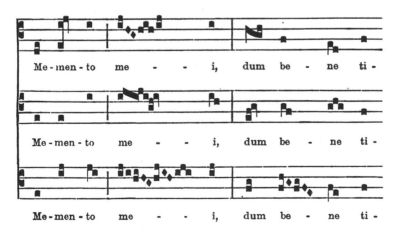

- bi fu - e - rit; ut sug - ge - ras

- bi fu - e - rit; ut sug - ge - ras

- bi fu - e - rit; ut sug - ge - ras

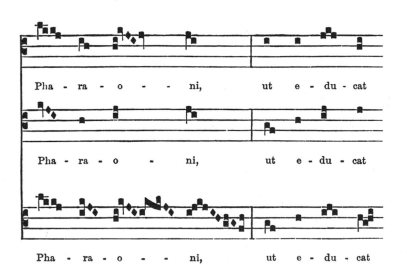

Pha - ra - o - ni, ut e - du - cat

Pha - ra - o - ni, ut e - du - cat

Pha - ra - o - ni, ut e - du - cat

The Respond in its Gregorian form belongs to a well-known type, and is made up largely of familiar phrases. The second and the last of the sections balance one another, for they end with two closely allied cadences. Each is properly one of three syllables, but it is extended here to four, by the insertion of an extra note, to carry the accent on the antepenultimate syllable, and to compensate for the shortness of the penultimate. Both these cadences constantly recur in this tonality. This balance between the two sections is maintained in the Ambrosian form, but the detail differs. It is not in the Old Vatican form.

Another familiar cadence is at the end of the fourth section on 'me': it is repeated at 'furtim' in the sixth section, and at 'innocens' in the eighth. The Old Vatican form has a corresponding figure at the end of the fourth and eighth sections, but not at the sixth. The Ambrosian corresponds only in the fourth section.

At the fifth section the cadence is the same in the Ambrosian form as at the second and at the last. In the Gregorian form it is a phrase which is often interchangeable with the one used in the second and the last sections. In the Old Vatican form, however, the cadence has no relation to others, but stands alone.

Such differences as these are characteristic, and they exemplify the similarity and dissimilarity of these three dialects in their treatment of the same text and musical theme. There are not very many points of contact at which Roman and Ambrosian lie so close to one another. More often they are separate both in words and music. But even then the differences which stand out from such a comparison as this remain characteristic of each dialect.

VIII

Hitherto we have been scrutinizing the traditional music itself. Internal criticism has alone been possible, for there are no materials available for the purpose of external criticism in the fifth, sixth, or the two following centuries.

In the ninth century a renascence began in music, as in many other branches of learning. This was probably helped by the coming to the West of musicians from Constantinople, who brought with them new ideas of music and musical theory. Unfortunately no Greek exposition of these views is extant. The Eastern masters are only known to us, at this stage, through their Western pupils. Forthwith there begins afresh a Latin literature on the subject of music after a long interval of darkness and dumbness. Aurelian is the earliest of these new writers of theory whose work we possess, and he is the precursor of a long series. Another sign of life is the development of musical notation. Out of the simple accents, which (apart from an alphabetic notation) had served hitherto as sole guide to the simple intonations of the reader, there develops in one form or another the elaborate notation of the neums. This clearly had its origin in the East, as its terminology shows, but it was seized and utilized quickly by the West in the ninth century, and adapted to the circumstances and taste of different *scriptoria* along a line of development which differs from that which was followed in the East. The earliest monuments of the notation that we have do not go back farther than this century. They are full and elaborate from the time of their first appearance. It became then possible to write down the traditional music and to preserve in some form, not only the chant itself, but the delicacies of phrasing and execution which the masters had inculcated. The fidelity with which the traditional chant had been handed on from singer to singer is attested by the very large measure of unanimity which the earliest manuscripts show, in spite of the wide diffusion and the independence of the existing music centres.

A new impulse also is given by this awakening to musical composition. From the middle of the seventh to the middle of the ninth centuries there had been comparatively little new work done, and that on traditional lines by inferior craftsmen. But now new ideas show themselves, and composition goes ahead. Some of this follows the old lines in a conservative way still, but some of it meets the new needs with a new spirit. The characteristics of the new output will be judged best from a part of the work which was new in form as well as in style.

A keen enthusiasm had arisen for a new class of melody, un-associated with words, and merely sung to a vowel sound. There was a freedom about such a method which was evidently valued. The Alleluia melodies in the Mass which had come down on the edge rather than in the full flood of tradition were of this type. It is significant that it was mainly in this class of composition that anything fresh was written, during the days of decadence, and any advance was made. But the traditional Alleluia melodies were not elaborate enough for the new school. Its most conspicuous product is a new series of Alleluia melodies, much longer than the existing ones, and divided into sections, each of which, normally, was repeated. The enthusiasm for this further development of wordless singing penetrated everywhere, and not only into the congenial class of Alleluias ; and so it came about that new phrases and new melodies were intruded at intervals into all the old music both of the Mass and of the Divine Service. The Greek origin of this queer fashion is shown in the name of *Trope* given to these interpolations. For the moment the tropes were ubiquitous. The fashion had

its day, and then was suppressed ; it vanished without leaving
much behind except in one respect.

The new Alleluia melodies seem to have been found both less
intrusive than other tropes and specially attractive.   As in the
case of other tropes, before long it was found convenient to
provide the long wordless melodies with words, and this was
done upon the dull plan of providing a word for each note.
The ' proses ' that resulted from this process proved to be the
chief survivors of the craze for tropes.   Of all the proses which
were written, those for the Alleluia melodies excelled the rest,
and under the name of ' Sequences ' they attained a permanence,
and a historical development, that was denied to most of the
other tropes.

The earliest type of Sequence melodies therefore stands as the
best representative of the art of musical composition, so far as it
flourished in the tenth and eleventh centuries.   In their original
form they bear witness to some interesting innovations.

The form is new : phrases, consisting of four to twelve groups
of perhaps ten to twenty-five notes, are each sung (without
words), and then normally repeated.   The compass is large ; it
extends often to a twelfth and sometimes further still.   The
demands laid upon the singer are as great as ever for agility, and
greater than hitherto for compass of voice.   But true musicianship
is lacking.   Nearly all the melodies belong either to the first
pair of modes or to the fourth pair :   there is little variation of
cadence ;   phrase after phrase ends monotonously in the same
way.   The chief one is a rise *portamento* from the subtonic to
the tonic, and one or other form of this cadence is repeated *ad
nauseam*.

EX AMPLE 10.   SHOWS THREE STAGES OF DEVELOPMENT

(i) Gregorian Alleluia, ' Dulce lignum '.

Al - le - lu   -   ia

(ii) The later and longer *jubilus* developed out of the above.

Al - le - lu - ia

In this the double bars imply the repetition of the preceding section, from the next single or double bar.

(iii) The same melody adapted to words, in the form of a Sequence, beginning with the Alleluia.

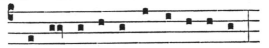

Sal - ve crux san - cta ar - bor de - co - ra, &c.

This example shows one of the most modest of these efforts. The new *jubilus* does not go far beyond the old Alleluia, and keeps close to it.

As this music is very little accessible, it may be well to add another specimen of a more ample kind. The music is more developed, but the words are clumsily adapted, without any real regard to the rhythm of the melody.

EXAMPLE 11

(i) Alleluia ' Hodie Maria '.—*Jubilus* and Sequence.

Al - le - lu - ia

(ii) Sequence, (part) beginning after the Alleluia has been sung.

A re - a vir - ga pri - me ma - tris E - vae flo - rens ro - sa
O - ri - tur ut Lu - ci - fer in - ter a - stra e - the - re - a

pro - ces - sit Ma - ri - a : ⎱ fra - gra - scit ul - tra om - ni - a
per - pul - chra ut lu - na. ⎰ pur - pu - re - a ut vi - o - la.

bal - sa - ma pig - men - ta et thy - mi - a - ma - ta ;
ro - sci - da ut ro - sa, can - dens ut li - li - a. &c.

IX

Three things, however, we owe to this rather dull epoch.
First, there is a further development of the themes and phrases,
and the value of musical logic seems to be felt more definitely.

Secondly, we observe a much more intelligent appreciation of
the tonic-dominant relationship. After several phrases ending
on the tonic the pitch shifts and a set of phrases end similarly
on the dominant; then a return is made to the tonic.
Thus some coming principles of later composition are fore-
shadowed.

Thirdly, the breaking up of *vocalises* into single notes, each
bearing one syllable of words, brought dire results. It was disas-
trous to monody, for soon the words gained the ascendancy over
the dismembered tune. They then, in later sequences, took a
metrical form; whereupon the older melodies, and the rhythmical
freedom that belonged to them, went out of fashion. For these
new metrical sequences new tunes had to be provided, which
were still hampered by the cruel restriction that a note must
go to each syllable. So the metrical sequence became, for the
most part, a dull sort of hymn, in which each even stanza
repeated the tune of the preceding odd stanza.

But harmony gained where monody lost. It was much easier
to set a counterpoint to a *canto fermo* of single notes than to any
other sort of tune. Consequently some of the earliest contra-
puntalists worked first upon these disintegrated tropes and
sequence melodies; then they learnt to disintegrate other plainsong phrases to serve as *canti fermi* for motets in the interests of
the budding art of harmony. The decline of plainsong was thus
still further advanced. Next the new harmony demanded that
strict time should supersede free rhythm, in order that part-
singers should be able to keep together; and so measured chant
became the fashion, and the freedom of plainchant was sacrificed.
Finally the triumphant progress of the art of harmony broke up
the modes and the sense of modality. The stages were slow, for
the modes made a long struggle to maintain existence, but at
last they disappeared, only to be recovered to some extent in
our own day, partly through the return to an interest in the
ancient plainchant, and partly through the channel of modal
folk-song.

X

Other signs of the times show that plainsong composition, as it revived in the ninth–tenth centuries, was not, as it had been, a superlative form of art. The new offices, which the service books now acquire, demand fresh music. The introduction of Trinity Sunday provides us with an early and a capital instance. The music so introduced—the work of Stephen of Liége—is decadent and insipid. The composers of these new offices still write in the old modes, but mechanically. In their pedantic way they often count it their duty to compose their sets of pieces impartially, taking each mode in turn. When they follow their bent it tends to the F modes, which, by the use of the B♭, can become what we call the major scale. Unpopular hitherto, these modes become popular now. The famous antiphon of Hermann Contractus *Alma redemptoris mater*, and the much-adapted antiphon in St. Nicholas's office *O Christi pietas*, may stand as favourable examples of a novel form of taste, tending towards the modern major.

A demand arose for new settings of the Ordinary of the Mass — *Kyrie, Sanctus*, &c. These, even at their best, are in a lower class than the older music. So the way was prepared for the fatuity of the so-called *Missa de Angelis*, and for even worse. A large amount of new music for new offices continues to be written throughout the twelfth century and into the thirteenth, but with less and less of the characteristics that make up the charm of classical plainsong. When a setting was required at the end of that century for the offices of the newly established Corpus Christi Day, it was provided mainly by adaptation from older models, many of them being of inferior quality,—and a clumsy adaptation too. The eclipse was then complete.

VII

FOLK-SONG

By A. H. Fox Strangways

It is notoriously difficult to give a definition of anything. Instead of defining folk-song let us enumerate its chief characteristics. A folk-song

(1) originates with the voice, not with an instrument ;

(2) its rhythm is affected by the words ;

(3) it is not written down ;

(4) it is conceived as melody without harmony.

We will discuss these points first generally and afterwards in detail.

(1) The voice as such takes melody downwards ; it finds descent more natural than ascent. In any cry, or call to attention, man and most of the animals spring to a high note and fall gradually to a low one. Song, as opposed to speech, dwells on this note or that, and so gradually defines its pitch. A sense of absolute pitch [1] plays a great part in this definition. Relative pitch is either (*a*) a judgement of distance, the perception of 'how far off' one note is from another, or (*b*) a judgement of interval which is based on a feeling for harmony. Whether as distances or as intervals, the first steps to appear are tone here or semitone there, not, as a rule, both together. Later comes the leap of the fourth, and more rarely of the fifth and octave. The tonic, as soon as it is felt, is high, since the upper register of the voice is the stronger. This tonic is usually the starting-point,

---

[1] It has been observed that the parrot starts always on the same note. The Hindus associated the notes of their scale with certain animals—C, peacock ; D, chātaka (bird of rainy season) ; E, goat ; F, crane ; G, coïl (cuckoo) ; A, frog ; B, elephant.

is fortified by repetition, and sometimes marked by a return to it or its lower octave. The singer has to begin by 'finding' his voice, and an initial recitative is common.[1]

(2) Rhythm is obviously as old as the possession of a pair of legs (two-time) and the tendency to press more heavily on one of them (three-time). Beyond that there is great divergence in the extent to which rhythm is developed by different peoples. Rhythm belongs to the dance. When it is applied to song, the question of breath delimits phrasing and 'barring', the formation of the verse affects the length of the 'strain', and the 'values' of the words and the dramatic situation are allowed to induce a *rubato* or an *ad libitum*, or even to distort the time (see Example 28).

(3) Notation is a late invention; it does not occur till music is made consciously, as an art. It is preceded by pictures, as writing was by hieroglyphics. The North American tribes make rude drawings of the situation which the music is to enhance. The Hindus still, after centuries of conscious art, and the acquisition of a notation, draw and paint, often most artistically, pictures (Rāgmāla) of the modes in which the songs stand. In the absence of any exact record the song depends for its permanence on intrinsic merit, whereas print makes no such discrimination.

(4) The advent of harmony has had various effects. It has caused us to feel a strong opposition between major and minor; there is no such opposition in folk-song. It has superseded grace notes, which were the chief resource of the unassisted voice for emphasizing one note at the expense of another. It has restricted the scale to a uniform intonation; it has, for instance, reduced the various thirds of folk-song to two, 5 : 4 and 6 : 5. Instead of five possible notes in the scale which could be utilized for a final close, it limits the singer to the tonic.

---

[1] In India the *ālāpa* is a definite form, sung to syllables—Na, Ma, Ta Ra, La.

There are certain difficulties in the way of discussing these points in detail. Folk-song sprouts spontaneously over the whole earth, and what happens in one place is no guide to what will happen in the next; or indeed, if it is, there may well have been some collusion—for music travels farther and faster than language—and the evidence is then not conclusive. Not only is it impossible to point to any common origin, but it is difficult, except in rare instances, to predicate even a before and after. Then, it is not easy to get either exact or complete evidence. There is very little before medieval times, and no certainty that what we do possess has been conscientiously recorded, and not 'improved'. Careful collection began a century ago, and increased in the last fifty years, but collectors vary much in their trustworthiness and comprehensiveness. Latterly the use of the phonograph has improved matters, and marks of pace and of dynamics are seldom omitted now. A fourth difficulty is the disinclination of the natives to divulge their oldest, and usually most sacred, songs, and of the members of a guild to communicate their theories and mysteries. And both the actual song and the musical theory which underlies it need to be studied together.

We will now take the four points again in order.

(1) Evidence for the tendency of the voice to sing downwards is copious. The Murray Islanders (Great Barrier Reef) guard jealously their 'Malu' songs, which are so sacred that 'no native woman or child may hear them and live'.[1] In these songs, which are old, free from external influence, and independent of instruments, the predominant 'distance' is the tone,[2] and the semitone is not known. Here are two out of five songs. The drum-beats are often late, as the asterisks indicate.

[1] *Reports of Cambridge Anthropological Expedition to Torres Straits*, vol. iv, chap. xii, on Music, by C. S. Myers; and, *Essays and Studies presented to William Ridgeway*, Cambridge Univ. Press, 1913, p. 560, by C. S. Myers.

[2] This tone is of three sizes, in the neighbourhood of 240, 198, 167 cents. (Our major tone is 204, and our minor 182.)

EXAMPLE 1

The rise of an octave which occurs in the middle of these songs is there merely because the song was going too low for the voice. In the next example the repeated note at the end and the rise of a fourth and drop of a fifth with a strong portamento remind us of the Irish 'Phillelew'.[1]

EXAMPLE 2

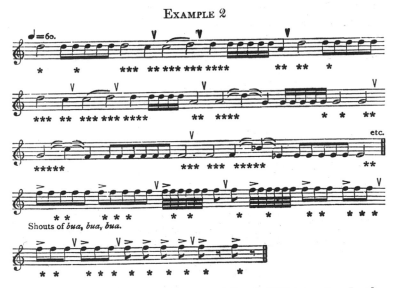

In both songs the tone is mean (about 195 cents.). In the first there are five of these followed by a large one (225), not, as

[1] See Stanford's edition of *Petrie*, no. 1027.

it necessarily appears in our notation, a minor third (316).   In
the second song the ascending fourth and descending fifth are
both very sharp (534 for 498, and 761 for 702), and are clearly
arrived at as 'distances' of three and four (small) tones, not as
'intervals' in their own right.

Caribs and bushmen [1] and Ojibbeways and Sioux [2] provide
other examples of songs which descend from a high note.   Also
the lettering of the Greek vocal scale downwards by Alypius in
the fourth century A.D., and the fact that the octave-scales of the
Indian system are quoted in descending order (C-mode first,
then B-mode, A-mode, &c.) by Bharata in the *Nāṭyaśāstra*, fifth
century A.D., point in the same direction.

Returning to the question of 'distance' *versus* 'interval', we
will look at the songs of the Veddas of Ceylon.   The first of
these examples consists of minor tone and mean semitone (187
and 102) ; the lowest note is tonic.

EXAMPLE 3

The next example is a tone between two semitones, the lowest
note but one being tonic.

EXAMPLE 4

The Poongi (snake-charmer) melodies of southern India consist of two semitones only, the middle note having the drone.

[1] See Parry's *Art of Music*, chap. iii.
[2] See Miss Densmore's publications in the Bureau of American Ethnology.

Example 5

This tune of two Pulaiyar women (Trivandrum), each taking
the other up and losing a beat in the process, combines the four
notes of No. 4 with the adjacent semitones of No. 5; the tonic
is the lowest note but one.

Example 6

In this next one, sung by boatmen at Alleppey, the distances
are nearly equal—about three-quarters of a tone.

Example 7

In this Malayan tune (near Paddikad) the drum rhythm
$(3+3+2)$ is the same as that of No. 4; and there is some
inversion.

Example 8

Two Malya men, at Trichur, sang the following, in which
not only is the diatonic tetrachord established, but we see a
hint of conjunct tetrachords.

z

EXAMPLE 9

We now turn to the Sarawak [1] territory of Borneo, and meet with something quite different. Here the tune consists of the

EXAMPLE 10

almost universal form of the tetrachord of the pentatonic scale—C B♭ G, the B♭ being taken as a passing note between C and G downwards. A drone is supplied an octave below

EXAMPLE 11

the starting note, and thus adds the 'instrumental' tonic to the 'vocal' tonic. In the process it develops passing notes E and F, E being the more important. Thus two tetrachords are formed, in effect—a diatonic and a chromatic F E C—and related disjunctly.

[1] See *A Study of Sarawak Music*, C. S. Myers, *I.M.S.*, vol. xv, 1914, pp. 296–307.

These examples (9 and 10) are to be found in *Essays and Studies*. Dr. Myers's observations are exact, and he took great pains to make them so. All the melodies were phonographed and the exact pitch afterwards determined by a Tonmesser (a harmonium with 64 notes between middle C and tenor C), and he took with him a kymograph, i. e. a revolving cylinder covered with smoked paper for the purpose of electrically recording drum-beats. He concludes thus:

It seems as if, at an early date in the development of Sarawak music, the large intervals of fourths and fifths received the greatest stress, and that at all events the latter were subsequently broken up into smaller intervals (of about 185 cents.). If this interpretation is correct we have two broad modes of the evolution of scale-notes, (i) by the synthesis of (small) 'distances' as among the Veddas, (ii) by the analysis of larger (consonant) 'intervals' as in Sarawak. In the Malu music the first method is the more pronounced, but octaves, fifths and fourths seem to have arisen independently and concurrently.

On a broad survey of the folk-song of the world we should all agree that it can be generalized into three forms of scale— pentatonic, diatonic, and chromatic—and that these scales are very various extensions of the single tetrachords which we may call by those names. These are—

EXAMPLE 12

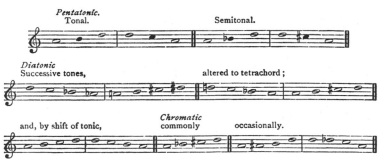

In the pentatonic tetrachord the fourth is, as we have seen, consonant, and the intermediate passing note is at tonal

distance from it. Dr. Myers alone has measured this tone,
and he makes it 185 cents., practically a minor tone; the
remaining interval in that case would be a true minor third.
This tonal pentatonic is found in Scotland, China, eastern
India, the Bantu tribes, and elsewhere. The semitonal pentatonic has not been measured, but it no doubt aims at being
similarly a diatonic semitone and a major third. It is common

EXAMPLE 13

in southern India and Japan. We may illustrate the tonal
from Ojibbeway music, and the semitonal from Japanese,

EXAMPLE 14

although this is instrumental music (for the Koto). But the
semitonal is eventually mixed with the tonal, either as in
Example 11, or with an 'accidental' as in this Sioux song.

EXAMPLE 15

The chromatic tetrachord originate doubtless in such songs as those of the Vedda and southern India. Its three forms are 'modes' of each other.

EXAMPLE 16

The first and third forms exhibit the Pyknon, of which the ancient Greeks made a point, and so does the second if another tetrachord is added above or below. The second form is common in Turkey, Asia Minor, and not unknown in Europe; it is the typical form for southern India, and looking back at Example 6 it is not impossible that such a form as Example 17 became Example 18 in course of time.

EXAMPLES 17 AND 18

Finally, two or more tetrachords are united conjunctly, disjunctly, or very occasionally by overlapping, to form the framework or 'mode' of the song. It is not worth while to pursue the fortunes of the modes, but a word may be said

about the diatonic modes found in Europe.   They are penta-
tones—that is, five 'strong' notes with two weak notes to fill
in the spaces [1]—and these two, if present, are variable (sharp or
flat).   The cadence of the 'strain', even of the whole song, may
be on any of the five, though one of them in particular is felt
as tonic.   One mode that is known as 'dorian' or '1st Tone'
is pre-eminent in most countries, and one reason for that may
be the symmetry of its tones and semitones, which are the same
in ascent and descent.   It is not, however, equally common, nor
is it pure everywhere; in Irish and Swedish dorian tunes the
7th is often sharpened; in French the 6th is flattened in
the second part of the song for pathetic effect.   English
(e. g. 'Tarry Trowsers', 'On board a ninety-eight') are usually
strict.

    After mode comes 'key'.   The feeling for contrast of pitch,
not merely of a note but of a phrase, which is what we mean
by key, appears in such a song as this.   A Gurkha mother and
son held a dialogue :

EXAMPLE 19

    The bagpipe scale,[2] known all over the world, is the expres-
sion of a desire for key and mode combined.   (The C is about
half-way between B and D, and the F between E and G.)   The
G scale is taken as one of three different modes according as C
and F are understood as natural, or the F as F♯, or the C also
as C♯; and similarly with the A scale.   The general effect on
the ear is that of a mixolydian, with some licences of intonation,
at two contrasting pitches.

    [1] In proportion as a folk-song is genuine, i. e. uncontaminated by harmony,
there is a tendency to fill in these spaces in descent rather than in ascent—
a further proof that melody was originally conceived downwards.
    [2] See Grove's *Dictionary*, s. v. Bagpipe.

EXAMPLE 20

Bagpipe tunes, Scotch or Irish, are commonly in $\frac{6}{8}$. 'What shall we do with a drunken sailor?' is an English instance in $\frac{2}{4}$.

EXAMPLE 21

The bagpipe is not the only instrument that was introduced as a servant of the voice and afterwards became its master. The Arab *al'oud* is another case, and the pianoforte another.

(2) Rhythm has even more to say to the vexed question of nationality than tune. We saw that the Murray Islanders liked to get in their note before the drum-beat (see Examples 1, 2). This is, in embryo, that syncopation which the Bantu (negro) tribes developed, as eventually in such a song as 'Joshua fit de battle of Jericho'.

EXAMPLE 22

Jer - i - cho, Jer - i - cho, Jer - i - cho.

Allied to this, though in essence the opposite of it, is the Hungarian snap $\frac{4}{4}$ | ♩. ♪♪♩. |, where the long note drags on after the beat. The object of both is cross-rhythm. Of this the Hindus are masters. Their elaborate drumming is devised so that two simultaneous rhythms shall always be felt; and, that these may be properly felt, ʳthey will meet several bars hence on the first of the bar.   Here are two simple examples of the way it is done.

EXAMPLE 23

In Example 23 the oboe states that $6 \times 2 = 12$, and the drum replies that $\dfrac{3+1+2}{2} \times 4 = 12$.   In Example 24 the oboe goes on to say that $6 \times 2 \times 2 = 24$, and the drum points out that $(3+3+2) \times 3 = 24$.   No doubt this is highly elaborate music, but it has been led up to by centuries of folk-song on the same principle (cf. Example 8).

The French have a delicate sense of rhythm.   They like to contrast different times and tempi.

EXAMPLE 25

The following shows a neat climax by anticipation; in the fifth and sixth strains the phrase is successively antedated by one crotchet

EXAMPLE 25 A

It is a good instance also of the small compass in which their songs usually lie, and there is an interesting suggestion of five-bar rhythm, of which the Irish, too, are fond, and of which the following is a complete example. (A pity, that G♯!)

EXAMPLE 26

And the following is in five-time, which, however, seldom occurs in Irish songs:

EXAMPLE 27

A a

When we English write in five-time it seems usually to be a compromise between two rhythms on which we have never been able to make up our minds. This is a garbled five-

EXAMPLE 28

So-vay, So-vay, all on one day, She drest her-self in man's ar-ray, With a

brace of pis-tols hanging by her side To meet her true love and a-way did ride.

time; a sixth beat is slipped in occasionally. But it represents, no doubt, an original $\frac{3}{2}$. If we restore that, are we to write it

$$\text{♩ | ♩ ♩ ♩.} \qquad \text{♩ ♩ ♩ | ♩.}$$

So-vay, So-vay,   or   So-vay, So-vay?

It depends on the way we read the verbal scansion. The same difficulty arises with 'Barbara Allen', 'In Bruton Town', 'Sweet, lovely Joan', 'The Robber', and others.[1] This sort of irregularity, and a rough and ready way of dealing with it, appeals peculiarly to the English, and we should not think of 'restoring' anything.

(3) It seems to us curious to draw a picture of a tune; but those who do so think not of a tune but of a mode. They conceive the tune as going in a general, not a particular, direction. When a peasant sings a folk-song with six variations, he speaks of them as six 'ways' of singing it. And if you then sing him a seventh variation he accepts it, provided it is in the same mode. Notation, therefore, would only hamper the unlimited power to vary. It would also be useless, because the songs are handed down and valued as being 'so-and-so's' song, with, of course, all his idiosyncrasies and mannerisms, which could not possibly be noted. Notation

---

[1] All in Sharp's *Folk-songs of Somerset*.

comes in with instruments. The earliest things, apparently, to be noted are grace notes. Time and tune, as far as they concern the player, can be sufficiently indicated by words at the beginning. These words are the names of the place where, or the man by whom, a song in that mode was known to have been sung, or else are descriptive of the mode itself— 'persuasive', 'angry', 'refined'—and of time, 'three time', 'jumping', 'crooked' time, &c.

(4) No folk-song anywhere recognizes harmony as a positive element. The drone, usually of one note, may add its neighbouring harmonics; voices in duet or chorus may overlap and, especially in pentatonic modes, harmonize for a moment; ancient Greeks magadized (sang in octaves); the valleys of the Niger and of the Severn hear some Gimel (singing in thirds). But harmony begins only when voices that have woven two tunes together mentally stop and admire the quality of the sound as such, and distinguish it from some other quality. Hence it is not surprising that folk-song makes little of the contrast between major and minor: there is even some reason to think (see Examples 3, 4, 6, 7, 8, 10, 11) that folk-singers preferred the minor third, which is an easier 'distance' than the major, and less of a plunge into the unknown; just as they preferred the fourth (which was the first place where the succession of 'distances' struck across an 'interval') to the fifth (which was the second place).

Example 29

The purpose of a grace note is to give prominence to some particular note of the melody, and so to assert or to point the rhythm. One purpose, at least, of harmony is to intensify the rhythm, as, for instance, by suspension and appoggiatura. To

some extent, then, ' grace ' did what harmony does. They both
bring the melody as it were out of the flat into the round.
Both are sometimes abused, as we see in the fiddler's vibrato
and the singer's tremolo, and in the complacent substitution of
harmonic complexity for melodic invention. A good instance
of vocal grace (as opposed to instrumental, which is more
elaborate) may be seen by comparing the two versions of ' La
Vierge ', from Spain.[1] The first phrase is here given : the
ornamented version is set to two lines of text where the plainsong is set to one.

EXAMPLE 30

Grace, as a singer understands it, is the continuous flow of
the voice round the graced note ; and this is quite indefinable
by notation which is confined to tones and semitones. Harmony,
for which that notation is devised, abolishes microtones. In
doing so it also abolishes mode ; for mode, in its prime, largely
depended on minute differences in the ' size ' of third, sixth,
and other intervals. Mode depended also on certain points of
rest, namely, on the pentatonic notes. Harmony can deal with
these, certainly, and in doing so it takes on a colouring which
has often a fascination ; but it also defines what the modal
singer left undefined, and thereby removes a certain wistfulness
and charm.

[1] Nos. I and XXIII, pp. 235 and 250, of Pedrell's article on the ' Festa
d'Elche ', in the *I.M.S. Sammelband*, ii.

If there are any who doubt that charm, it is probably because they have not heard folk-song in its native haunts. Being itself a perfectly sincere thing, its charm does not survive publicity, nor the treatment of the song as something quaint, still less as something to be exploited. Folk-song is like a hedgerow flower, which, when plucked, withers more quickly than one from a garden. If we are to get at its real beauty we must do with it what the singer himself has done—we must sing it all through and many times. Its merit comes from its having run the gauntlet of the best kind of criticism, that of the singers themselves. It has always been judged by results. If it did not move these singers, they either altered it or dropped it. It is, and can only be, the work of time.

Time is endless in thy hands, my lord. There is none to count thy minutes.
Days and nights pass and ages bloom and fade like flowers. Thou knowest how to wait.
Thy centuries follow each other perfecting a small wild flower . . .
It is the most distant course that comes nearest to thyself, and that training is the most intricate which leads to the utter simplicity of a tune. *Gitanjali*, 82 and 12.

Somebody, of course, started a folk-tune on its way, just as somebody started the legend of Faust. We do not know about the folk-tune. We know about Faust. A certain ' Magister Georgius Sabellicus, Faustus junior' existed. He learned the black art at Cracow, and exhibited his powers and his villainy in Germany, amongst other places at Gelnhausen, forty miles from the abbey at Würzburg. The abbot heard of him and tried to see him, but Faust took fright. The abbot scourged him, however, in Latin, in a letter to Joh. Virdung the astronomer, August 20, 1507. In 1587 a rhymed version of Faust's iniquities was current as a folk-song; and in that year J. Spies collected the various rumours in a publication of which five copies exist, one at the British Museum. His book went through four impressions in that year, and was pirated by somebody every year for the next five years. Ackermann rewrote Spies in 1596, Widmann in 1599. Marlowe dramatized the story in 1604, and his English players took it back to Germany, where it became more popular than ever, and influenced the folk drama during the seventeenth and eighteenth centuries. Lessing printed in 1759 a scene of a projected drama, and Goethe saw a marionette show of Dr. Faust when he was nineteen. In the last two decades of the century four plays and two novels were written on this theme. Goethe published in 1808 and 1831, Berlioz in 1846, Gounod in 1859, and Boïto in 1868; and Spohr, Lindpaintner, Liszt, Wagner, and Kaulbach the painter may be mentioned in parenthesis.

We may take this story of well-known names as an allegory of the anonymous folk-song. Our idea of Faust is made up of the plot, some memorable scenes and phrases, and the music. A folk-song, similarly, is an intimate fusion of words and tune. Although this is not the place for discussing anything but the music, words and tune cannot be separated, if only for the reason that they proceed by exactly the same methods. Both are made up of stock phrases and of everyday wisdom that has passed into proverb or melisma. Neither aims at originality. It is not new facts which startle the imagination that people want to sing about, whenever they have free leave to sing about anything they like, but old ideas that have worn a groove in the mind and reached the feelings. No doubt there was a time when the death (May 1824) of Maria Marten was news that was purveyed by itinerant chapmen; but the purchasers of this news took care to have it sung over to them, to see if it agreed with their feelings, before they bought it. And as she passed from history into legend, the edge of the horror was taken off by modifying place and date and circumstance, until it seemed at last a not impossible leap from 'Come all you thoughtless young men, A warning take by me' to 'Come all you worthy Christians, That dwell within this land'; and in like manner the tune, that had begun as a plangent dorian, sojourned a while as a plaintive aeolian and ended life as a placid mixoly-dian.[1] Yet the facts are not got rid of. The thing did happen, and might happen again. And the singer, as he tells of the murderer's feelings in the first person, and piles up the horrors in the third, is giving by his song all the solemnity he can, not to his own view but to the just judgement and common sense of the country-side.

[1] See *Folk-song Society Journal*, vol. vii, pp. 117–23.

VIII

SOCIAL ASPECTS OF MUSIC IN THE MIDDLE AGES

By Edward J. Dent

The difficulty which all students experience in arriving at a coherent understanding of medieval music is due very largely to the lack of the written music itself and to the uncertainty of its correct interpretation. The difficulty is increased rather than diminished by the comparatively large number of theoretical treatises which have come down to us, for the more these treatises are compared with the actual music which has survived the more apparent it becomes that during several centuries the theory of music and its actual practice were separated by a gulf which it often seems hopeless to bridge. The main purpose of this chapter is to consider the more directly human aspects of medieval music, but it will be well to begin by an inquiry into the origins of this strange separation of theory from practice.

PAGAN PHILOSOPHERS AND CHRISTIAN FATHERS

Plato and Aristotle had considered music mainly in its relation to the State: as a factor in education its function was to make men good citizens. In the days of the Roman Empire the philosophers were concerned with religion rather than with politics, and in so far as they treated of music, they regarded it as a factor in religious experience. What 'music' actually meant to them it is impossible to say. The fact that the Romans themselves made no great contribution to the art of music is here a matter of small moment. English musical life in the nineteenth century offers a very fair parallel. Music was regarded simply as an amusement, and it was provided mainly by foreigners; but there was plenty of it in actual practice, whatever its artistic merits may have been. Comedy and tragedy degenerated into Mimus and Pantomimus, which appear to have corresponded roughly to such entertainments as we should now call respectively musical farce or *revue* and pantomime ballet, appealing respectively to 'popular' and 'intellectual' audiences. There is nothing inherently inconceivable in the idea that philosophers such as Plotinus should in this social and artistic environment have theorized about music from a moral and religious point of view. We can imagine them as genuine lovers of music but not living in the thick of the professional musical world, susceptible to some particular musical appeal, brooding over it in memory and finally writing —writing, too, with high literary skill—about it not as a practical fact but rather as a spiritual ideal.

The Neo-Pythagoreans, of whom the chief representative was Nicomachus of Gerasa (second century A. D.), reduced music and its acoustical facts to a series of theological and metaphysical symbols. The familiar doctrine of 'the music of the spheres' illustrates the remoteness of their speculations from all that we now regard as music. They refused to regard music as an end in itself; they viewed it solely as a means to religious experience. The Jew Philo of Alexandria accepted a good deal of their teaching, but went even farther in his rejection of music as a pleasure of the senses. A view of music more intelligible to modern minds is that of the Neo-Platonist Plotinus, who accepted the sensuous pleasure of music as a stepping-stone towards the ideal beauty through which the ideal good is eventually to be attained. Music was also intimately associated with prayer and with magic. The doctrines of Plotinus were further developed by Porphyry, Iamblichus, and Proclus, all of whom exercised a considerable influence on early Christian thought. What is important for us to notice here is that it was these non-Christian philosophers who maintained the principle that music was to be regarded not as an end in itself, nor as a pleasure of the senses, but only as a means of attaining to the Divine through a condition which they call 'ecstasy' or 'enthusiasm'.

This pre-Christian teaching explains the ascetic view of music held by Augustine and by practically all the Christian Fathers. It is evident that they were intensely susceptible to the emotional appeal of music—Augustine more than any of them—and from the vast number of allusions to music in patristic literature it is evident that the early Christian Church regarded music as by far the most important of the arts.   The Fathers evidently preach to congregations who are thoroughly familiar with music and indeed with musical instruments, although it is very uncertain to what extent instruments were permitted in Christian worship during this period.   The general theory of the Fathers is that music is to be tolerated only in so far as it is the servant of Christian doctrine.   This was a natural enough point of view for a community that was bent upon keeping itself apart from all the moral evils associated with pagan society in general and the theatre in particular. Penitence was the first requirement of an early Christian convert, and the primary function of music was to awaken the *compunctio cordis*.   Any idea of music as an art in itself was utterly rejected.   For those who were already within the fold music had a further practical use.   Religious doctrine was easier to assimilate when sung than when only spoken.   A tune impressed the words on the memory, and like the honey with which the physician disguised the unpleasant taste of his medicines the sweetness of melody made doctrine more palatable.   The Fathers agree in holding that music is a concession of God to the weakness of human nature.   God has no more need of singing than of sacrifice.   Women were allowed to sing in church to prevent them from chattering; but the permission had to be withdrawn when it was found that they were enjoying the music as if they were at the theatre.

As Christianity spread to a more educated class after it became the official religion of the Empire, music developed more freely. Ascetic teachers were always afraid of it, and attempted, as they have attempted in all periods of Christian history, to bar the Church's door to every modern artistic development. But the will to sing could not be denied. The Greek Churches had always kept more closely in touch with the classical tradition than the Latin, and it was the Greek Christians who first introduced the practice of hymn singing. The hymns were definitely musical compositions in which the music, as a work of art, was the main thing. It has been suggested by some authorities that the hymns may have been originally secular melodies. The Church of Rome for a long time refused to allow the admission of hymns, but was eventually forced to accept them. It was the Greek Church too that brought about the elaborate musical developments of the later plainsong, the *jubilus* and all the florid *coloratura* which ultimately led ecclesiastical music far away from the penitential spirit of the earlier centuries and made plainsong an art-product of singular complexity and subtlety.

A curious illustration of the early medieval attitude to music is to be found in the symbolical interpretation of musical terms and of musical instruments. The Fathers condemned instrumental music as being associated with paganism, but that did not prevent them from attaching a mystical significance to the instruments themselves. This shows that they were preaching to hearers who were thoroughly familiar with the instruments. It was a doctrine of the Neo-Platonists that man is the instrument on which God Himself plays. St. Gregory speaks of the angels who came down from heaven bearing instruments :

Cum descendunt, ante se psalterium, tympanum, tibiam et citharam deferunt. Psalterium quippe habent, quia regnum coelorum annunciant, tympanum habent, quia praedicant mortificationem carnis, tibiam habent, quia flere subditos jubent pro acquisitione aeternae laetitiae, citharam quoque habent, quia gaudere pios pro certitudine aeternorum bonorum edocent.

This passage probably accounts for the strange choice of
instruments placed in the hands of angels by Fra Angelico and
other painters. The *psalterium* (called in Italy the *testa di
porco*) symbolized the body of Christ, the *cithara* the cross; it
was for this reason that David's *cithara* drove out Saul's evil
spirit. The *tympanum*, being made of a stretched animal
membrane, represented the crucifixion of the flesh. The
trumpet stands for the Word of God and those who preach it;
others, among them Augustine, often compare it with those
who like Job bear suffering patiently, because the trumpet is
made of metal subjected to prolonged beating.

THE TEACHING OF MUSIC

Pope Sylvester I (d. 335) is said to have been the founder of
the first school of church singers at Rome. In any case, boys,
both in the East and in the West, were trained for church
singing in special schools as *lectores*; they were taught by the
priests, and many of them rose eventually to high ecclesiastical
positions. An African inscription of the early sixth century
mentions a *lector* who was only five years old. John the
Deacon ascribes the foundation of the Roman *Schola Cantorum*
to Gregory I; but it is clear that from the fourth century
singing by boys was the general practice throughout the
Church. Gregory appears to have taught the Roman boys
himself, for John the Deacon says (*c.* 872) that in the school
buildings there was still shown the couch on which he reposed
while giving his lessons, and that the whip with which he
threatened the boys was still preserved and venerated as a
relic. The boys were mostly orphans, chosen for their voices,
and the school was also known as *orphanotrophium*. In the
sixteenth and seventeenth centuries the orphanages of Naples,
called *conservatori*, developed into schools of music—thus the
word *conservatoire* has come to be the traditional name for a
music school.

In an age when books were few and musical notation hardly

existent it is evident that all music must have been learned by
ear. It has been generally supposed that the monochord was
employed for teaching the correct intonation of the intervals,
but there seems to be very little evidence for its practical use.
Guido of Arezzo recommends its use, but only in the elementary
stages. In the earlier centuries the amount of music which had
to be committed to memory was comparatively small, but as the
art of plainsong developed, musical education must have become
a very laborious matter. We obtain a glimpse of it from Bede,
who tells us that in 680 Benedict Biscop on returning to
England from Rome was allowed to take with him the Abbot
John, who was a singer of great skill,

> that he might teach in his monastery the system of singing
> throughout the year as it was practised at Saint Peter's at Rome.
> The Abbot John did as he had been commanded by the Pope,
> teaching the singers of the said monastery (i. e. Wearmouth) the
> order and manner of singing and reading aloud, and committing to
> writing all that was requisite throughout the whole course of the
> year for the celebration of festivals; and these writings are still
> preserved in that monastery and have been copied by many others
> elsewhere. The said John not only taught the brothers of that
> monastery, but such as had skill in singing resorted from almost all
> the monasteries of the same province to hear him, and many invited
> him to teach in other places.

John remained two years in England. In the northern part of
the Continent the most important school was that of Metz,
founded by Bishop Chrodegang in 762. Charlemagne took
energetic measures to secure uniformity in church music
throughout his dominions. The practical difficulties involved
in this undertaking are well illustrated by the story of how the
Pope, at Charlemagne's request, sent twelve of his best singers,
who were to proceed each to a different part of France, and
there teach the true Gregorian chant. There being much
jealousy between the Romans and the Franks on the subject
of church singing, these Roman musical apostles are said to
have conspired among themselves to make the confusion of the

French churches worse by each teaching an entirely different method. Charlemagne in the course of his travels found out what they had done, and complained to the Pope, who sent for the offending teachers and punished them severely. Charlemagne, in spite of assiduous effort, was never able to learn to write with his own hand; but if the foregoing story is true, it speaks well both for his interest in music and his knowledge of it. The Romans were very contemptuous of the barbarous ignorance of the Germans and Gauls, as well as of their physical inability to sing properly; the northerners were correspondingly resentful of the self-conceit of the Romans. But the Romans were not without justification; the Italians had kept up an old Roman tradition of secular education, while in the north literary culture was purely ecclesiastical.

> Solis Teutonicis vacuum vel turpe videtur,
> Ut doceant aliquem nisi clericus accipiatur.

The practical difficulties of learning music are further illustrated by the famous *Sequences* of Notker, who began by inventing words, with a syllable to every note, to fit the *longissimae melodiae* which, in their original purely vocalized form, the boys could never commit to memory. The medieval choir-boy must have had good cause to bless the memory of Guido of Arezzo, for his education was a painful one. The holiest relic of Gregory the Great appears to have been his rod, and the rod was seldom out of the hand of the medieval school-master. The Custumal of St. Benigne at Dijon, more or less contemporary with Guido, gives us a picture of the choir-school:

At Nocturns, and indeed at all the Hours, if the boys commit any fault in the psalmody or other singing, either by sleeping or such like transgression, let there be no sort of delay, but let them be stripped forthwith of frock and cowl, and beaten in their shirt only . . . with pliant and smooth osier rods provided for that special purpose. If any of them, weighed down with sleep, sing ill at Nocturns, then the master giveth into his hand a reasonably great

book, to hold until he be well awake.   At Mattins the principal
master standeth before them with a rod until all are in their seats
and their faces well covered.   At their uprising likewise, if they
rise too slowly, the rod is straightway over them. . . . In short, me-
seemeth that any King's son could scarce be more carefully brought
up in his palace than any boy in a well-ordered monastery.

Another characteristic picture is given in the life of St.
Stephen of Obazine, near Limoges :

Stephen was strenuous in discipline, and most severe to correct
the failings of delinquents.   For if any raised his eyes but a little
in church, or smiled but faintly, or slumbered but lightly, or negli-
gently let fall the book which he held, or made any heedless sound,
or chanted too fast or out of tune, he received forthwith either
a rod on his head or an open hand upon his cheek, so loud that the
sound of the blow rang in all men's ears ; a punishment that was
especially inflicted on the younger boys, to their own correction and
the terror of the rest.

Guido's systematization of the stave and his method of
solmization made it possible for the first time in the history
of Christian music to read music at sight from the written
page.   He claimed himself that by his method boys could
learn in a month what it had formerly taken them ten years
to learn.   It is interesting to note that Guido included in his
method not only the singing of an unknown cantus from the
notes but also the writing down of a cantus already known by
ear.   His invention of the ' musical hand ' seems to us of to-day
less valuable ; but in those days when books were rare it may
well have been useful for class teaching, much in the same way
as ' manual signs ' are used by modern Tonic Sol-fa teachers.[1]

But it may well have taken several generations before the
habit of sight-singing became general or even thought generally
desirable.   Records of episcopal visitations in the thirteenth

[1] Readers familiar with Tonic Sol-fa methods must be warned that
Guido did not indicate the notes of the scale by different positions of the
whole hand ; each joint of the left hand was given a separate note, and the
teacher pointed the notes with his right hand on the finger-joints of his left
just as the Tonic Sol-fa teacher points the notes on the ' modulator '.

century disclose a very low standard of education, both musical
and literary, among the parish clergy, both in England and in
France. The Archbishop of Rouen in 1253 was dissatisfied
with a priest because 'examined in chant, he could sing nothing
without solfeggio or note'. This looks as if the archbishop
attached more importance to memorizing than to sight-reading.
Singers were human, even in the ages of faith ; Bishop Grandison
of Exeter complained in 1330 that among other offences committed in the cathedral

those who stand at the upper stalls in the choir, and have lights
within their reach at mattins, knowingly and purposely throw drip-
pings or snuffings from the candles upon the heads or the hair of
such as stand at the lower stalls, with the purpose of exciting
laughter and perhaps of generating discord.

And again,

Item, whereas some ministers do sometimes (and, as we grieve to
say, too often) commit plain faults in singing or reading incorrectly,
then others who know better (and who should rather have com-
passion on the ignorant and bewail the defects of their brethren),
break out, in the hearing of many, into this speech of imprecation
and derision in the vulgar tongue : 'Cursed be he who told the last
lie !'

Hawkins quotes some curious verses on bad singers ascribed
to St. Bernard :

Detestatio contra perverse psallentes,

Qui psalmos resecant qui verba rescissa volutant
Non magis illi ferent quam si male lingue tacerent.
Hi sunt qui psalmos corrumpunt nequiter almos,
Quos sacra scriptura damnat, reprobant quoque jura,
Janglers cum Japers, Nappers, Galpers, quoque Drawers,
Momlers, Forskippers, Overrenners, sic Overhippers,
Fragmina verborum Tutivillus colligit horum.

Hawkins supposes Tutivillus to have been a writer whose
works have been lost. Mr. Hughes-Hughes says that it was the
typical name given by the monks to Lollards ; but Mr. Coulton

has shown that he was a devil whose especial duty it was to collect dropped notes and syllables in a large sack.

THE LITURGICAL DRAMA

Notker's inseparable friend Tutilo was the inventor of Tropes, which, like the Sequences, were new words written syllabically to those florid passages which had come into the plainsong through the Byzantine influences which were prevalent at the court of Charlemagne. Many of these were in the form of dialogues, the most famous of which is known as the *Quem quaeritis* from its opening words :

> Quem quaeritis in sepulchro, Christicolae?
>
> Iesum Nazarenum crucifixum, o caelicolae.
>
> Non est hic, surrexit sicut praedixerat.
> Ite, nuntiate quia surrexit de sepulchro.

From these Tropes there gradually developed in the course of the eleventh, twelfth, and thirteenth centuries a number of religious dramas, of which the most widespread appears to have been that which dealt with the Resurrection. Their musical history is still very obscure. Coussemaker in 1861 printed twenty of them, chiefly from French sources, with their music ; later researchers have discovered over two hundred, but they have not added much to our knowledge of the music. Yet it is clear that these dramas were primarily of musical origin. They seem to have begun more in the fashion of oratorio than of opera, but as the symbolical acts which accompanied them were elaborated, the transition to drama with dramatic costume and action, with even some sort of scenery as well, was an easy one. They were part of the liturgy and were acted in church, the actors being always clerics, priests, or nuns ; but eventually they were transferred to places outside, and acted in the vernacular instead of in Latin by lay actors. When the religious drama became established in the vernacular it ceased to be sung and was entirely spoken ; from that point therefore it does not belong to the history of music.

The ceremonial of the Mass itself is in a certain sense dramatic. The *Concordia Regularis* of Ethelwold, Bishop of Winchester (second half of the tenth century), gives elaborate directions for the *Quem quaeritis* at the third Nocturn at Matins on Easter morning.

While the third lesson is being chanted, let four brethren vest themselves.   Let one of these, vested in an alb, enter as though to take part in the service, and let him approach the sepulchre without attracting attention and sit there quietly with a palm in his hand. While the third respond is chanted, let the remaining three follow, and let them all, vested in copes, bearing in their hands thuribles with incense, and stepping delicately as those who seek something, approach the sepulchre.   These things are done in imitation of the angel sitting in the monument, and the women with spices coming to anoint the body of Jesus.   When therefore he who sits there beholds the three approach him like lost folk and seeking something, let him begin in a dulcet voice of medium pitch to sing *Quem quaeritis*.   And when he has sung it to the end, let the three reply in unison *Ihesum Nezarenum*.   So he, *Non est hic, surrexit sicut praedixerat.   Ite, nuntiat? quia surrexit a mortuis*.   At the word of this bidding let those three turn to the choir and say *Alleluia ! resurrexit Dominus !* This said, let the one, still sitting there and as if recalling them, say the anthem *Venite et videte locum*.   And saying this, let him rise and lift the veil, and show them the place bare of the cross, but only the cloths laid there in which the cross was wrapped. And when they have seen this, let them set down the thuribles which they bare in that same sepulchre, and take the cloth and hold it up in the face of the clergy, and as if to demonstrate that the Lord is risen and is no longer wrapped therein, let them sing the anthem *Surrexit Dominus de sepulchro*, and lay the cloth upon the altar.   When the anthem is done, let the prior, sharing in their gladness at the triumph of our King, in that, having vanquished death, He rose again, begin the hymn *Te Deum laudamus*.   And this begun, all the bells chime out together.[1]

Here we have a little musical drama, though without special costume and with purely symbolical 'properties'.   The body of Jesus is represented by a cross, wrapped in a cloth and hidden

---

[1] Translated by Sir E. K. Chambers in *The Mediaeval Stage*, ii. 14.

by a curtain until the appropriate moment. Similar ceremonies were in use in many other parts of Europe. They were practised chiefly in Benedictine monasteries, though the Cistercians and Carthusians apparently disapproved of them; in England they were used also in the Cathedrals of Salisbury, York, Lincoln, Hereford, and Wells, and probably in many parish churches besides. The drama eventually passed through three stages of scenic development: the first introduces only the angel and the women, the second brings in the apostles Peter and John, and in the third the risen Christ appears *in similitudinem hortolani*. Versions further exist of a play representing the journey to Emmaus and the incredulity of Thomas. Another step towards real drama is marked by the introduction of an *unguentarius* from whom the women buy their spices. He is at first a *persona muta*; in the fourteenth century he obtains a speaking part, and in a still later stage he becomes a comic character.

The plays printed by Coussemaker are as follows:

ELEVENTH CENTURY. *The Wise and Foolish Virgins*. This is partly in Latin and partly in French. It begins with a chorus:

> Adest sponsus qui est Christus: vigilate virgines.
> Pro adventu ejus gaudent et gaudebunt homines.

There are ten lines of this, each couplet being sung to the same melody. The next number is assigned to the *Prudentes* in the manuscript, but from the words (French) it was evidently sung by the angel Gabriel. He warns them not to sleep (five stanzas with recurrent refrain). A *Fatua* begs the wise virgins for oil (three Latin stanzas with French refrain); the *Prudentes* reply in the same stanza (Latin, with the same French refrain), advising them to buy oil of the *Mercatores*. Next come two stanzas for the *Fatuae* in Latin and one for the *Prudentes* in French, all with the same French refrain. The *Mercatores* refuse politely in French, and the *Fatuae* express their despair

in Latin, again with the French refrain.   Here the music ends.
The Bridegroom appears (*modo veniat sponsus*) and addresses
them, beginning in Latin and ending in French, after which
Modo accipiant eas demones et precipitentur in infernum.   From
the metrical structure of the Bridegroom's words it seems
probable that they were intended to be sung, and that the
absence of the notes is due to some accidental omission.

As to the music of the play, which is all in plainsong, we
may note its regular arrangement in rhythmic stanzas.   Each
person or group of persons has a different melody which is
repeated for all the stanzas in that particular part.   The French
refrain is the same for both groups of·Virgins, and adds to the
sense of musical form and unity.   It cannot be said that there
is any appreciable attempt at musical characterization or
dramatic expression.

The Prophets of Christ.   After an introduction of three
couplets set to the same melody, the precentor calls in turn
upon Israel, Moses, Isaiah, Jeremiah, Daniel, Habakkuk, David,
Simeon (who sings a paraphrase of the *Nunc dimittis*—music
missing), Elizabeth, John the Baptist, Virgil, Nebuchadnezzar,
and finally the Sibyl to prophesy of Christ.   This play, if it
can be so called, is all in Latin ; there are no stage directions,
and it is more in the manner of an oratorio.

TWELFTH CENTURY.   *The Resurrection.*   This is unfortunately
incomplete both at the beginning and later on.   As it is, it is
a long and elaborate play, with liberal stage directions.   It
begins with Pilate summoning his soldiers, who proceed to the
tomb.   The next direction is interesting :

Modo veniat Angelus et injiciat eis fulgura.   Milites cadant in
terra, velut mortui.   Tunc tres parvi vel clerici, qui debent esse
Marie : due vero deferunt vas cum unguento pro manibus, tercia
autem turribulum.   Tunc veniant ante hostium ecclesie et dicant
hos versus.

It has been suggested that the words *ante ostium ecclesiae*
imply a performance outside the church, but Chambers points

out that there is no need to take them in this sense, especially
as later directions clearly point to performance inside. The
three Marys buy spices of a merchant to the weight of *quasi
centum libras* for which they pay *mille solidos*, and then go to
the tomb, where they meet the angel. The soldiers return
to Pilate, explain what has happened, and are given money by
him. Here a stage direction seems to have been set to music
by some error—

> Milites simul respondeant ad Pilatum ; tunc exit.
> (The last two words have notes.)

—unless possibly *tunc exit* rather bluntly ends the statement
which they made about the angel before Pilate interrupted
them. If so, it is a curious and noteworthy attempt at dramatic
realism. If not, probably something is missing. At this point

Maria Magdalene in sinistra parte ecclesie stans, exurget inde et
eat quatenus sepulcrum et plausis manibus plorando dicat :

She sings a very long and expressive solo, at the end of which
Jesus appears with the words *Mulier, quid ploras ?* Next comes
a scene with the angel, at the end of which Mary Magdalene
falls fainting and is lifted up by the other two Marys. Peter
enters followed by disciples ; Mary Magdalene starts the hymn
Tristes erant apostoli, which is taken up by the disciples and
sung to the end. Then comes the scene with Thomas, in which
Jesus appears *indutus sacerdotalibus vestimentis candidis*. After
this Thomas and the disciples sing the *Victimae paschali* ; Mary
points out in turn sepulchre, angels, *sudarium*, and cross ; and
the play concludes with the *Te Deum* in chorus.

The music of this play shows considerable musical elaboration. Rapid dialogue is contrasted with stretches of *planctus*,
strophic song, and hymn-tunes. The part of Mary Magdalene
is so prominent as to make her almost comparable to an operatic
heroine.

Daniel is another curious mixture of Latin and French.
It shows Belshazzar's feast, the arrival of Darius, and Daniel in

the lions' den.   Like the other plays it ends with the *Te Deum*, and was evidently a Christmas play.   It seems to require a very large number of performers ; as it was written by the students of Beauvais—

> Ad honorem tui Christe
> Danielis ludus iste
> in Belvaco est inventus
> et invenit hunc juventus

—they perhaps planned it to bring in as many of them as possible. There is considerable humour in the characterization of the various choruses, and Darius appears to have been escorted by minstrels with all sorts of instruments.

To the same century belong several plays on the miracles of St. Nicholas.   The music of these is mostly uninteresting, with frequent repetitions of the same strophic melody ; but we may probably see here the origin of the later English farces called *jigs* or *drolls*, in which the whole play was sung to some such tune as *Brave Lord Willoughby*.   Other plays of St. Nicholas are extant, written by one Hilarius, a pupil of Abelard (twelfth century), who was still better known by his Goliardic poems (see *infra*), and it is supposed that some of these formed the repertory of *clerici vagantes*, strolling players in minor orders, who acted them in any monastery that would engage them.

The manuscript from which the St. Nicholas plays are taken (in the Orleans Library) contains also plays with music on the Epiphany, the Massacre of the Innocents, the Resurrection, the Supper at Emmaus, the Conversion of St. Paul, and the Resurrection of Lazarus.   The general character of the music is similar to that of the Resurrection play described above.   Stage directions are copious, and it is evident that these plays were acted in church as part of a service.   A certain tendency towards operatic elaboration, if the expression may be used of such primitive dramas, may be noted in the parts of Rachel (Innocents' play) and Mary Magdalene (Resurrection).   The Lazarus play is all sung to repetitions of a single short strophic tune.

THIRTEENTH CENTURY. Three short plays on the Nativity, the Epiphany, and the Resurrection. These plays are obviously made short because they are in the first two cases to be followed immediately by the Mass, in the celebration of which some of the chief characters are to take part, presumably still wearing their play costumes. The Resurrection play ends as usual with the *Te Deum*.

FOURTEENTH CENTURY. A Resurrection play which is of especial interest as coming from a nunnery. It is almost all in French, with a little Latin, and all the stage directions are in French. The manuscript also supplies copious information (in French) as to the preparation of the play and subsidiary details of ceremony. The three Marys were to be represented by nuns, the male parts (including the angel) by priests.

The last four plays printed by Coussemaker are from manuscripts at Cividale. The Annunciation play is very short, and was represented out of doors during a procession which preceded the service inside the church. The most interesting of them is a Resurrection play in which directions are given for gestures and movements at almost every line of the text. The following quotation will give some idea of the effects aimed at:

Maria Major
Hic vertat se ad populum manibus apertis
O vos omnes qui transitis
Hic ad oculos suos ponat manus
per viam simul mecum flete,
Hic ostendat Christum
et meum dulcem filium
pariter lugete et videte
Hic se percuciat
si est dolor similis
Hic se percuciat
Sicut dolor meus.
Hic se percuciat
Heu me! Heu me! misera Maria!

Similar plays have recently been found in Austria and

Germany. The Austrian type shows at times (e. g. in the familiar quasi-comic scene between Mary Magdalene and the *unguentarius*) melody of a frankly secular cast. In Germany there were in the eleventh and twelfth centuries no less than four distinguished female composers, of whom the most famous is Hrostwitha of Gandersheim; musically more interesting is St. Hildegard (d. 1179), Abbess of Eibingen and Rupertsberg, among whose numerous musical works is a play *Ordo Virtutum*. This work also shows the influence of popular song. A curious feature of it is that the Devil is the only one of the characters who does not sing.

Hymns, Sequences, Tropes, and Liturgical Dramas all show that during this period music was acquiring an increasingly sharp definition of form. It becomes gradually more and more evident that music, with or without ecclesiastical approval, was asserting its right to exist as an independent art. How far ecclesiastical music was influenced by folk-song it is difficult if not impossible to say; but it is clear that the development of musical form is intimately connected with the development of poetry based on accent and rhyme instead of on quantity. The more we study the life of the Middle Ages the more inextricable appears the confusion between the categories of 'sacred' and 'secular' music, which were never clearly separated until the Reformation and the Council of Trent.

THE CLERICI VAGANTES OR GOLIARDS

To the modern reader it may seem strange to learn that the Tropes, which formed part of the church service, were in some cases trivial, indecent, or profane. The authorship of these is ascribed to the *goliardi*. The goliards were young men in minor ecclesiastical orders, who wandered all over Western Europe during the twelfth and part of the thirteenth centuries. They appear to have arisen about the time of Charlemagne, and they are not much heard of after about 1225, the period at which the great medieval universities became systematically organized. They were of all nationalities, united by the common use of Latin as an international language. As far as is at present known, they seem to have been mostly German and English, but there is probably a large quantity of material from other countries which has not yet been thoroughly investigated. Although technically ecclesiastics, and vigorously conscious of their superiority to the uncultured who knew no Latin, they were classed socially with the minstrels, actors, and acrobats who descended from the Roman *mimus*, and were generally regarded as vagabonds and notoriously immoral persons. But the goliards could read and write, and could express themselves—with no respect for bishops—in masterly Latin verse. They derived their name from a Bishop Golias, who was probably an imaginary prelate; they seem to have regarded themselves as a definite order or confraternity of whom Golias was the head. The most famous collections of their poems are the *Carmina Burana* (so called from the monastery of Benediktbeuern, whence the MS. of about 1225 passed into the Munich Library), the collection in the British Museum attributed to Walter Mapes, and the song-book in the Cambridge University Library. Their favourite subjects are either wine and women or satire of ecclesiastical authority.

Some of their songs were set to music, and others are interesting on account of their musical allusions. It is mainly to the goliards that we owe the first notation of secular music. As early as the ninth century we find classical poems set to music (in neums)—odes of Horace and passages from Virgil and Statius—as well as contemporary songs on historical subjects. The Cambridge MS. (eleventh century) has neums to a few songs only. The earliest decipherable melody is that of a pilgrims' song in praise of Rome—

O Roma nobilis orbis et domina
cunctarum urbium excellentissima

D d

—which appears also to have been sung to the well-known love-song

O admirabile Veneris ydolum,

which is provided with neums in the Cambridge MS.   Another interesting song is one to the nightingale, which starts off with learned musical allusions :

Aurea personet lyra clara modulamina ;
Simplex chorda sit extensa voce quindenaria
primum sonum mese reddat lege hypodorica.

The monochord is to be divided into the fifteen notes o the scale from A to A (*gamma ut* being at this time not included), and the song is to begin on the *mese* A according to the Hypodorian Mode.   The tune is very similar in style to those of the Church hymns.

THE MINSTRELS

Medieval literature is full of allusions to the minstrels.   They were descended on the one side from the comic actors and singers of the theatre of the Roman Empire, and on the other from the Celtic and Teutonic bards who sang the deeds of heroes to their harps.   They were perpetually condemned by the Church, and it was laid down over and over again that to give anything to a minstrel was equivalent to robbing the poor. They were homeless outcasts, but they found a warm welcome everywhere, not excluding the monasteries, in spite of repeated prohibitions.   The wandering minstrel (under which term may be classed not only musicians, but acrobats, jugglers, story-tellers, and entertainers of all kinds) was indispensable to a society that possessed neither books nor newspapers and which rarely left its home except for wars and pilgrimages.   They were always in demand for weddings, and would at once con-gregate wherever they heard that a wedding was to take place. They were the normal and necessary accompaniments of social entertaining.   Thus Bartholomaeus Anglicus (*c.* 1250), speaking ' of the suppar ', says :

Many thynges bene necessarye and worshyppe (i. e. honour) the supper . . . the viii is myrthe of songe and of Instrumentes of Musike. Noble men use not to make suppers without harpe or symphony.

The advance of civilization made a gradual change in the status of the minstrel. A great many obtained permanent posts at the courts of princes. Froissart gives an interesting picture of Edward III listening to music before the naval battle of Winchelsea (29 August 1350)—

Si se tenoit li rois d'Engleterre ou chief de sa nef, vestis d'un noir jake de veluiel . . . Et faisoit ses menestrelz corner devant lui une danse d'Alemagne, que messire Jehans Chandos, qui là estoit, avoit nouvellement raporté. Et encores par esbatement il faisoit ledit chevalier chanter avoech ses menestrelz, et y prendoit grant plaisance. Et à la fois regardoit en hault, car il avoit mis une gette ou chastiel de sa nef, pour noncier quant li Espagnol venroient. Ensi que li rois estoit en ce deduit, et que tout li chevalier estoit moult liet de ce que il le veoient si joieus, li gette, qui perçut nestre la navie des Espagnolz, dist : ' Ho ! j'en voi une venir, et me semble une nef d'Espagne.' Lors s'apaisièrent li menestrelz.

Much information about music is to be found in the household accounts of Philip the Bold (b. 1342, Duke of Burgundy 1363). He maintained ' ménestrels de bouche ', i. e. singers of both sexes, as well as boys for his chapel at Dijon, and players on the gittern, harp, psaltery, and ' eschiquier '. Others played viols and rebecks ; wind instruments were represented by an organist, and two players each of ' challemelle ' and ' cornemuse '. The trumpeters were still more important people, but their functions were probably more ceremonial and military than artistic. Wherever the Duke went he was surrounded by minstrels, and there are frequent records of his hearing and rewarding those of other princes, including the Emperor of Constantinople. Towns also had their permanent minstrels ; in Germany they formed very important corporations.

Some idea of musical organization at this date may be gathered from the frequent mention of the so-called schools of

minstrelsy—*escoles de menestrandie*—which, however, must not be
regarded as medieval equivalents of the modern *conservatoire*.
They could be more accurately described as international con-
gresses.   They were held in Lent, as the minstrels would not
be required for service during that season, and seem to have
taken place for the most part in Flanders and North Germany.
The princes paid the travelling expenses of their musicians
when they attended them.   No doubt a minstrel who went to
meet his fellow minstrels from other parts at one of these
'schools' learned something new; but the word 'school' is not
to be taken as meaning a course of instruction.   It is the
common medieval word for a corporate assembly.   These
meetings led eventually to the recognition of music as an
honourable profession.   Thus Henry VI in 1449 appointed a
commission of royal minstrels with authority to supervise and
punish all minstrels throughout the realm, in order that the
genuine professional musician should not suffer by the com-
petition of unskilled persons who might well be earning their
normal living in some other trade.   The minstrels of England had
already existed as a guild for a century.   The unincorporated
musician plied for hire as late as the days of Ben Jonson, for
we see them at the wedding in *Epicoene*; but the spread of
reading and writing throughout a wider class of the popula-
tion, and the general use of a practical musical notation for
secular music as well as sacred, put an end to the *jongleur* of
the thirteenth century.   Some lines attributed to Dr. John
Bull pointedly express the views of a respectable professional
musician :

> When Jesus went to Jairus' house
>   (Whose daughter was about to dye),
> He turned the minstrels out of doors,
>   Among the rascal company :
> Beggars they are, with one consent,
> And rogues, by Act of Parliament.

TROUBADOURS, TROUVÈRES, MINNESÄNGER, AND MEISTERSINGER

Among the noble patrons of the minstrels and *jongleurs* were some who had artistic abilities and ambitions of their own. The poetry of chivalry, represented first by the *troubadours* of Provence and later by the *trouvères* north of the Loire, covers a period from about 1150 to 1300. Some of these noble amateurs composed their own melodies as well as the words; but they seldom played or sang them. Performance as a rule was left to the professional *jongleur*, who in some cases composed the music himself. The musical importance of *troubadour* songs lies in the fact that they were independent of the musical art of the Church. Plainsong was by no means a dead language at this period; new additions were constantly being made to services and new plainsong music being composed for them. But the *troubadours* developed an art that was purely secular, and based on a different rhythmical principle. They brought into music the metrical accent of the dance and its rhythmical balance of phrase; we see in this music the germ of what we may roughly sum up in the words *classical form*. From a social point of view the *troubadours* are important, because their art gradually led to the acceptance of music as an independent art, to its cultivation among the leisured classes, and so to a wider sphere of influence than could ever be permeated by an art of music which remained subservient to ecclesiastical ritual.

Historians of literature have proved conclusively that this Provençal poetry was greatly influenced by Arabic models. It is also a matter of common knowledge that the lute, as its name shows, was originally an Oriental instrument. It has therefore been suggested that medieval Western music must have had a much closer contact with Eastern music than we have hitherto been led to believe. The Moors in Spain, the Saracens in Sicily and South Italy, might well be expected to have influenced

European music, and the Crusades offered further opportunity for the musical approach of East and West. But in the absence of any Arabic musical notation it is impossible to obtain direct evidence. It has not been possible even to ascertain 'the influence of the Moors on Spanish folk-song, although a Moorish tune, *Qalbí qalb a'rabi,* is frequently mentioned in Spanish litera- ture from the time of the Archpriest of Hita (contemporary with Chaucer) to the seventeenth century, and four bars of it were recorded in our notation by Francisco Salinas, Professor of Music at Salamanca in the sixteenth century. It has been suggested that some of the *cantigas* collected by Alfonso the Sage in the thirteenth century may have been Moorish in origin, and the theory is supported by the fact that at his learned court Jews and Muslims met Christians on equal terms, and that the very manuscripts of the *cantigas* are illustrated with miniatures representing Muslim musicians playing on Muslim instruments.

The earliest known *troubadours* were Guillaume, Count of Poitiers and Duke of Aquitaine (*fl.* 1087–1127), and Marcabru, whose activity seems to have come to an end in 1147. The earliest of the northern trouvères were Chrétien de Troyes and Gautier d'Épinal (second half of twelfth century). The develop- ment of the art in the north of France is ascribed to the influence of the wandering *jongleurs,* who probably contributed much to the sense of national unity between the different regions of France. Towards the beginning of the thirteenth century we find some odd characters among the *troubadours* : the Monk of Montaudon, a somewhat Rabelaisian personality, who was richly rewarded by the great for his music, but handed over all their gifts to his priory, and Gaucelm Faidit, son of a *bourgeois,* who became a *jongleur* after losing all his fortune by gambling, married a lady of the same class, and became enormously fat. Some idea of the *troubadour's* life may be gained from occasional biographical notices; we read of one Guiraut de Borneil, who was called the 'master of the *troubadours'*, that he passed the whole winter at school and learned (? taught), and during the summer went from court to court taking with him two singers who sang his songs. In the course of the thirteenth century the social distinction between *trouvères* and *jongleurs* seems to have been largely obliterated; the minstrels became more respectable, the nobility better educated. The head of the aristocratic school was Thibaut de Champagne, King of Navarre (1201–53); the most eminent of the *bourgeois* school of Arras was Adam de la Hale.

In Germany the *Minnesänger* practised a similar art; but although such names as Wolfram von Eschenbach and Frauenlob are famous in the history of German poetry, the musical records of them are very sparse and the interpretation of their notation has given rise to much controversy. There is not much music of this type available before the days of Oswald von Wolkenstein (1377–1445). The *Meistersinger* flourished from about 1430 to 1600. Wagner's opera, apart from its music, gives a very good general idea of what they were. They were amateur musicians of the middle class, believing themselves to be the artistic heirs of the *Minnesänger* and cultivating that style of music under a number of pedantic and old-fashioned rules. They were the sort of people who in a German town to-day would be members of the local *Liedertafel*. Their musical outlook was entirely reactionary. It must be admitted that they pursued their art with an extraordinary devotion and idealism; and both in spirit and in practice they had their place in the musical history of the Reformation. After the Council of Trent they could exist only in Protestant cities, for the German Bible was the chief source of their inspiration.

ANTICIPATIONS OF THE RENAISSANCE

During the fourteenth century there developed an increasing sense of the advantages of domestic comfort and of privacy. The old patriarchal life, in which the nobles and all their dependants, down to the humblest, lived and ate together in the great rush-strewn hall, gradually disappeared as people took to building separate living-rooms. Langland describes the change regretfully in *Piers Plowman*:

> There the lord ne the lady · liketh noughte to sytte,
> Now hath uche riche a reule · to eten bi hym-selve
> In a prive parloure · for pore mennes sake,
> Or in a chambre with a chymneye · and leve the chief halle,
> That was made for meles · men to eten inne.

England was a good deal behind other countries in these respects. The Italy of Dante, Petrarch, and Boccaccio, where the new art of Francesco Landini was growing up, shows 'is a cultured society that was already looking forward to the Renaissance. Dante was a great lover of music, and is recorded to have been a capable performer; but the musical allusions in his works, numerous as they are, do not suggest that he had much intellectual appreciation of the art. He certainly must have studied the theory of music as it was studied in the Middle Ages in the works of Boëthius; but that theory was a thing curiously separate from actual musical practice. In his Hell there is no music; it is in Purgatory that the poet first hears singing. How Dante was accustomed to listen to music is shown by such a passage as this (*Purg.* ix. 139):

> Io mi rivolsi attento al primo tuono,
>   E *Te Deum laudamus* mi parea
> Udir in voce mista al dolce suono.
> Tale imagine appunto mi rendea
>   Ciò ch' io udiva, qual prender si suole
>   Quando a cantar con organi si stea:
> Che or sì or no s'intendon le parole.

> ·At the first peal I turned around attentive
>   And seemed to me that *Te Deum Laudamus*
> I heard in voices blended with sweet music.
> That which I heard the very same impression

Produced on me as one is wont to gather
When we are present where they chant with organs,
And now the words are, now are not, distinguished.[1]

and still more in the following passage (*Par.* xiv. 118) :

E come giga ed arpa, in tempra tesa
Di molte corde, fa dolce tintinno
A tal da cui la nota non è intesa,
Così dai lumi che lì m'apparinno
S'accogliea per la croce una melode,
Che mi rapiva senza intender l'inno.
Ben m'accors' io ch'ell' era d'alte lode,
Perocchè a me venia ; *Risurgi e vinci*,
Com'a colui che non intende ed ode.

And, even as, strung in pitch, a harp and fiddle
With multitude of strings make a sweet tingling
To one by whom the tune is not distinguished,
So from the Lustres that showed there before me
Along the Cross a melody was swelling,
That, though the hymn I not distinguished, rapt me.
I well perceived it was of lofty praises,
Because there came to me ' Arise and Conquer ',
As to a man who hears, not comprehending.[1]

It is what we might now call an impressionist's idea of
music—voices and organ at a distance, the words sometimes
heard, sometimes not—the tinkling of harps and lutes with no
clear perception of definite values. A more poignant impression
of music is that of Casella singing (*Purg.* ii) and holding Dante,
Virgil, and the suffering souls enthralled. We should note, too,
the description of the birds singing at dawn (*Purg.* xxviii.
16–18):

Ma con piena letizia l'ore prime
Cantando, ricevièno intra le foglie,
Che tenevan bordone alle sue rime.

But with full-throated joy they drank in, singing,
The matutinal airs amid the foliage,
That to their lays kept up a drone incessant.[1]

---

[1] From Sir S. W. Griffith's translation of Dante's *Divina Commedia* (Oxford
University Press).

This allusion to high voices singing against a bass will be further illustrated by a passage from another author to be quoted later. What Dante tells us about music is chiefly the overpowering effect that it had upon him ; and he is particularly susceptible to singing (*Par.* xxvii. 2–3) :

> Cominciò *Gloria* tutto il Paradiso
> Si che m'inebriava il dolce canto.

> 'Glory !' began all Paradise in such wise
> That the sweet song with rapture made me drunken.[1]

Boccaccio gives us more concrete information about music in the social life of his time. Every day the young people of the *Decameron* sing and dance to lute and viol, and we note that while the man plays the lute, the viol is the lady's instrument. They sang to their instruments, they danced to singing, and they had purely instrumental music as well—Boccaccio mentions the *stampita*, a favourite dance of the Provençal troubadours (*estampida*) which was popular in Germany as well. In the Latin treatise of Johannes de Grocheo it is called *stantipes*. Besides the lute and viol, Boccaccio mentions the rebeck and the bagpipe, and on the evening of the Fifth Day, when Dioneo is maliciously offering to sing a number of popular songs, the words of which were not to the ladies' taste, he says that if he had a *cembalo* he would sing certain songs named, but as he has none he proposes others. It must not be supposed that this instrument was a *clavicembalo* ; it was either a tambourine or (as Arnaldo Bonaventura suggests) a psaltery. Boccaccio, like Dante, insists on the overpowering emotional effects of music.

Even more interesting than the *Decameron* is Giovanni da Prato's *Paradiso degli Alberti* (1389). Like the *Decameron*, it describes a cultured country-house party near Florence ; but it includes philosophical discussions as well as stories, and it has the additional interest of introducing real historical personages, among whom we meet Francesco Landini, the blind organist and composer. Landini, we are told here, was not merely an

[1] From Sir S. W. Griffith's translation of Dante's *Divina Commedia* (O.U.P.).

accomplished player ; he was a man who had studied the philosophy of music and all the liberal arts, although blind from
early childhood.   At that period blindness would be much less
of an impediment than now to the acquirement of learning, for
the lecture system of medieval universities, still perpetuated in
our own, had a basis of common sense when books were all
in manuscript and rarities beyond the purse of any student.
At Alberti's villa Landini was among men of distinction in
theology and science, but his music made him a link with the
younger generation as well.   The author spares no words in
his description of the beauties of the house and garden as well
as of the sumptuous hospitality daily provided.   We pass
through the courtyard, its *loggia* furnished with hangings
and couches, into the garden, where a table is set out with
refreshments in silver dishes and precious wines in exquisite
glass against a background of cypresses, pines, oranges, pome-
granates, laurels, and olives.   The seniors sit down, and
Francesco, who, though he can see nothing, is ' very cheerful ',
asks for his little portative organ, and begins to play his love-
songs so sweetly that for the sweetness of this most sweet
harmony (*si dolcemente . . . che per dolcezza della dolcissima
armonia*) there was none who did not feel that his heart was
bursting for superabundance of happiness.   Whenever he plays
the author reiterates that *dolcemente, dolcissima, dolcezza*—

       If music be the food of love, play on—

A troop of girls come in and dance ; they sing a song in two
parts, to which Messer Biagio di Sernello take the bass (*tenendo
loro bordone*—compare the lines quoted from Dante) ; the
examples printed by Wooldridge in vol. i of this History will
show us the sort of thing they sang.   On another day the girls
and the musicians sang *qualche madriale*, and they chose those
made in Padua by Frate Bartolino, *sì famoso musico* (cf. Wooldridge, new edn., i. 258, note).   And when they had finished
there was singing and playing for a very long space.

The importance of these pictures of Florentine life is that they show us artistic secular music as one of the most intense pleasures of a highly cultured society—a society which in its general character has much more affinity to our own than the medieval society described in previous sections of this chapter. But it is a musical appreciation which is absolutely direct, sensuous, and concrete ; it is neither romantic nor—as we might nowadays say—intellectual.

MUSIC IN THE UNIVERSITIES

Music in its theoretical aspect was an indispensable item in medieval university education as one of the so-called seven liberal arts. The degree of *Magister Artium* was based on the *Trivium* and *Quadrivium* ; the former included the three lower arts of Grammar, Rhetoric, and Logic, the latter the four higher arts of Arithmetic, Geometry, Music, and Astronomy. From a modern point of view there is nothing so very odd about the position here given to music, if by music we imply the mathematical theory of sound, which may well form part of a course of higher mathematical studies. Nor is there anything inherently illogical in the distinction between *cantus*, the actual practice of music, and *musica,* its theoretical principles. This distinction is apparent in the often quoted verses of Bede :

> Musicorum et cantorum magna est distantia,
> Illi dicunt, isti sciunt quae componit musica ;
> Nam qui facit quod non sapit, diffinitur bestia.

The inadequacy of musical notation, which lasted for some considerable time after the days of Guido of Arezzo,[1] may well have aggravated the natural stupidity of singers, and the

---

[1] The Guidonian system did not become universal in Europe for some centuries. In German churches people were still singing from neums as late as 1300, and the result was that in German Switzerland plainsong was ridiculed under the name of *cantus confusus*. Towards the end of the thirteenth century the Bishop of Regensburg, the Abbot of Einsiedeln, and the Bishop of Breslau employed monks from Austria to teach their clergy the Guidonian notation.

rarity of books of any kind naturally assisted the petrifaction of theoretical studies.

Students were instructed in singing and in plainsong, and in English universities the colleges had their musical foundations for the service of the Church. But as far as can be ascertained the function of a Bachelor in Music was to lecture on Boëthius. The Doctorate was given apparently to musicians of distinction ; the earliest records date from 1463 at Cambridge and 1511 at Oxford. In 1515 there appears the first notice of any conditions imposed on candidates for the Mus.D. degree : Robert Perrot was required to compose a Mass. But 'these Doctors of Music were in no way connected with the university as teachers'.[1] The professorships at both Oxford and Cambridge date from the seventeenth century. No other universities conferred degrees in music, and the only ones which seem to have had special musical professorships were Salamanca, where there was a Master of Music from 1313 down to the nineteenth century, as well as a Master of the Organ, established by Alfonso the Sage in 1254, and Coimbra, where there was a Chair of Music from 1323. The most distinguished Professor of Music at Salamanca was Salinas (d. 1590), who studied in Rome and Naples.

It is evident from Chaucer and other writers that there was a fair amount of amateur music in the universities, and that medieval tutors, like those of the present day, were often inclined to regard it as 'a dangerous snare'.

THE MUSICAL LIFE OF THE RENAISSANCE

The exaggerated importance attached by many writers on music to Palestrina has caused a false view to be taken of the position of music in the period of the Renaissance. The revival of Greek studies was only a small part of the change which is generally held to mark the end of the Middle Ages, and that

---

[1] C. F. Abdy Williams, *Degrees in Music.*

change makes its appearance in music in the epoch of Josquin des Près. In the practical life of music the application of the new art of printing is an important landmark. Although a certain amount of music was printed during the last quarter of the fifteenth century, music-printing as a commercial enterprise may be said to have begun with Petrucci of Fossombrone in 1501. We are accustomed to think of printed books as contributing greatly to international intellectual intercourse, but in the world of music it is surprising how much actual travelling was done by musicians in earlier medieval days. English harpers were in demand as far away as Spain ; in 1384 Charles the Bad of Navarre rewarded several English harpers and *juglares* of both sexes, and in 1442 the Prince of Viana paid 10 florins to Maestre Johan de Londres, *arpero*. Germans were engaged as players of wind instruments by King John of Aragon ; at Ferrara there were German trumpeters, and from 1472 to 1475 a choir of German singing-boys. Petrucci's first music-book was a collection of motets of the Netherland school. A curious tribute to Josquin and his school is paid by the somewhat disreputable macaronic poet Teofilo Folengo (1519). Folengo, after a comic description of the village priest Jacopinus and his hurried performance of Mass, goes on to describe a special festival at which Jacopinus undertakes a Mass in counterpoint :

> Inde Iacopinus, chiamatis undique pretis,
> Coeperat in gorga Missam cantare stupendam ;
> Subsequitant alii, magnisque cridoribus instant.
> Protinus Introitum spazzant talqualiter omnem,
> Ad Chyrios veniunt, quos miro dicere sentis
> Cum contrappunto, veluti si cantor adesset
> Master Adrianus, Constantius atque Iachettus.

and regrets that Josquin is not there to hear it. He calls Josquin 'the glory of the senate of Phoebus', happy are the singers of Pope Leo X who sings his works—

> Quos Deus auscultans coelum mostrabit apertum !

works which the poet must forthwith enumerate—

Missa super voces Musarum, lassaque far mi,
Missa super sextum, Fortunam, missaque musque,
Missaque de Domina, sine nomine, Duxque Ferarae—
&c.

calling finally on his pupils to adore him and on Franchino
Gafurio to draw up the principles of modern musical composition:

Magnus adorabit tua tunc vestigia Brumel,
Iannus Motonus, Petrus de Robore, Festa
Constans, Iosquinus qui saepe putabitur esse.
Tuque pater Franchine novas componere normas
Incipe, et antiquas remove squallore sepultas.

A new age in music has begun, and the music-printers must
have given increasing assistance to the spread of practical
interest in music throughout the rising middle classes as well as
amongst the aristocracy. Castiglione tells us in the *Cortegiano*
how necessary it was in good society that a man should know
something of music. He quotes an amusing remark made by
a lady to a man who refused to dance or listen to music on
the ground that he was a soldier and that his business was
fighting:

I should think that as you are not at the war, nor in any likelihood
of fighting, it would be a good thing if you were to have yourself
thoroughly well oiled and put away in a cupboard with all your
fighting gear until you were wanted, so as not to get more rusty
than you are already.

One of those taking part in the discussion suggests that music
is a diversion for ladies only, but he is at once talked down by
Count Lodovico da Canossa, the chief speaker of the book, with
what he himself calls 'a sea of argument' from ancient history
as to the manly virtues of music. How universal was the love
of music can be observed from the minor varieties of secular
music—*laudi spirituali* which were nothing but popular folk-
tunes to which devout words had been set in place of the
original poems, *frottole* and all their tribe, the *canti carnascia-*

leschi, madrigals on street cries, madrigals on children's games, descriptive madrigals such as those of Jannequin, semi-dramatic madrigals such as Striggio's *Cicalamento delle donne al bucato* which lead us on to the *Amfiparnaso* of Orazio Vecchi. Some of these have their parallels in England too.

MUNICIPAL AND MILITARY MUSIC

On the Continent, especially in Germany and Italy, music was much encouraged by the multitude of small princely courts, and also by the independent free cities. The towns had their musicians for ceremonial purposes as well as the dukes, bishops, and electors ; they had even what might be called a musical heraldry. Trumpeters had from early times possessed special privileges. They were supposed to serve princes only ; in war-time, if they were taken prisoner, they could be exchanged for officers ; at the christening of a prince of Württemberg in 1596 they claimed the right to sit at table with the nobility on the ground that they were not 'musicians' but 'trumpeters'. The towns kept other wind instruments, including trombones, but were not supposed to have trumpeters except by special concession from the emperor. Such permission was granted to Augsburg in 1426, and about the same date to Nürnberg and Ulm. Cologne always claimed the right to have trumpeters as the seat of a prince-archbishop. Princes and cities, whether they had trumpets or not, all had their own particular fanfares which were blown on ceremonial occasions, just as their coats of arms could be displayed. A few of these have been preserved, and attempts have been made in Germany to form a collection of them.

Municipal music was very strictly regulated in Germany, and the records of it are often curious. The night-watchman with his horn was a familiar figure ; he still blows from St. Lambert's tower at Münster. Hornblowers accompanied the criminal to the gallows at Hamburg ; at Strasburg, up to 1791, a horn was blown every evening between eight and nine to warn the Jews to leave the town. In the sixteenth century the German merchants at Antwerp were escorted daily to the Exchange by a band of music. Weddings and other domestic festivities were classified according to the social position of the parties, and the number of instruments for each class clearly fixed. A first-class wedding at Bremen might have trumpets and trombones to lead the procession; a second-class bride might have them to salute her with a fanfare at her father's door, but for the procession she was only allowed the town pipers; for weddings of the third and fourth classes trumpets, trombones, *Zinken,* and *Dulcianen* were all forbidden. Serenades with a band of instruments, such as eventually developed into the serenades and *cassations* (the word is said to be derived from *gassatim,* 'through the streets'), were frequent in Germany in the sixteenth century, and something of the kind is described as early as 1325.

The history of the Middle Ages is a continuous record of wars, and we have ample evidence of the presence of musicians in all military operations. As to the music which they actually played we know next to nothing. Almost up to the days of Louis XIV the drum was the main accompaniment of marching. Trumpets were used for fanfares and signals, but the earliest recorded marching tunes seem to be those of Byrd's 'Battle'. Arbeau describes in great detail the various drum-rhythms used. The fife appears to have been introduced by the Swiss about 1500, but Arbeau says the fifers may play what they like as long as they keep time with the drums. They probably played the popular songs and dance-tunes of the day. Some of the songs in the early German manuscript collections bear the heading 'to be sung on the march', and it is clear that most of the military music in Elizabeth Rogers's Virginal Book (1656) is of this character. It is agreed even by German authorities that the quick march in $\frac{6}{8}$ time came from England, and the earliest English examples are obviously country dances. In view of the popularity of the fife for marching in the days

of Henry VIII it is fairly safe to assume that folk-dances were
what the fifers played, and it is probable that some of them
have survived down to modern times as traditional regimental
marches.

Of the origins of the art of the Troubadours nothing need
be added to what Professor Dent has written. Descended
originally from the Church by means of the Sequences of Notker
and the Tropes of the Goliards, it was nevertheless essentially
secular in development and achievement. At the same time it
must be clearly understood that, in spite of certain points of
contact with popular music, particularly in the ' Reverdies ' and
' Chansons de Danse ', it was an aristocratic and intricate art
with none of the haphazard characteristics of folk-music.

The history of secular music still remains to be written. The
patient labours of several generations of scholars have succeeded
in tracing more or less completely the development of religious
music from the earliest times, but the history of the secular art
still remains a series of disconnected episodes. Thus the great
Elizabethan school of madrigal- and song-writers seems to have
sprung from nowhere and to have vanished as suddenly as it
appeared. The ancestry of the Virginalists is equally hard to
trace, and in just the same fashion the Troubadours and
Trouvères practised for nearly two centuries a highly-developed
and intricate art whose origin is still a matter of conjecture.

The Troubadours and Trouvères were a race of knightly
poets and musicians who flourished from the beginning of the
twelfth to the end of the thirteenth century, the Trouvères in
the north of France and the Troubadours in the south. The
names are essentially the same, being derived from the French
trover and the Provençal *trobar*, to find or to invent. Although
the Troubadours, who, as their name implies, wrote in
Provençal, were first in point of time, they seem to have been
outnumbered by the Trouvères, who wrote in French. At any

rate we possess nearly 2,000 songs by some 200 Trouvères as against 260 songs by 40 Troubadours. These have been preserved in a variety of forms, ranging from the most sumptuous illuminated volumes to the modest song-books of the itinerant Jongleurs. The songs are usually classified by authors; but there are exceptions, and in one case they are arranged more or less in alphabetical order.

The system of notation is always the same. The music is written on a stave of four or five lines in square neums and ligatures, which show clearly the pitch of the notes but give no indication of value or rhythm. The words of the first verse are written under the notes, the other verses following below.

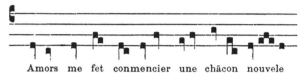

Amors me fet conmencier une chãcon nouvele

From this example it will be seen that the pitch of the notes and the 'underlaying' of the words are quite clear. The clef is always C or F, and when more notes than one are to be sung to a syllable they are bound together by a ligature. The only missing factor is the value of the notes, and this problem remained unsolved until the researches of M. Jean Beck and M. Pierre Aubry [1] proved that the rhythm of the music is to be found in the verse, and that once this is established the melodies can be interpreted by means of the Rhythmic Modes (see *O. H. M.*, vol. i, p. 64). The rules for the carrying out of this process are too long and complicated to be included here, but a detailed account of them can be found in the works quoted above.

The poetry of the Troubadours is not so much new wine poured into old bottles as the reverse; its originality lies in the

---

[1] Jean Beck, *La Musique des Troubadours* (Les Musiciens Célèbres: Laurens, Paris). Pierre Aubry, *Troubadours et Trouvères* (Les Mâitres de la Musique: Alcan, Paris). Engl. version trans. by C. Aveling, Schirmer, N.Y. and London.

form of expression rather than in the thought expressed. With the exception of the rule that the rhythm of the verse, iambic, trochaic, or dactylic, must remain constant, the strophic form was quite free and was the subject of considerable ingenuity. Indeed it was a point of honour with the Troubadour never to copy exactly the versification of an existing poem, even if the difference was only a matter of finding a new rhyme. On the other hand the matter of the poetry is essentially conventional. Not only do the same phrases and clichés occur over and over again, but the various types of poem are quite clearly defined, and almost the whole mass of Troubadour poetry can be classified in this manner.

There are two main classes of poem : subjective, in which the Troubadour speaks in his own person, and objective, in which he describes events in which he is not involved. Under these two headings the two types can be ranged as follows :

A. *Subjective.*

1. The 'Chanson d'amour' or 'Canso', expressing the devotion of the Troubadour to his lady in terms of the 'théorie de l'amour courtois', the formal and idealistic code of knightly passion.

2. The 'Sirventes', a political or moral satire.

3. The 'Tenson' or 'Jeu Parti', a philosophical, moral, or political dialogue between the Troubadour and some other person or persons.

4. Religious songs, including the 'Chansons de Croisade'.

B. *Objective.*

1. The 'Chanson d'Histoire', also called 'Chanson de Toile' from the fact that the heroine ('Belle Doette', 'Belle Oriolant', and so on) is always described as spinning or sewing.

2. The 'Chanson d'Aube', not, like the much later 'Aubade', a morning serenade, but a song of warning, in which the Watcher ('guetteur'), like Brangaene in her tower, calls to the lovers that dawn is at hand and they must part. A charac-

teristic feature of this type of song is the use of the word 'alba' (aube) in the last line of each strophe.

3. Dramatic Songs: little domestic dramas, involving usually three characters, the husband, the wife, and the lover.

4. The 'Reverdie', an idyll of love in springtime.

5. The 'Pastourelle', dealing with the loves of knight and shepherdess.

6. The 'Chanson de Danse' or 'Estampie', a song for dancing and a dance for singing.

GERALD COOPER.

BIBLIOGRAPHY

Compiled by M. D. Calvocoressi,
with assistance from the authors

TO CHAPTER I

Athenaeus. The Deipnosophists (Bohn's Library, 3 vols.). London, 1854. (Transl. by C. D. Yonge: see Chapter XIV.)

Bellermann, F. Die Hymnen des Dionysios und Mesomedes. Berlin, 1840.

Anonymi Scriptio de Musica. Berlin, 1841.

Die Tonleitern und Musiknoten des Griechen. Berlin, 1847.

Boethius, A. M. S. De Musica Libri V, edidit H. Glareanus. Basel, 1546. (Modern reimpression, Teubner, Leipzig.)

Denniston, J. D. Some recent theories of Greek modes. In *Classical Quarterly*, 1913.

Emmanuel, M. La Danse Grecque Antique. Paris, 1896.

La Musique Grecque, in *Encyclopédie Musicale et Dictionnaire du Conservatoire*, vol. i. Paris, 1913.

Fleischer, O. Reste der altgriechischen Tonkunst. Leipzig, 1899.

Fortlage, K. Das Musikalische System des Griechen in seiner Urgestalt. Jena, 1847.

Gevaert, F. Histoire et Théorie de la Musique dans l'Antiquité. Gand, 1875-81.

La Mélopée antique dans le chant de l'Église Latine. Gand, 1895.

Gevaert and Vollgraef. Problèmes musicaux d'Aristote. Gand, 1903.

Graf, E. De Graecorum Veterum Re Musice. Leipzig, 1885.

Greif, F. Articles in *Revue des Études Grecques*. Paris, 1909.

Hero (of Alexandria). The Pneumatics (translated by Bennett Woodcroft). London, 1881.

Jan, K. von. Musici Scriptores Graeci et melodiarum veterum quidquid exstat. Leipzig, 1895.

Excerpta Neapolitana. Leipzig, 1895.

Laloy, L. Aristoxène de Tarente et la musique de l'Antiquité. Paris, 1904.

Macran, H. C. The Harmonics of Aristoxenus. Oxford, 1902.

Marnold, J. Les fondements naturels de la musique grecque antique. (In *Sammelbände der I. M. G.*, Leipzig, 1909.)

Meibomius, M. Antiquae Musicae Auctores Septem (2 vols.). Amsterdam, 1652.

Monro, D. B. Modes of Ancient Greek Music. Oxford, 1894.

Mountford, J. F. Greek Music and its relation to modern times. (In *Journal of Hellenic Studies*, 1920.)

The Musical Scales of Plato's *Republic*. (In *Classical Quarterly*, 1923.)

The Harmonics of Ptolemy and the Lacuna in ii. 14. (In *Transactions of Amer. Phil. Association*, 1926.)

PAUL, O. Boetius und die Griechische Harmonik. Leipzig, 1872.

PERRETT, W. Some Questions of musical theory (2 vols.). Cambridge, 1926-8.

REINACH, Th. La Musique Grecque. Paris, 1926.

REINACH, Th., and WEIL, H. Plutarque, de la Musique — édition, traduction, commentaire. Paris, 1900.

ROSSBACH, A., and WESTPHAL, R. Theorie der Musikalischen Kunst der Hellenen. Leipzig, 1886-9.

RUELLE, Ch. E. Études sur l'Ancienne Musique Grecque. Paris, 1875-1900.

TANNERY, P. Les Intervalles de la Musique Grecque. (In *Revue des Études Grecques*, Paris, 1902.)

THÉON DE SMYRNE. Des Connaissances mathématiques utiles pour la lecture de Platon, traduit par J. Dupuis. Paris, 1892.

THEOPHRASTUS. De Historia et Causis Plantarum. Leipzig, Teubner, n. d.

VINCENT, A. J. H. Notices sur divers manuscrits grecs relatifs à la musique (Notices et extraits des mss. de la bibliothèque du Roi, vol. xvi, pt. ii). Paris, 1847.

WALLIS, Dr. John. Opera Mathematica. Oxford, 1693-9.

Vol. iii contains the Harmonics of Claudius Ptolemy, with commentary by Porphyry and Manuel Bryennius.

WESTPHAL, R. Geschichte der Alten Musik. Leipzig, 1865.

Harmonik und Melopoe der Griechen. Leipzig, 1863.

Plutarch über die Musik. Breslau, 1865.

Aristoxeni fragmenta harmonica, with comments. Leipzig, 1883-93.

See also various articles in *Congrès International d'Histoire de la Musique*. Paris, 1900.

TO CHAPTERS III–VI

ABDY WILLIAMS, C. F. The History of Notation. Newcastle, 1903.

AUBRY, P. Le Rhythme tonique dans la poésie liturgique, etc. Paris, 1903.

Estampies et Danses Royales. Paris, 1907.

Cent Motets du 13ᵉ Siècle. Paris, 1908.

Trouvères et Troubadours. (Contains a full bibliography.) Paris, 1908.

BAS, G. Manuale de Canto Gregoriano. Düsseldorf, 1906.

BECK, J. La Musique des Troubadours. (Contains a full bibliography.) Paris, n.d. (1908).

BOURDON, A. Méthode du Chant Grégorien. Tours, 1920.

BRIGGS, H. B. A Manual of Plainsong. London, 1895.

BRIGGS, H. B., and others. Elements of Plain Song. London, 1902.

COMBARIEU, J. Histoire de la Musique (vol. i). Paris, 1912.

DAVID, E., and LUSSY, M. Histoire de la Notation Musicale. Paris, 1882.

DAVID, L. Méthode pratique du Chant Grégorien. Lyon, 1922.

EMMANUEL, M. Histoire de la Langue Musicale (2 vols.). Paris, 1911.

FRERE, W. H. Bibliotheca Musico-liturgica. London, 1901.

(Editor) The Historical Edition of Hymns Ancient and Modern. London, 1902.

GASTOUÉ, A. Paléographie Musicale Byzantine. Leipzig, 1906.

Cours théorique et pratique de plain-chant Grégorien. Paris, 1904.

L'Art Grégorien. (Contains a full bibliography.) Paris, 1911.

Nouvelle méthode pratique de Chant Grégorien. Paris, 1920.

Les Origines du Chant Romain. Paris, 1907.

Le Graduel et l'Antiphonaire Romain. Lyons, 1913.

GATARD, A. La Musique Grégorienne. Paris, 1913.

JAKOBSTHAL, G. Die Chromatische Alteration im Liturgischen Gebrauch, etc. Berlin, 1897.

LAPEYRE, J. La Notation Aquitaine, etc. Paris, 1882.

LUDWIG, F. Repertorium organorum recentiorum ac motettorum vetustissimi stili. Halle, 1911.

MACHABEY, A. Histoire et évolution des formules musicales du Iʳ au XVᵐᵉ siècle. Paris, 1928.

MOCQUEREAU, A. Le nombre musical Grégorien (2 vols.). Tournai, 1908, 1927.

NISARD, Th. Études sur les anciennes notations musicales. Paris, 1891.

PALÉOGRAPHIE MUSICALE DE SOLESMES. Tournai, 1889–1925.

PLAIN SONG, a grammar of. By the Benedictines of Stanbrook.

RIEMANN, H. Geschichte der Musiktheorie (2nd ed., Berlin, 1920). Leipzig, 1898.

Kompendium der Notenschriftkunde. Regensburg, 1910.

Studien zur Geschichte der Notenschrift. Leipzig, 1878, 1910.

SUNYOL, G. M. Introducció a la paleografía musical Gregoriana. (Contains an invaluable bibliography.) Montserrat, 1925.

Método de Canto regoriano. Barcelona, 1925.

THIBAULT, P. J. Monuments de la notation ekphonétique et hagiopolite de l'Église Grecque (2 vols.). Petersburg, 1913.

Origine Byzantine de la Notation Neumatique. Paris, 1907.

TILLYARD, H.J.W. Greek Church Music, *Musical Antiquary*. Oxford, 1911.

Studies in Byzantine Music. ib., 1913.

Byzantine Music and Hymnography. London, 1923.

VIVELL, C. Initia Tractatuum Musices. Gras, 1912.

WAGNER, P. Neumenkunde. (Further Bibliography in Wellesz, v. *infra*.) Leipzig, 1913.

Einführung in die Gregorianischen Melodien (3 vols.). Freiburg, 1901.

WELLESZ, E. Die Byzantinische Musik. (Contains an extensive bibliography.) Breslau, 1927.

WOLF, J. Handbuch der Notationskunde. Leipzig, 1913.

PERIODICALS

SAMMELBÄNDE DER INTERNATIONAL MUSIKGESELLSCHAFT. Leipzig.
ZEITSCHRIFT DER I. M. G. Leipzig.
MONATSHEFTE FÜR MUSIKGESCHICHTE. Leipzig.
ARCHIV FÜR MUSIKWISSENSCHAFT. Leipzig.
ZEITSCHRIFT FÜR MUSIKWISSENSCHAFT. Leipzig.
VIERTELJAHRSCHRIFT FÜR MUSIKWISSENSCHAFT. Leipzig.
PROCEEDINGS OF THE MUSICAL ASSOCIATION. London.
REVUE DU CHANT GRÉGORIEN. Grenoble.
REVUE GRÉGORIENNE. Tournai.
TRIBUNE DE ST-GERVAIS. Paris.
MUSICA SACRA. Bruges.
RASSEGNA GREGORIANA. Rome.
RIVISTA MUSICALE ITALIANA. Torino.
REVUE D'HISTOIRE ET DE CRITIQUE MUSICALES. Paris.
REVUE MUSICALE. Paris.

TO CHAPTER IV

ABELE, H. The Violin. (Translated by Broadhouse.) London, 1907.
ABERT, HERMANN. Musikanschauung des Mittelalters. Halle, 1905.
 Die Lehre vom Ethos in der griechischen Musik. Leipzig, 1899.
AGRICOLA, MARTINUS. Musica instrumentalis Deudsch. Wittenberg, 1528, 1529.
 Reprint Ges. f. Musikforschung, Bd. xx. Berlin, 1873, etc.
ALTENBURG, W. Die Klarinette. Heilbronn. a. N., 1904.
ANDERSSON, OTTO. Strå Kharpan (The Bowed-Harp). (Engl. Transl. in preparation.) Stockholm, 1923.
BUHLE, EDVARD. Die Musik. Instrumente in den Miniaturen d. frühen Mittelalters. I. Die Blasinstrumente. Leipzig, 1903.
CHAPPELL, WILLIAM, F.S.A. The History of Music. London, 1874.
CLÉDAT, JEAN. Le Monastère et la Nécropole de Baouït. Caire, 1904.
COUSSEMAKER, C. E. H. Scriptorum de Musica Medii Aevi (Tomi IV). (Many other works.) Paris, 1864–76.
DAY, CAPT. C. R. Descriptive Catalogue of the Musical Instruments at Roy. Mil. Exhibition, Lon. 1890). London, 1891.
DEGERING, HERMANN. Die Orgel, ihre Erfindung u. ihre Gesch. bis zur Karolingerzeit. Münster, 1905.
DIETTRICH-KALKHOFF. Geschichte d. Notenschrift. Jauer in Schlesien, 1907.
EICHBORN, H. L. Das alte Clarinblazen. Leipzig, 1894.
ENCYCLOPÉDIE DE LA MUSIQUE ET DICTIONNAIRE DU CONSERVATOIRE (Part II, vols. 2 and 3 : Technique Instrumentale). Paris, 1926, 1927.

ENGEL, CARL. Researches into the Early Hist. of the Violin Family. London, 1883.

The music of the most ancient nations. (Reprint by Reeves.) London, 1864, 1909.

EUTING, F. Die Blasinstrumente. Berlin, 1899.

FLEISCHER, OSKAR. Neumen-Studien (Mittelalterliche Gesangstonschriften), 3 vols. Plates. Leipzig, 1895, 1897 ; Berlin, 1904.

FRIEDLAENDER, ARTHUR M., A.R.C.M. Facts and Theories relating to Hebrew Music. (*Royal Asiatic Soc. Jrnl.*, 1923, reprint.) Harold Reeves, London, 1924.

GALILEI, VINCENTIO. Dialogo della Musica. Florence, 1581.

GALPIN, FRANCIS W., M.A. Old English Instruments of Music. London, 1911.

GERBERT, MARTIN. De Cantu et Musica Sacra. San Blasius, 1774, 1784. Scriptores Ecclesiasticis de Musica (2 vols.). Medieval treatises. San Blasius, 1784.

GROSSET, JOANNY. La Musique de l'Inde, in *Encycl. de la Mus. et Dictionnaire du Conservatoire.* Paris, 1913.

HERMESDORFF, MICH. Micrologus *Guidonis* de disciplina artis musicae. (Latin and German text.) Trier, 1876.

D'HARCOURT, R. and M. La Musique des Incas. (Texte et atlas de 39 planches and bibliogr.) Paris, 1925.

HIPKINS, A. J. The Pianoforte and Older Keyboard Instruments. London (Novello), 1906.

HOPE, ROBERT C., F.S.A. Medieval Music. London, 1894.

HORNBOSTEL, E. M. VON. African Negro Music. (Int. Inst. of African Languages and Culture. Memo. IV.) Oxford Univ. Press. London, 1928.

HOTTETERRE-LE-ROMAIN. Principes de la Flûte Traversière, de la Flûte-à-Bec, et du Haut-Bois. Paris, 1707.

JEANNIN, DOM, O.S.B. Mélodies Liturgiques Syriennes. Paris, 1924.

KIESEWETTER, R. G. Die Musik d. neuern Griechen. Leipzig, 1838.

Die Musik d. Araber. Leipzig, 1842.

KINSKY, GEORG. Doppelrohrblatt-Instrumente mit Windkapsel (16th and 17th cent.). *Archiv f. Musikwissenschaft*, vii. Juni, 1925, pp. 253–96. Leipzig.

KIRBY, P. R., M.A., F.R.C.M. Some Problems of Primitive Harmony and Polyphony (Bantu Practice). *S. African Journal of Science*, vol. xxiii, pp. 951–70. Johannesburg, 1926.

KIRCHER, ATHANASIUS. Musurgia Universalis. 2 tom. fol. Rome, 1650.

KOSEGARTEN, J. G. L. Alii Ispahanensis, Kitāb-al-Aghāni. (Latin Translation. Arabian Theorists, x. cent.) Greifswald, 1840.

LORET, VICTOR. Anciennes Flûtes Égyptiennes. *Jrnl. Asiatique,* 8e série, tome xiv, pp. 111–42 and 197–237. Paris, 1878.

LORET, VICTOR. La Musique de l'Égypte, in *Encycl. de la Mus. et Diction-naire du Conservatoire*. Paris, 1913.

MACLEAN, CHARLES, Mus.Doc. The Principle of the Hydraulic Organ. (Chronol. Bibliographical Notice, *Int. Mus. Ges.*, Sbd. vi, 2, pp. 183–236. 1905.

MAHILLON, C. VICTOR. Le Trombone ; le Cor ; la Trompette. (Series of Handbooks.) Brussels and London, 1907, &c.

MERSENNE, MARIN. Harmonie Universelle. (2 tomes fol., illusts.) Paris, 1636-7.

PANUM, HORTENSE. Middelalderens Strengeinstrumenter og deres Forløere i Oldtiden. (Ills.) Copenhagen, 1915.

PAREIA, BARTOLOMEI RAMI DE. Musica Practica. (Edited by Dr. Joh. Wolf. Publ. d. Int. Mus. Ges. Leipzig, 1901, Beiheft ii.) Bologna, 1482.

PEDRELL, FELIPE. Emporio . . . de Organographia musical antigua española. Barcelona, 1901.

PRAETORIUS, MICHAEL. Syntagma Musicum et Theatrum Instrumentorum. (Reprinted *Ges. f. Musikforschung*, xiii, Berlin, 1885.) Wolfenbüttel, 1618.

Syntagmatis Musici. (Reprint by Dr. Eduard Bernouilli, Leipzig, 1916.) Tomus Tertius, Wolfenbüttel, 1619.

QUANTZ, J. J. Versuch einer Anweisung die Flöte Traversière zu spielen. Berlin, 1752.

RIAÑO, JUAN F. Notes on Early Spanish Music. Quaritch, London, 1887.

RIEMANN, Dr. HUGO. Geschichte der Musiktheorie im ix–xix. Jahrhundert. (2nd ed.) Berlin, 1920.

Handbuch der Musikgeschichte. Leipzig, 1904.

Studien zur Geschichte der Notenschrift. Leipzig, 1878.

Die Byzantinische Notenschrift. Leipzig, 1909.

ROCKSTRO, RICH. S. A Treatise on the Construction . . . of the Flute. London, 1890.

ROUANET, JULES. La Musique des Arabes, in *Encycl. de la Mus. et Diction-naire du Conservatoire*. Paris, 1922.

RÜHLMANN, Dr. JULIUS. Geschichte d. Bogeninstrumente. (With atlas of Plates.) Braunschweig, 1882.

SACHS, Dr. CURT. Handbuch der Musikinstrumentenkunde. Leipzig, 1920.

SCHLESINGER, KATHLEEN. Articles in *Ency. Brit.* (126). All very fully documented.

Bibliography of Works on Musical Instruments, Archaeology, and Antiquities. (100 pp.) W. Reeves, London, 1911.

Musical Instruments. (Under separate headings in *Ency. Brit.* xi, xii, xiii. Editions 1911, &c.: see Aulos, Cithara, Crowd, Rotta, Buccina, Horn, Sackbut.)

Researches into the Origin of the Organs of the Ancients. *Intern. Mus. Ges.*, Sbd. ii (1901), ii, p. 177.

The Precursors of the Violin Family. (Bibliography, pp. 501–600. Out of print.) William Reeves, London, 1910.

STAINER, JOHN, M.A., Mus. Doc. Oxon. The Music of the Bible. (New ed. with Supplementary Notes by Rev. F. W. Galpin, M.A.) London, 1914.

STRAETEN, EDMOND VAN DER. La musique aux Pays-Bas, Documents inédits. (8 vols.) Gand, 1867, &c. Bruxelles, 1888.

TZETZES, Dr. JOH. Über die Altgriechische Musik in d. Griech. Kirche. Munich, 1874.

VIRDUNG, SEBASTIAN. Musica getutscht und aussgezogen. (Reprint, *Ges. f. Musikforschung*, Bd. xi, Berlin, 1873, &c.) Strassburg, 1511.

WASIELEWSKI, J. W. VON. Geschichte d. Instrumentalmusik im xvi. Jhrt. Berlin, Jena, 1878.

ZAMMINER, FRIEDRICH. Die Musik u. die musikalischen Instrumente in ihrer Beziehung zur . . . Akustik. Giessen, 1855.

TO CHAPTER VII

There is here neither room nor call for a full bibliography of folk-music and books concerning it. A number of the most useful sources of information are given below, classified according to countries, and special attention is called to books in which bibliographies are provided. The following bibliographies deserve special mention :

AUBRY, P. Esquisse d'une bibliographie de la chanson populaire en Europe. Paris, 1905.

BAUDRY, J. Notes sur la Musique Populaire Française. (In *Le Guide du Concert*, Paris, 1926–8.)

KNOSP, G. Bibliographia Musica Exotica. (In monthly *Mercure Musical & S. I. M.*, Paris, 1910–11.)

TIERSOT, J. Bibliographie de la Chanson Populaire Française. (In *La Revue Musicale*, Paris, 1904.)

BRITISH ISLES

(Extensive bibliographies in Grove's *Dictionary*, under headings ' SONG ', ' ENGLISH FOLK-SONG ', ' IRISH MUSIC ', ' WELSH MUSIC ', &c.)

SOMERVELL, A. Songs of the Four Nations. London, 1892.

ENGLAND

BARING-GOULD AND SHEPPARD. Songs and Ballads of the West (4 vols.). London, 1889–91.

BROADWOOD, J. Old English Songs as now sung by the peasantry of Surrey and Sussex. London, 1893.

Broadwood, C. E., and Fuller Maitland, J. English Country Songs. London, n.d.

English Traditional Songs. London, 1908.

Chappell, W. Popular Music of Olden Times. London, 1893.

Fuller Maitland, J. English Carols of the Fifteenth Century. London, n.d.

Gill, W. H. Songs of the British Folk. London, 1917.

Hill, G. Wiltshire Songs and Carols. London, 1904.

Kidson, F. Traditional Tunes (chiefly Yorkshire and South Scotland). Oxford, 1891.

Moffat, A. Minstrelsy of England. London, n.d.

Sharp, C. J. The English Folk-song. London, 1924.

Folk-songs of Somerset (5 vols.). London, 1905.

Book of British Folk-song. London, 1902.

(Complete bibliography of Cecil Sharp's collections and writings in the quarterly *Music and Letters*, Oct. 1924.)

Stokor, J. Songs and Ballads of North England. Newcastle, n.d.

Whittaker, W. G. North Country Songs, Ballads, and Pipe Tunes (2 vols.). London, 1921.

ISLE OF MAN

Gill, W. H. Manx National Songs. London, 1896.

Moor, A. W. Manx Ballads and Music. Douglas, 1896.

SCOTLAND

Balfour, D. Ancient Orkney Melodies. Edinburgh, 1885.

Glen, J. Early Scottish Melodies. London, 1900.

Kennedy-Fraser, M. Songs of the Hebrides (3 vols.). London, 1909-21.

Macbean, L. The Songs and Hymns of the Gael. London, 1900.

Moffatt, A. The Minstrelsy of the Scottish Islands. Glasgow, 1907.

The Minstrelsy of Scotland. London, 1895.

Pittman and Brown. The Songs of Scotland. London, n.d.

WALES

Brinley Richards. The Songs of Wales. London, 1884.

Moffat, A. The Minstrelsy of Wales. London, n.d.

Parry, Joseph. Cambrian Minstrelsie (6 vols.). Edinburgh, n.d.

Thomas, S. Welsh Melodies (4 vols.). 1862-74.

Williams, M. J. Ancient National Airs of Gwent and Morganwg. London, 1844.

IRELAND

Hannagan, M., and Clandillon, S. Songs of the Irish Gaels. London, 1927.

Hughes, H. Irish Country Songs (2 vols.). London, 1927.

BIBLIOGRAPHY

Moffat, A.   The Minstrelsy of Ireland.   London, n.d.

Petrie, G.   The Petrie Collection of Ancient Music of Ireland.   Dublin, 1855.

A Complete Collection of Irish Music, edited by C. V. Stanford (2 vols.). London, 1902.

Wood, Ch.   Irish Folk-song.   1897.

See also the publications of the English, Welsh, and Irish Folk-song Societies, and Scottish National Song Society, and of English Folk Dance Society.

FRANCE

Arbaud, D.   Chants populaires de Provence (2 vols.).   Aix, 1862–4.

Beauquier, Ch.   Chansons populaires recueillies en Franche-Comté. Paris, 1894.

Bourgault-Ducoudray, L.   30 mélodies populaires de Basse Bretagne Paris, 1885.

Bujeaud, J.   Chants et chansons populaires des provinces de l'Ouest (2 vols.).   Niort, 1862–4.

Canteloube, J.   Chants populaires de la Haute Auvergne (2 vols.). Paris, 1907.

Chants d'Auvergne (3 vols.).   Paris, 1923–7.

Duhamel, M.   Chansons populaires du Pays de Vannes.   Paris, 1910.

Emmanuel, M.   Trente chansons Bourguignonnes.   Paris, n.d.

Indy, Vincent d', and Tiersot, J.   Chansons populaires recueillies dans le Vivarais et le Vercors.   Paris, 1892.

Meyrac, A.   Traditions des Ardennes (vol. iii).   Charleville, 1890.

Millien, A., and Penavaire.   Chants et Chansons du Nivernais.   (2 vols.) Paris, 1906.

Moullé, E.   Cinquante chants populaires de Basse Normandie.   Paris, 1890.

Rolland, E.   Recueil de chansons populaires (6 vols.).   Paris, 1883–90.

Simon, Fr.   Chansons populaires de l'Anjou.   Angers, 1921.

Tiersot, J.   Chansons populaires recueillies dans les Alpes Françaises. Paris, 1903.

Mélodies populaires des provinces de France (3 vols.).   Paris, n.d.

Noëls Français.   Paris, n.d.

Chants de la Vieille France.   Paris, n.d.

Vidal. F.   Le Tambourin (pt. iii : Tunes from Provence).   Aix, 1864.

Weckerlin.   Chansons populaires des provinces de France.   Paris, 1860.

Chansons populaires de l'Alsace (2 vols.).   Paris, 188ʻ.

L'ancienne chanson populaire en France (bibliographical).   Paris, 1887.

SPAIN

Calleja, R.   Canciones populares de la provincia di Santander.   Madrid, 1901.

Capmañy, A.   Cançoner popular (3 vols.).   Barcelona, n.d.

Falla, M. de. 7 canciones populares Españoles. Paris, 1920.

Inzenga, J. Cantos y Bailes populares de España (3 vols., devoted to Galicia, Murcia, Valencia respectively). Madrid, n.d.

Ocon, E. Cantos Españoles. Malaga, 1874-1906.

Pedrell, F. Cancionero musical popular Español. Valls, 1918-19.

Torner, E. M. Cancioniero musical de la lirica popular Asturiana. Madrid, 1920.

Trend, J. B. Luis Milan. London, 1925.

BASQUE COUNTRY

Bordes, C. H. Cent chansons populaires Basques. Paris, 1894.

12 Noëls Basques anciens. Paris, 1897.

12 chansons amoureuses du pays Basque Français. Paris, 1910.

Salabery, J. D. Chants populaires du pays Basque. Bayonne, 1870.

PORTUGAL

Dasneves, C., and Campos, G. de. Cancioneiro de musicas populares. Porto, 1893-8.

Keil, A. Tojos e Rosmaninhos (songs from Beira). Lisbon, n.d.

Salvini, G. R. Cancioneiro musical Portugues. Lisbon, 1884.

Thomas, P. Fernandes. Velhas canções e romances populares Portugueses. Lisbon, 1913.

Canções populares de Beira. Lisbon, 1893.

ITALY

Fara, Giulio. L'anima musicale d'Italia. Roma, 1920. Contains a full bibliography, to which the only needful addition is:

Gavino, Gabriel. Canti di Sardegna. Milano, 1923.

RUMANIA

Bartok, B. Die Volksmusik der Rumänen. Berlin, 1925.

Chansons populaires Romaines du département Bihar. Bucarest, 1913.

Volksmusik der Rumänen von Maramures. Munich, 1923.

GREECE

Bürchner, L. Griechische Volksweisen. (In Sammelb. der I. M. G., vol. iii.) Leipzig.

Bourgault Ducoudray, L. Trente mélodies populaires de Grèce et d'Orient. Paris, 1876.

Lampadarios, L. Collection de Mélodies Grecques. Constantinople, 1842.

Matsa, P. 80 Mélodies Grecques (in Greek). Constantinople, 1883.

Pakhtikos, G. 260 Greek songs (in Greek). Athens, 1905.

PERNOT, H. Mélodies populaires de l'Île de Chio. Paris, 1902.

The following are mentioned in P. Aubry's Bibliography, but are not otherwise traceable: Vlachopulos, S., Harmonia ou Chants Grecs et Turcs, Constantinople, 1848; Georgiadis, P., Calliphonos Sirène, Chants populaires, Constantinople, 1859. [Sigala's *Ethnika Asmata* (Athens, 1880) contains few genuine folk-songs.]

RUSSIA

Full up-to-date bibliography of Great-Russian folk-music (mentioning 108 collections and 71 books or pamphlets) in:

FINAGHIN, A. Russkaya Piesnia. St. Petersburg, 1923.

Good studies of Russian folk-music are to be found in:

KASTALSKY, P. Osobennosti Narodnoï Russkoï Muzykalnoï Sistemý. Moscow, 1923.

SOKALSKY, P. Russkaya Narodnaya Muzyka. Kharkof, 1888.

LINEVA, E. Peasant Songs of Great-Russia (2 vols.). (First volume contains introduction in English; second volume, an English translation appeared at Moscow, 1912.) Petrograd and Moscow, 1905-9.

Chief collections:

BALAKIREF, M. 30 piesen Russkavo Naroda. Petersburg, 1901.

Recueil de chants populaires Russes. (First published 1866.) Leipzig, n.d.

ISTOMIN and DUTSCH. Piesni Russkovo Naroda. (Songs from Archangel and Olonets.) Petersburg, 1894.

ISTOMIN and LIAPUNOF. 35 Piesen Russkovo Naroda. (Songs of the Vologda, Vialka, and Kostroma provinces.) Moscow, 1901.

ISTOMIN and NEKRASSOF. 50 Piesen Russkovo Naroda. Moscow, 1901.

KIREJEFSKY and BEZSONOF. Russkiye Piesni. Moscow, 1862-78.

LIADOF, A. 50 Piesen Russkovo Naroda. (For voice and piano.) Petersburg, 1901.

35 Piesen Russkovo Naroda. Petersburg, 1903.

Various useful books of songs and arrangements by this composer have appeared (publishers, Belaief, Jurgenson, Gutheil, Leipzig and Moscow).

MELGUNOF, S. Russkiye Piesni (2 vols.). Petersburg, 1879-85.

RIMSKY-KORSAKOF. Sbornik 40 Russkikh Narodnikh Piesen. Moscow, 1882.

100 Russian Folk-songs. (With English translations. First published 1877.) Paris (Bessel), 1926.

SLAVONIC (General Collections)

KUBA. Das Slaventum in seinen Liedern (collection of Czech, Slovakian, Polish, Wend, Moravian, Slovene, Montenegrian, Croatian, Dalmatian, Serbian, and Bosnian tunes), 14 vols. Prag, 1920-7.

H h

234 BIBLIOGRAPHY

KUHACS, F. S. Chansons nationales des Slaves du Sud (Serbian, Croatian, Montenegrian, Dalmatian, and Bosnian tunes), 4 vols. Agram, 1878–81.

YUGOSLAVIA

DADJUREK, B. Pisne Cernohorske. Prag, 1890.
Pisne Slovinske. Prag, 1890.
Pisne Charvatske. Prag, 1892.
GEORGEVITCH, V. Mélodies Nationales Serbes. Belgrade, 1896.
Mélodies populaires Serbes (Serbie du Sud, introduction par E. Closson). Skoplje, 1928.
KOCORÁ. 15 chants nationaux des Serbes Lusaciens. Prague.
PARLOVIĆ. Serbian Songs. Agram.
See also the monthly *Sveta Cecilija*, published at Zagreb since 1906.

BULGARIA

PEÏTAVI, S. Les chansons populaires Bulgares, in *Le Mercure Musical*. Paris, 1905.
STOYANOF and RATCHOF. 24 chansons populaires notées. Varna, 1887.
VASILEF, G. 225 chansons populaires Bulgares. Tirnovo, 1891.

UKRAINE

ARTEMOFSKY. 55 chants de l'Ukraine. Kief, 1883.
GEMTCHUNOF, A. and V. Chants des Cosaques de l'Oural. Petersburg, 1899.
LISSENKO, M. Receuil des chants de l'Oukraïna (5 vols.). Petersburg, 1878–92.
MIKHAILOF, F. Chansonnier populaire de l'Oukraïna. Kharkof, 1887.
RUBETS, A. 216 chants populaires de l'Oukraïna. Moscow, 1872.
Recueil de chants populaires de l'Oukraïna. Petersburg, 1872.
DE VOLLAU. Rutheno-Galician Folk-songs. Petrograd, 1885.

LITHUANIA, LATVIA

BARTSCH, Ch. Dainu Balsai, Melodien Litauischer Volkslieder. Heidelberg, 1886–9.
JUSZKIEWICZ. Mélodies populaires Lituaniennes. (Exceptionally valuable.) Cracow, 1900.
KOLBERG, O. Piesni ludu Litewskiego. Cracow, 1879.
NAST, L. Die Volkslieder der Lithauer. Tilsitt, 1893.
NESSELMANN. Littauische Volkslieder. Berlin, 1853.

POLAND

GOLOVATSKY. Narodniya piesni Galitskoï i Ugorskoï Russi. Petrograd, 1878.
GLOGER and NOSKOVSKI. Chants du peuple. Cracow, 1892.
KOLBERG, O. Piesni ludu Polskiego. Warsaw, 1890.

CZECHOSLOVAKIA

BARTÓK, B. 2600 Slovakian Folk-tunes. Curciansky St. Martin, 1924–5.

BARTOŠ, F. Národni Pisne Morawske. Brunn, 1889.

Moravska Svatba. Brunn, 1892.

BARTOS, F., and JANÁČEK. Národny Písne Moravske. Prag, 1901.

ERBEN. Nápěvy prostonárodních písní českych. Prag, 1886.

FRANCISCI, J. Travnici, 100 Slovenskich Národnich Pjesni. Turocz Szt. Marton, n.d.

FRANCISCI, J., and others. Spevy Slovenske. Turocz Szt. Marton, 1880–93.

MALAT, J. Český Národni Poklad. Prag, 1866–95.

HUNGARY

BARTALUS, I. Magyar Népdalok (7 vols.). Budapest, 1873-96.

BARTÓK, B. Das Ungarische Volkslied. (Contains 320 songs and bibliography.) Berlin, 1925.

BARTÓK, B., and KODÁLY, Z. Magyar Népdalok. Budapest, 1906.

Nepdalok. (Transylvanian Hungarian folk-tunes, preface in English.) Budapest, 1923.

LÁSZLÓ, K. 1000 Népdalo. Budapest, 1905.

FINLAND, ESKIMOS

KAJANUS, R. Suomen Kansan Sävelmiä. (Edited by Ilmari Krohn. 3 vols.) Helsingfors, 1888–1904.

LAGUS, E. Nyländska Folkvisor. (2 vols.) Helsingfors, 1887–1900.

THALBITZER, W. A phonetical study of the Eskimo language and a new collection of Greenland songs and music. Copenhagen, 1904.

SCANDINAVIA

BERGGREEN, A. P. Folkesange og melodier. (T. i. Danish music ; T. ii. Norwegian music ; T. iii. Swedish music ; T. xi. additions to the above three.) Copenhagen, 1860.

(1) DENMARK

ABRAHAMSON. Udvalgte Danske Viser fra Middelalderen. Copenhagen, 1812–14.

NIERUP and RASMUSSEN. Udvalg af Danske Viser. (2 vols.) A sequel to the foregoing. Copenhagen, 1821.

KRISTENSEN, E. T. Gamle Jyske Folkeviser. (Songs from Jutland.) Copenhagen, 1876.

LAUB, T. Danske Folkeviser. Copenhagen 1899.

236   BIBLIOGRAPHY

(2) SWEDEN

AHLSTRÖM, J. N. 220 Svenska folkdanser. Stockholm, n.d.
    300 Svenska folkvisor. Stockholm, n.d.
CARLHEIM GYLLENSKIÖLD, V. Visor och Melodier. Stockholm, 1892.
DYBECK, R. Svenska vallvisor och hornlaton. Stockholm, 1846.
    Svenska visor. Stockholm, n.d.
LAGUS, E. Nyländska Folkvisor. (Songs of the Nyland Swedes.) 2 vols.
    Helsingfors, 1887-93.
LUNDQVIST. 100 Svenska Folkvisor. Stockholm, 1866.

(3) NORWAY

AHLSTRÖM, J. N. Nordiska Folkvisor. Stockholm, n.d.
GARBORG, H. Norske Folkevisor. Stockholm, 1903.
LANDSTAD. Norske Folkevisor. (With an appendix by Lindeman.) Chris-
    tiania, 1852-3.
LINDEMAN, L. Aeldre og nyere Norske Fjeldmelodier. Christiania, 1840.

GERMANY

BOEHME, F. Altdeutsches Liederbuch. Leipzig, 1877.
    Volkstümliche Lieder der Deutschen im 18. und 19ten Jahrhundert.
    Leipzig, 1895.
ERK, L., and BOEHME. Deutsches Liederhort. 3 vols. Leipzig, 1893-5.
(These three give a complete bibliography up to date of publication.
Further information in Grove's *Dictionary* and P. Aubry, *op. cit.*)

AUSTRIA

NECKHEIM, H. 222 Echte Kaerntnerlieder. Wien, 190?.
POMMER, J. Volksmusik der Deutschen Steiermark. Wien, 1901.
SCHÜSTER, F. W. Siebenbürgisch-Sächsische Volkslieder, &c. Hermann-
    stadt, 1865.
SPAUN, A. VON. Die Oesterreichischen Volksweisen, &c. Wien, 1845.
TSCHISCHKA and SCHOTTKY. Oesterreichische Volkslieder. Pest, 1844.
    Further bibliography as above.

SWITZERLAND

HUBER, F. Schweizerliederbuch. Aarau, 1824.
    Recueil de Ranz des Vaches. Aarau, 1830.
KUELLA. Chansonnier Suisse. Zürich, 1882.
KUHN, G. Sammlung von Schweizer Kuhreihen und Volksliedern. (New
    edition, revised by Wysz and Huber.) Bern, 1826.
KURZ, H. Schlacht- und Volkslieder der Schweizer. Zürich, 1860.
WYSZ, J., and HUBER, F. Der Schweizersänger. Lucerne, 1883.

Chansons et Coraules Fribourgeoises. Fribourg, 1894.
Chants et Coraules de la Gruyère. Leipzig, 1894.
Chansonnier des Zofingiens de la Suisse Romande. Lausanne, 1894.

NETHERLANDS

(1) FLANDERS

BOLS, J. Honderd oude Vlaamsche Liederen. Namur, 1897.
CLOSSON, E. Chansons populaires des provinces Belges. Brussels, 1905.
COUSSEMAKER, E. DE. Chants populaires des Flamands de France. Ghent, 1856.
GEVAERT, E. Versameling van acht oude Vlaemsche Liederen. Ghent, 1854.
LOOTENS and FEYS. Chants populaires Flamands recueillis à Bruges. Bruges, 1879.
VAN DUYSE, F. Het oude Nederlandsche Lied. Antwerp, 1905.
Dit is een sunverlijck Boecxken inhoudende oude Nederlandsche (geestelijke) Liederen. Ghent, 1899.
6 Oude Nederlandsche Liederen. Ghent, n.d.
WILLEMS, J. F. Oude Vlaemsche Lieder. Ghent, 1848.

(2) HOLLAND

BRANDTS-BUYS, M. A. Liedjes van en voor Nederlands volk. Leyden, 1875.
COERS, F. R. Liederbook van Groot-Nederland. Amsterdam, 1898–1902.
LANGE, RIEMSDIJK, and KALFF. Nederlandsch Volksliederenbook. Amsterdam, 1896.

MISCELLANEOUS

ARMENIA

BOYADJIAN, G. Chants populaires arméniens. Paris, 1904.
EGHISARIAN, L. Recueil de chants populaires Arméniens. Paris, 1900.
KOMITAS KERVORKIAN. La Lyre Arménienne. Paris, 1907.
Armenische Dorflieder (2 vols.). Leipzig, 1913.
ANON. Mélodies Kurdes. (In Armenian.) Moscow, 1904.

ARABY

RIBERA, S. Historia de la Música Árabe medieval. Madrid, 1927.
ROUANET, J. Histoire de la Musique Arabe en Algérie. Alger, 1905.
ROUANET, J., and YAFIL, E. N. Répertoire de Musique Arabe et Maure. Alger, 1905-11.

GEORGIA

GROSDOF. Chansons populaires des Mingréliens. (Privately printed.)
KARGARETELLI. Chants populaires Georgiens. Tiflis, 1899.
TSCHIKWASCHWILI. Salamouri. (Georgian tunes.) Tiflis, 1896.

Various

RYBAKOF. Songs of the Ural Moslem. Petrograd, 1897.

USPENSKY, V., and BELAIEF, V. Turkmenskaya Muzyka. Moscow, 1928.

India

FOX STRANGWAYS, A. H. *Music of Hindostan.* Oxford, 1914.

North America

ALLEN, W. F., and others. Slave Songs of the United States. N.Y., 1867.

BROCKWAY, H., and WYMAN, L. Twenty Kentucky Mountain Songs. Boston, 1920.

CAMPBELL, O. D., and SHARP, C. S. English Folk-songs from the Southern Appalachians. N.Y., 1917.

DENSMORE, F. Teton Sioux Music. Washington, 1918.

North American Tribes, in *Bulletin of Bureau of American Ethnology,* nos. 45, 53, 61, 75, 80.

FENNER, T. P. Cabin and Plantation Songs. N.Y., 1874.

GAGNON, E. Chansons populaires du Canada. Quebec, 1865; n. ed., 1894.

HAGUE, E. Spanish American Folk-songs. Lancaster, Pa., 1917.

HUGHES, R., and STURGIS, E. B. Songs from the Hills of Vermont. N.Y., 1919.

The fifth volume of *Encyclopédie Musicale et Dictionnaire du Conservatoire* (Paris, 1920) contains a wealth of information on the folk music of Araby, Turkey, Persia, Burmah, Cochinchina, Cambodge, Dutch Indies, Africa, and America (North and South).

TO CHAPTER VIII

ABERT, HERMANN. Die Musikanschauungen des Mittelalters. Halle a. d. S., 1905.

ADLER, GUIDO. Handbuch der Musikgeschichte. (Edited by G. A.) Frankfurt a. M., 1924.

AUBRY, PIERRE. Trouvères et Troubadours. Paris, 1910.

BRENET, MICHEL. La Musique Militaire. Paris, 1917.

Musique et Musiciens de la vieille France. Paris, 1911.

BREUL, KARL. The Cambridge Songs. Cambridge, 1915.

CHAMBERS, E. K. The Medieval Stage. Oxford, 1903.

COULTON, G. G. A Medieval Garner.

COUSSEMAKER, E. DE. Drames Liturgiques du Moyen Âge. Paris, 1861.

DENT, EDWARD J. The *Laudi Spirituali*. Proceedings of the Musical Association. London, 1917.

FARMER, H. G. The Rise and Development of Military Music. London, 1912.

JUSSERAND, J. J. English Wayfaring Life in the Middle Ages. London, 1925.

MOSER, HANS JOACHIM. Geschichte der Deutschen Musik. Stuttgart, 1923.

POWER, EILEEN. Medieval English Nunneries. Cambridge, 1922.

SYMONDS, JOHN ADDINGTON. Wine, Women, and Song. London, 1907.

TREND, J. B. The Music of Spanish History. Oxford, 1926.
Alfonso the Sage. London, 1926.

WAGNER, PETER. Introduction to the Gregorian Melodies. London, Plainsong and Medieval Music Society.